HUMAN KINETICS ONLINE STUDENT RESOURCE

How to access the supplemental online student resource

We are pleased to provide access to an online student resource that supplements your textbook, *Introduction to Teaching Physical Education.* This resource offers case studies, worksheets, templates, and more.

Accessing the online student resource is easy! Follow these steps if you purchased a new book:

1. Visit **www.HumanKinetics.com/IntroductionToTeachingPhysicalEducation**.
2. Click the first edition link next to the book cover.
3. Click the Sign In link on the left or top of the page. If you do not have an account with Human Kinetics, you will be prompted to create one.
4. If the online product you purchased does not appear in the Ancillary Items box on the left of the page, click the Enter Key Code option in that box. Enter the key code that is printed at the right, including all hyphens. Click the Submit button to unlock your online product.
5. After you successfully enter your key code, your online product will appear in the Ancillary Items box. On future visits to the site, all you need to do is sign in to the textbook's Web site and follow the link!

➜ Click the Need Help? button on the textbook's Web site if you need assistance along the way.

How to access the online student resource if you purchased a used book:

You may purchase access to the online student resource by visiting the text's Web site, **www.HumanKinetics.com/IntroductionToTeachingPhysicalEducation**, or by calling the following:

800-747-4457	U.S. customers
800-465-7301	Canadian customers
+44 (0) 113 255 5665	European customers
08 8372 0999	Australian customers
0800 222 062	New Zealand customers
217-351-5076	International customers

For technical support, send an e-mail to:

support@hkusa.com	U.S. and international customers
info@hkcanada.com	Canadian customers
academic@hkeurope.com	European customers
keycodesupport@hkaustralia.com	Australian and New Zealand customers

HUMAN KINETICS
The Information Leader in Physical Activity & Health

S: 03-2011

Product: Introduction to Teaching Physical Education online student resource

Key code: SHIMON-UUMEUL-OSG

This unique code allows you access to the online student resource.

Access is provided if you have purchased a new book.
Once submitted, the code may not be entered for any other user.

Introduction to TEACHING PHYSICAL EDUCATION

Principles and Strategies

JANE M. SHIMON, EdD, ATC
Boise State University

Human Kinetics

Library of Congress Cataloging-in-Publication Data

Shimon, Jane M.
Introduction to teaching physical education : principles and strategies / Jane M. Shimon.
p. cm.
Includes bibliographical references and index.
ISBN-13: 978-0-7360-8645-5 (hard cover)
ISBN-10: 0-7360-8645-5 (hard cover)
1. Physical education and training--Study and teaching--United States. 2. Physical education teachers--Training of--United States. I. Title.
GV361.S466 2011
796.07'7--dc22
2010034153

ISBN-10: 0-7360-8645-5 (print)
ISBN-13: 978-0-7360-8645-5 (print)

The Web addresses cited in this text were current as of December 2010, unless otherwise noted.

Acquisitions Editor: Scott Wikgren; **Developmental Editor:** Bethany J. Bentley; **Assistant Editors:** Elizabeth Evans, Derek Campbell, and Tyler Wolpert; **Copyeditor:** Patsy Fortney; **Indexer:** Alisha Jeddeloh; **Permission Manager:** Dalene Reeder; **Graphic Designer:** Bob Reuther; **Graphic Artist:** Angela K. Snyder; **Cover Designer:** Keith Blomberg; **Photographs (interior and cover):** © Human Kinetics, unless otherwise noted; **Photo Asset Manager:** Laura Fitch; **Photo Production Manager:** Jason Allen; **Art Manager:** Kelly Hendren; **Associate Art Manager:** Alan L. Wilborn; **Illustrations:** © Human Kinetics; **Printer:** Sheridan Books

Printed in the United States of America

10 9 8 7 6 5 4 3 2 1

The paper in this book is certified under a sustainable forestry program.

Human Kinetics
Web site: www.HumanKinetics.com

United States: Human Kinetics
P.O. Box 5076
Champaign, IL 61825-5076
800-747-4457
e-mail: humank@hkusa.com

Canada: Human Kinetics
475 Devonshire Road Unit 100
Windsor, ON N8Y 2L5
800-465-7301 (in Canada only)
e-mail: info@hkcanada.com

Europe: Human Kinetics
107 Bradford Road
Stanningley
Leeds LS28 6AT, United Kingdom
+44 (0) 113 255 5665
e-mail: hk@hkeurope.com

Australia: Human Kinetics
57A Price Avenue
Lower Mitcham, South Australia 5062
08 8372 0999
e-mail: info@hkaustralia.com

New Zealand: Human Kinetics
P.O. Box 80
Torrens Park, South Australia 5062
0800 222 062
e-mail: info@hknewzealand.com

E4925

Dedicated to Marianne L. Woods, EdD,
a wonderful physical educator and friend.

CONTENTS

PREFACE

The extensive amount of information physical education majors need to know about teaching and learning can be overwhelming. As such, it's important to focus on the basics of instruction and develop a solid foundation of teaching skills. That foundation, built on the nitty-gritty, must-have concepts and skills of teaching physical education. The purpose of *Introduction to Teaching Physical Education* is to provide the key principles of teaching physical education, a starting block to quality teaching at the K-12 level. Additional upper-level elementary and secondary methods courses in your program of studies will refine and add to the core information found in this textbook.

Introduction to Teaching Physical Education is intended for students entering the field. Each chapter begins with a list of chapter objectives to provide a general idea of the material presented. In addition, key terms are provided to further specify chapter content. Each chapter ends with helpful discussion questions. Throughout each chapter are sidebars and questions to encourage further reflection on certain concepts or issues.

Organization

Overall, this text is designed to take you through progressive steps in developing a basic understanding of teaching and the critical pedagogical skills needed by all physical education teachers. *Introduction to Teaching Physical Education* is divided into four parts and 11 chapters.

Part I, Behind the Scenes of Physical Education, commences in chapter 1 with a general outline of the history of physical education, including the two main systems that served as the foundation of the profession, as well as influential concepts and people who paved the way to physical education as we know it today. Chapter 2 addresses the purpose of physical education, including the current National Standards for Physical Education. The chapter concludes with a description of various philosophical views on education and their applications to physical education. Chapter 3 highlights the many teaching and nonteaching duties physical education teachers assume, along with current issues and concerns facing physical educators today.

Part II, Teaching Physical Education, presents the nuts and bolts of teaching physical education. Chapter 4 outlines a sequence of steps for setting a foundation for quality classroom organization and instruction in the gymnasium. This chapter provides basic core concepts of teaching. Chapter 5 outlines general strategies for motivating children and adolescents to move and enjoy physical activity, and chapter 6 addresses considerations for preventing misbehavior and positively managing student behavior in the classroom.

Part III, Lesson Planning and Outcomes, includes basic information needed for planning lessons and assessing student outcomes. Chapter 7 focuses on the concepts of scope (content) and sequence (progressions) at the elementary and secondary levels, and chapter 8 describes how to develop appropriate performance objectives for lessons as well as quality lesson plans. General components of a lesson plan format are described, along with helpful lesson planning tips. Finally, Chapter 9 addresses basic concepts of assessment, describes how to create rubrics and written tests to assess learning outcomes, and provides information on Fitnessgram and grading considerations.

Part IV, Beyond the Classroom, includes the final two chapters. Chapter 10 directs you to current fitness and instructional technology, as well as online resources you can access to help enhance your content knowledge and instructional skills. Chapter 11 concludes part IV with information about other career options you may consider if teaching positions are hard to find or if you decide that teaching is not your long-term career choice.

Accompanying Online Ancillary Materials

The online student resource, found at www.HumanKinetics.com/IntroductionToTeachingPhysicalEducation, includes a variety of practical worksheets, lesson plan templates, short situational studies, and Web links to supplement the content found within the textbook. Throughout the book, you will notice thumbnail-size screen captures that will alert you to check out the accompanying materials online. You can either complete them online or print them out. Note that some of the case studies included in the online student resource were derived from actual events, while others are modifications to case studies found in *Case Study Workbook for Physical Education Teacher Preparation* by Arbogast and Kizer (1996).

For instructors, a detailed instructor guide with a sample course syllabus, chapter summaries, key terms, discussion questions, and more is included; along with a test package with 187 test questions in a variety of formats (multiple choice, true or false, essay, etc.); and a PowerPoint presentation package to accompany each chapter.

Teaching physical education is a wonderful career choice. Just think, you will be contributing to the health and well-being of students you teach; and you will be educating the next generation on the skills, knowledge, and attitudes needed to be active for a lifetime. I hope the information found in this textbook will enhance your understanding of physical education and help you build a solid foundation of teaching skills as you continue your quest to become a physical education teacher. Happy trails!

ACKNOWLEDGMENTS

A huge thank-you goes out to Dr. Paul Brawdy at St. Bonaventure University. You made me think, Paul! Also, thanks to Dr. Terry-Ann Gibson, Dr. Laura Jones-Petranek, and Dr. Tyler Johnson at Boise State University; Kathy Clemons of AAHPERD; John Bale, Corinne Morgan, Steve Morgan, and Sharon Boland, K-12 teachers in the Boise School District; and Scott Wikgren, Bethany Bentley, and all the folks at Human Kinetics who helped with this project.

Finally, to my parents, Jim and Beverly Shimon: Thanks for your continued support and confidence. Mom, thanks for the chapter comments—you would have made a great physical education teacher. Thanks, also, for supporting my latte habit with those chapter returns!

PART I

BEHIND THE SCENES OF PHYSICAL EDUCATION

Have you ever wondered what physical education was like before it became an accepted subject in its own right? What was important to people back then? Did they consider physical education as a vital component of education? Did they believe it was essential to live a healthy and physically active lifestyle? More specifically, how did the values and attitudes of early leaders in physical education help shape our current profession?

The three chapters comprising part I present a window into past events and ideologies that have helped shape the profession, along with an examination of beliefs and attitudes of physical education that currently exist, yet are often shielded from view. As you begin your studies in teaching physical education, it is helpful to be mindful not only of how the past affects the present, but also of how modern behind-the-scenes topics affect teaching physical education today.

CHAPTER 1

History of Physical Education

CHAPTER OBJECTIVES

After reading this chapter, you will be able to:

- ☐ Identify the names and contributions of early influential leaders in the profession.
- ☐ Explain how initial systems and early events shaped current physical education programs.
- ☐ Describe the impact of past and recent federal mandates on physical education.
- ☐ Discuss how past issues and concerns in physical education are mirrored in current views.
- ☐ Identify present challenges and trends.

KEY TERMS

American gymnastics
anthropometric measurements
concepts-based model
fitness education model
German gymnastics
hygiene
Individuals With Disabilities Education Act (IDEA)
movement education
new physical education
No Child Left Behind (NCLB)
normal schools
PETE
physical training
responsibility model
sport education model
Swedish gymnastics
tactical games approach
Title IX

When most students know they have to read a chapter on history, their eyes begin to mist and usually roll upward, and they let out a big sigh of resignation. However, the history of physical education is interesting and relevant because it shows how past events and people have paved the way to today's physical education. History measures the progress of the past and present; thus, an understanding of the past helps influence and shape the present and future. As Gerda Lerner, an author, historian, and pioneer of women's history, said:

> *What we do about history matters. The often repeated saying that those who forget the lessons of history are doomed to repeat them has a lot of truth to it. But what are the "lessons of history"? The very attempt at definition furnishes ground for new conflicts. History is not a recipe book; past events are never replicated in the present in quite the same way. Historical events are infinitely variable and their interpretations are a constantly shifting process. There are no certainties to be found in the past. (Lewis 2009)*

We are about to take a step back in time and travel the path of the development of physical education. As presented in this chapter, the path may appear linear; however, the history of physical education was affected by an array of intertwined and parallel events and movements. An overview of main events and influential people will provide a general sense of how physical education evolved to what it is today. Such terms as ***physical training***, *exercise, gymnastics, physical culture,* and *calisthenics* imply the essence of physical education at a given time in history.

The Beginning

When did physical education begin? Actually, forms of physical education have been present for as long as people have existed. Even though primeval people did not go to school or take physical education classes, their children were educated physically every day. They were taught survival skills, games, dances, and the ways of their people by their elders. Learning to hunt for food, manage a water vessel in a river, make or repair clothing, or shoot arrows and throw spears were some of the practical skills children had to learn. More than likely children practiced those skills over and over until they could perform them instinctively.

Similarly, just as we dance and play games today, the people of early civilizations also played games and used dance as part of their social gatherings to celebrate special occasions and perform religious ceremonies and rituals. These customs and traditions were passed on from generation to generation. Even the great civilized cultures of the past, such as the flourishing ancient societies of Egypt, China, and India, practiced forms of physical education (Van Dalen and Bennett 1971). Although some societies emphasized physical activities more than others did, all placed some kind of value on physical exercise, dance, or game play.

Evidence suggests that the concept of physical education in the Western world began in ancient Greece (800-300 BC) (Leonard and McKenzie 1927). Exercise was a vital component of the educational program in this society. In the city-state of Sparta, extensive exercise, or physical training, was required for boys and men to help develop strong, dominating armies, whereas girls exercised to bear strong, healthy children. Today's children go to gymnasiums for physical education classes, and adults travel to local fitness centers; in ancient Greece boys attended private wrestling schools called *palestras,* and men continued with their training in public outdoor gymnasiums. Physical education at *palestras* and gymnasiums focused on courage, strength, form, grace, and well-proportioned physiques as the foundation for intellectual development (Weston 1962). In today's educational structure, we also believe that physical education plays an important role in developing the whole child.

What do you know of in today's society that uses the mind/body connection?

The Renaissance period (14th to 17th centuries) and the Age of Enlightenment (17th to 18th centuries) resurrected a belief in the importance of physical activity and health after the lengthy, stagnant period of the early Middle Ages, often referred to as the Dark Ages. The Renaissance was a time of cultural and intellectual transformation that revived an appreciation for literature, the fine arts, science, and the gradual reformation of education. The bond between the concepts of mind and soul was central to the philosophy of the Renaissance; it was important to develop the mind as well as the body because both were intertwined and interacting (Weston 1962). The concept of mind and body, or body and soul relationships, would remain important to future leaders of physical education in the New World.

During the Age of Enlightenment of the 18th century, new lands were being discovered across the seas, while along the crossways of Europe, scientific inquiry and experiments were being conducted; various philosophical ideologies of life and education were recognized; and issues of medicine, health, and the body were of particular interest. The impact of these changes in the Old World played an important role in the development of physical education in the New World.

Physical Education in the United States

The Pilgrims arriving on the northeastern shores of North America in the early 1600s paid little attention to play or any form of physical education. Early New England colonies existed under the influence of the Puritans, who emphasized hard work and attention to the church. Although there is a long history of games among the Native Americans during this time (Carbarino 1976), early colonists often viewed play as a snare of the devil (Woody 1929).

As more immigrants arrived in the New World, new colonies developed and an increased focus on education, play, physical activity, and dance began to take root. Although physical education had not yet developed during the late 1600s and into the early 1700s, several people asserted a belief in the need for physical activity and physically educating colonial youth. Benjamin Franklin was one such early pioneer for physical education and physical activity for children (McKenzie 1936), and Thomas Jefferson reasserted that belief, expressing a need for physical exercise to be included in general education. Keep in mind, however, that these early educational beliefs and physical education concepts were developed, in large part, from the religious and conservative foundations of the time.

Early American Period: Mid-1700s to 1900

During the Early American period (mid- to late 1700s to 1900), which included the American Revolutionary War through the Civil War, the shaping of America was underway. Lewis and Clark began their exploration in 1804, and by the late 1820s, the Great Western Expansion and Reform had begun. Scores of wagon trains and pioneers began making their way west. The California gold rush of 1849 helped ignite the western push. Short-line rail systems began around the 1830s along eastern cities, and by the 1860s, the continental railroad system was completed, connecting the East and West Coasts. By the 1920s, Ford's Model T was a popular gas-powered automobile.

Also underway during the Early American period were situations not favorably discussed. While the country was expanding, the significant culture of Native Americans was being suppressed, including their traditions and forms of physical activity. By the 1830s, Native Americans had been erased from virtually all the territory between the Atlantic Ocean and the western border of Missouri (Gibson 1969). The vast history of dances and games of Southern slaves also was largely deleted from the development of physical education in the United States.

Nonetheless, American physical education was under construction. Physical training, or gymnastics, was the first step, introduced by both European immigrants and American-born citizens. Of the many physical education systems and programs evolving during this time, two prominent systems were derived from Europe: **German gymnastics** (the Turnverein: Old-country German Gymnastics Society) and **Swedish gymnastics**.

German System

German gymnastics keyed on developing strong, healthy men by implementing vigorous calisthenics with heavy hand weights and clubs, using apparatuses such as ropes, ladders, parallel and horizontal bars, rings, and poles for vaulting, and activities that worked on balance. Endurance activities such as marching, running, and swimming were also required. Music and rhythm (e.g., drumbeats) would accompany the strenuous exercises, which initially were conducted mainly outdoors (Leonard and McKenzie 1927).

The German, or Turner, system of gymnastics set the stage for physical education and became the prominent system in the development of physical education in the United States during the early 1800s, and in the mid-1880s in larger Midwestern towns inhabited by German immigrants (Van Dalen and Bennett 1971). Many pieces of equipment that were used for this system can still be found in school gymnasiums and playgrounds today, such as climbing ropes, balance beams, ladders and climbing apparatuses, rings, and dumbbells. This equipment allows children to explore their world in a way that aids in the development of strength and balance. One could argue that the German system was responsible for the initial construction of gymnasiums in this country, where equipment could be set up and used all year long.

Charles Follen, one of the early immigrant leaders of German gymnastics, taught German at Harvard College. Because gymnastics, or physical training, was not yet embraced at the college level, he organized German gymnastics activities for students, using campus lawns as his classroom. His program became so popular that eventually Harvard College offered Dr. Follen a vacant hall so he could conduct his activities indoors (Van Dalen and Bennett 1971). While at Harvard College, he was responsible for opening the first college gymnasium in the United States. Soon thereafter, other colleges took note, and outdoor and indoor gymnasiums were built on college campuses to accommodate physical training and gymnastic exercises. In 1826, Dr. Follen also was responsible for opening the first public gymnasium in Boston (Leonard and McKenzie 1927). In conjunction with the opening of the Boston Gymnasium, Francis Lieber, another German gymnastics leader, opened the first swimming school in the United States, where he also taught (Van Dalen and Bennett 1971). Because the German system was the system of choice for physical training early on, it became the system to challenge in later years, which indirectly ignited an array of research on physical training and the development of other systems and teacher training programs.

Pratt Gymnasium at Amherst College. This example of an early gymnasium is from 1884.
Photo courtesy of Amherst College

One other important leader of German gymnastics in the United States was Charles Beck. Considered the first teacher of physical education in the United States, he taught Latin and German gymnastics at the private Round Hill School in Massachusetts in 1823. Although it was becoming generally recognized that exercise (gymnastics) and games were important for the growth and well-being of children, the concept of physical education as part of a school's educational program was not yet accepted. For that reason, Charles Beck and the Round Hill School are considered an important first step in the history of physical education in the United States.

Swedish System

The Swedish system of the late 1880s was also popular during the early development of American physical education. Dr. Hartwig Nissen introduced the Swedish gymnastics system to the Boston schools and served as their director of physical training. He followed the original Swedish system, which included a more scientific and therapeutic approach to gymnastics (medical gymnastics) that focused on developing the heart and lungs through enhanced bodily movements and specific developmental movement patterns (Enebuske 1890). These systematic and well-defined movements progressed from easy to strenuous and were done on strict commands from the teacher. Body positions were maintained over a period of time until the teacher indicated a new position (see figure 1.1 on page 8). In addition to these body positions, the Swedish system also used apparatuses such as ladders, rings, and bars, and exercises were not done to music, as was common with the German system (Enebuske 1890). Perhaps the current command style of warm-up

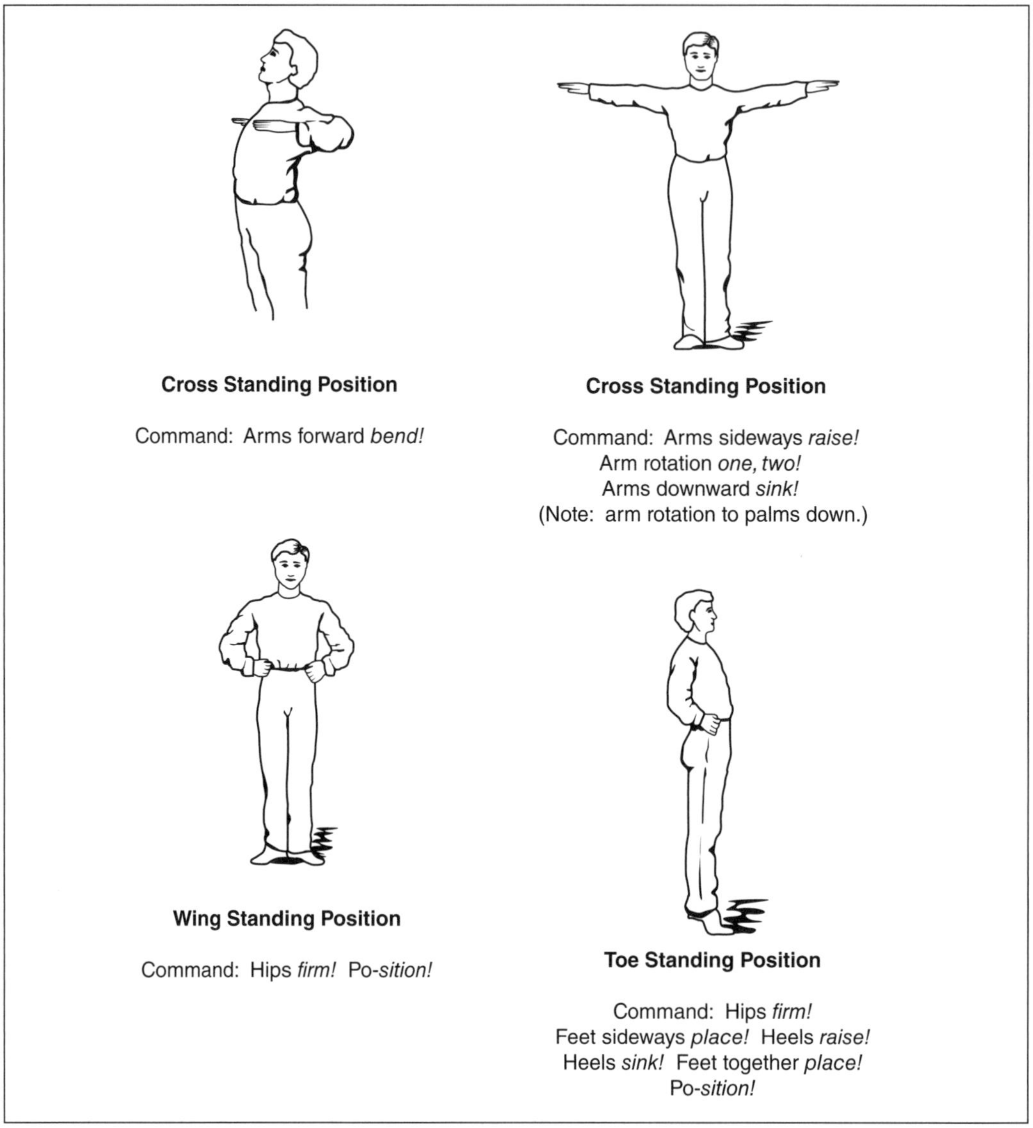

Cross Standing Position
Command: Arms forward *bend!*
Cross Standing Position
Command: Arms sideways *raise!*
Arm rotation *one, two!*
Arms downward *sink!*
(Note: arm rotation to palms down.)
Wing Standing Position
Command: Hips *firm!* Po-*sition!*
Toe Standing Position
Command: Hips *firm!*
Feet sideways *place!* Heels *raise!*
Heels *sink!* Feet together *place!*
Po-*sition!*

FIGURE 1.1 An example of teacher commands and body positions from *Progressive Gymnastic Day's Orders.*

From Enebuske 1890.

exercises, with a teacher or coach calling out the exercises and the count, evolved from the Swedish gymnastics system of the past.

In addition to Hartwig Nissen, several other people were responsible for developing the Swedish system in the United States. By 1890, Nils Posse was instrumental in leading instruction (teacher training) of Swedish gymnastics. He taught at the Boston Normal School of Gymnastics and started the Posse Normal School. At the time, **normal schools** were schools devoted to the training of teachers. These schools served an important role in the development of the training of physical education teachers. Those who wanted to teach went to normal schools to receive training. Eventually, normal schools became colleges or departments of physical education within colleges and universities across the country.

Amy Morris Homans also helped introduce the Swedish system to the Boston public schools. She directed the Normal School of Gymnastics, which later became the Department of Hygiene and Physical Education at Wellesley College. Many future physical educators received Swedish gymnastics training under Amy Morris Homans (Halsey 1961).

Did your college or university begin as a normal school?

Normal schools trained teachers in what was then called physical training, and those teachers then went and taught the program to children or adults. We follow a similar progression today: After taking an instructor training course in CPR or first aid from the American Red Cross or the American Heart Association, the person then teaches the content and skills to others. This is how early gymnastics systems of physical education were spread across the country.

Although the idea of a free, public education was growing during the Early American period, physical education in the public schools was slow to develop. It wasn't until 1866 that California passed a law requiring physical exercise as part of the school's program. By the 1880s, several larger cities had introduced physical education into their schools' programs, and by 1892, the state of Ohio required public schools to include physical education by law (Van Dalen and Bennett 1971). Currently, states may set minimum physical education requirements; however, it's usually up to local school districts within each state to determine specific physical education requirements. Currently, not all states require physical education in school programs (NASPE and AHA 2010).

American Gymnastics Systems and Influential People

American gymnastics systems were also beginning to influence the scope of physical education in the United States during the mid-1800s to early 1900s. Early on, however, the systems were mainly offered to men through private gymnasiums or schools. The North American Young Men's Christian Association (YMCA) was one successful private organization that provided gymnasiums and physical training, and helped develop the all-around man (Morse 1913). Central to the mission of the YMCA was the desire to better the environment of young men through a blend of religious influence and social and civic service to the community—specifically so they wouldn't brawl and carry on in local taverns. The YMCA in Boston began in 1851; by 1861, there were around 200 YMCAs across the country (Morse 1913). However, only 60 associations survived through the Civil War. The Young Women's Christian Association (YWCA) began in Boston in 1866 (Weston 1962).

Influential people of the Early American period began to make their mark on American systems of physical education, often modifying or adapting the German or Swedish systems.

Catharine Beecher

Catharine Beecher, an important American pioneer in physical education, modified the Swedish gymnastics system to create her own system. Her concerns about physical inactivity and the poor health of women and children drove her to develop and teach a less rigorous system of gymnastics that did not require extensive apparatuses or special rooms. At that time, it was not considered proper for girls and women to participate in any type of gymnastics or physical training. Beecher began to change that belief. She developed a system of calisthenics for girls that concentrated on performing beautiful and strong movements to music to help produce good posture, strength, and grace (Beecher 1867). Many of her exercises involved holding a body position for a period of time, similar to the isometric exercises of today (see figure 1.2 on page 10).

Catharine Beecher was adamant in her belief that daily calisthenics should be required for children and taught at every school. She wrote several books (*A Course*

FIGURE 1.2 Examples of Catharine Beecher's system of calisthenics.
From Beecher 1867.

of Calisthenics for Young Ladies and *Physiology and Calisthenics for Schools and Families*) that were widely distributed to the general population and helped foster a belief in the need for physical training in schools (Halsey 1961). By all accounts, Beecher could be considered the first women physical education leader in the United States (Goodsell 1931; Halsey 1961).

Dio Lewis

Another Early American leader in physical education was Dio Lewis. His "new gymnastics" was a combination of Beecher's calisthenics program and components of the Swedish system. His systematic program involved the use of handheld implements moved in a precise way according to the command of the teacher; the purpose of the exercises was to develop strength, flexibility, agility, and grace of movement (Lewis 1864). Exercises were performed to the rhythm of music or the beat of a drum in graceful and flowing repetitions to help increase heart rate.

Dio Lewis designed his own exercises (Leonard and McKenzie 1927), which involved the use of weighted beanbags, wooden rings, wands, dumbbells, and clubs (see figure 1.3 on page 12). His beanbag exercises are similar in concept to the medicine ball exercises used today. Wooden hand rings were used between partners as they pushed and pulled the rings against each other in various movements and patterns. A current stretching protocol that involves pushing and pulling with a partner is PNF (proprioceptive neuromuscular facilitation). The use of tubing or exercise bands is another example of a current exercise form that contracts muscles in a similar fashion to Lewis's ring exercises.

Lewis developed a series of exercises using 4-foot (1.2 m) wooden dowels (wands) to help improve flexibility in the upper and lower body. Wooden dowels are currently used in physical therapy settings and strength training facilities to improve flexibility and range of motion, especially for the shoulder. Lewis also believed that lighter wooden dumbbells (2 to5 lb, or 1 to 2.3 kg), lifted more often, were more beneficial than the heavy metal weights used in the German system. He believed that lifting lighter weight many times through a number of movements was better for the nerves and muscles than lifting heavy weights, and that it helped enhance accuracy and flexibility for daily labor and work (Lewis 1864). His concept is found in muscular endurance training in today's strength training programs.

Robert Roberts

One of Dio Lewis's students was Robert Roberts, MD. Roberts was particularly interested in applying the sciences of physiology, anatomy, and **hygiene** (health) to his work of physical training. In 1869, at the young age of 18, he began employment at the YMCA, where he eventually became the leading director for the North American YMCA and one of the pioneers of physical training in the United States. The YMCAs during this time were important avenues to develop moral, intellectual, and religious qualities in men through fitness and sports (Mechikoff and Estes 1993).

Roberts believed that everyone needed to make exercise part of a daily regimen; in other words, it was essential to form an exercise habit while young. His premise was that all exercises must be safe, short, easy, beneficial, and pleasing (Brink 1916). He sided with Dio Lewis and developed a training program that involved the use of lighter weight resistance. More importantly, Roberts made sure his program of strength training and stretching developed balance and symmetry in muscles and body parts to help counteract the cramped chest and slumping shoulders of men who lifted heavy weights to increase chest size.

The current training protocol of strengthening opposing muscles (e.g., include back extension exercises with abdominal crunches, add triceps extensions to biceps curls, and strengthen the hamstrings along with the quadriceps) to foster muscle symmetry and balance can be traced back to the ideals of the ancient Greeks and the instructions of Robert Roberts.

Robert Roberts also had a huge interest in the science of hygiene (health) and in exploring how to live a healthy life, which was a part of his physical training program (see figure 1.4 on page 13). In addition, his concept of including physical activity and health as part of a daily routine was an important component of his program that is currently recommended for children and adults today. Roberts was a significant leader of physical training in the United States and in the development of the YMCA in North America.

Edward Hitchcock

Edward Hitchcock, MD, was a prominent early leader in the development of physical education. He became the director of the Department of Hygiene and Physical

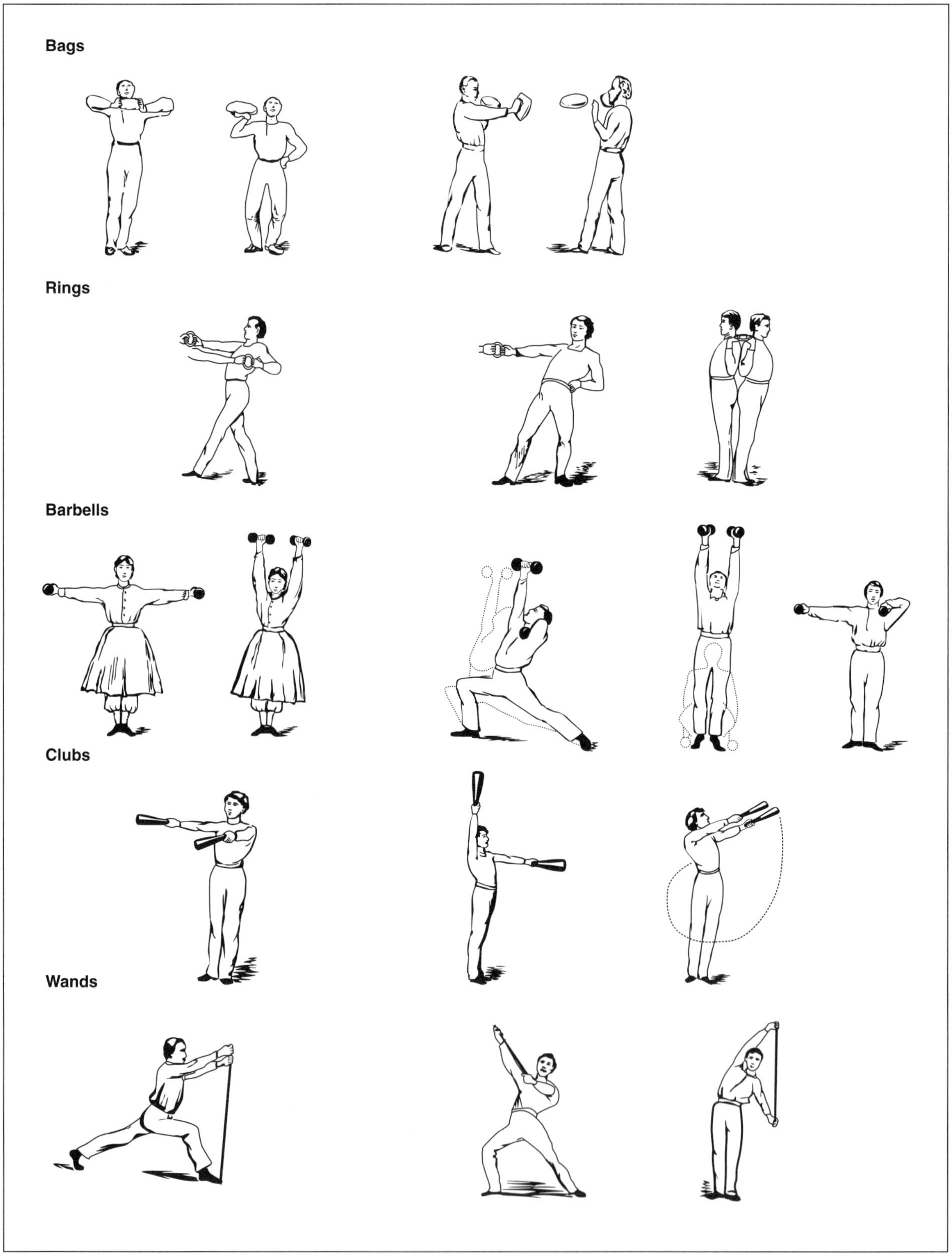

FIGURE 1.3 Sample exercises from *The New Gymnastics for Men, Women, and Children*.
From Lewis 1864.

FIGURE 1.4

Robert J. Roberts' Health Recommendations from the Late 19th Century

1. See that the body is in a sound and healthy condition.
2. Live on a wholesome, nourishing diet.
3. Give the system [the body] sufficient amount of rest in sleep at regular hours. Eight hours is usually sufficient.
4. Take exercise. Muscles grow in strength and size by using [them]. Begin moderately, never overdo.
5. Develop all parts symmetrically. Each will help the other. Stop exercise before feeling tired.
6. Use plenty of patience and perseverance. You can't change your form in a day.
7. Avoid all stimulants. There is nothing in them that builds up muscular tissue.
8. Bathe sufficiently after muscular exercise to remove perspiration. Take short cool baths.
9. Do not overeat; it only clogs the system.
10. Be pure in imagination, body, and practice.

From Brink 1916.

Culture at Amherst College in 1861, where he taught for over 50 years. This was the first such department in the United States. Hitchcock believed in a healthy mind and body so that one could maintain full activities of both daily duties and college life, in addition to living a longer life (Leonard 1915). Along with running, light gymnastics exercises were included to enhance personal hygiene. These activities were required of his students four days per week.

Do you see any comparisons in figure 1.4 to what are considered to be the qualities of leading a healthy life today?

To develop a personalized hygiene program for each student, he used his scientific background as a medical doctor to collect **anthropometric measurements** on his students: height, weight, girth of the chest and arms, and strength of the upper arms (Leonard and McKenzie 1927). He would record preliminary measurements, prescribe exercises, and gather post measurements at the end of the term to determine whether students improved. Hitchcock's measurement system was the foundation for what other leaders began using in their systems. Currently, most physical education teachers administer various tests to determine whether their students are improving in health-related fitness components or reaching personal fitness goals, such as getting faster or becoming stronger.

Dudley Sargent, MD, 1849-1924.

Courtesy of the Library of Congress

Dudley Sargent

Perhaps the most influential leader of the Early American period was Dudley Sargent, MD. He believed his eclectic system afforded the well-rounded development of muscular, respiratory, and circulatory functions. His program emphasized hygiene as an important component of physical education and included education, recreation, and individual remedial or corrective measures (Bennett 1984). In addition to collecting anthropometric data on his students, he also modified and developed exercise machines that could accommodate people comfortably and safely. Some of his equipment used pulley systems to lift or pull weights (Sargent 1927). The strength training machines found in weight rooms across the country today were based, in part, on the devices he developed.

Dudley Sargent became the assistant professor of physical training and director of the Hemenway Gymnasium at Harvard College in 1879. This was an important appointment at the time, because the rank of assistant professor with faculty status in the area of physical education was very uncommon. Scholars at Harvard did not consider the area of physical training an academic subject worthy of the efforts of an educated man (Sargent 1927). Throughout his professional career, Sargent fought to raise physical education to a standard equal to other subject areas in the college curriculum (Bennett 1984). His status at the university level was critical in the development of physical education as an accepted academic discipline in colleges and universities across the United States. To this day, physical education still struggles to maintain a high level of acceptance as an important academic discipline in both public school curricula and institutions of higher learning.

According to Sargent, his most outstanding accomplishment was the creation of the Harvard Summer School for Physical Education (training school for teachers), which began in 1887 (Sargent 1900). Even though he taught at Harvard College, his summer school was independent of the college; course credit for physical training at Harvard College was not recognized at the time. Because Sargent offered his program during the summer, he was able to attract and train people from across the United States, many of whom became leading physical educators of their time.

Delphine Hanna

One final notable early leader in physical education was Delphine Hanna, MD. She also used her medical background to enhance physical education, both as a teacher in the public schools and at the university level. Beginning in 1885, she taught and prepared physical education teachers at Oberlin College in Ohio. During her 35-year tenure, she was responsible for creating the first college-level teacher preparation program in physical education for credit in the United States. By1900, Oberlin College offered a two-year certificate in physical education, with a bachelor's degree available in another field; this eventually led to a major in physical education. Dr. Hanna and Oberlin College set the stage for future collegiate degrees in physical education. Similar to Edward Hitchcock, she used scientific principles including anthropometric measurement and corrective procedures as part of her program, the first women to do so (Secretary, Department of Physical Education for Women, Oberlin College 1941).

In 1903, Hanna became the first woman to be appointed to the rank of full professor of physical education. This was a huge feat at that time, because the profession was dominated by men. Hanna broke the barrier into a male-dominated profession and paved the way for future female physical educators at the university level. Many future leaders in physical education graduated from her program, including Drs. Thomas Wood (page 17) and Luther Gulick (page 18) and will be discussed later.

Some of the early physical training programs for women in the late nineteenth century involved performing exercises in "squad lines," or structured rows.

Courtesy of the Library of Congress

Important Events

Two important conferences that had a tremendous impact on the future of physical education occurred during the Early American period: the Adelphi and Boston conferences. In 1885, Dr. William Anderson organized a meeting of leading physical directors at Adelphi University in Brooklyn. The current American Alliance for Health, Physical Education, Recreation and Dance (AAHPERD) was born at that meeting, first named the Association for the Advancement of Physical Education (AAPE). Edward Hitchcock was elected its first president. Table 1.1 on page 16 shows how the name of the national association has changed over time.

The other conference occurred in Boston in 1889. Speakers at the conference included many medical doctors and professionals from the various systems of gymnastics, physical training, and calisthenics to discuss the scope and purpose of physical education. Because of the controversy over what system was best to use, central to Dudley Sargent's message at the conference was that the type of gymnastics system used was not most important; rather, people should first think about the results they wanted to accomplish, and then select activities, techniques, and methods to reach those results (Sargent 1927). That comment by Sargent and the proceedings of the conference marked a critical turning point in American physical education.

Summary of the Early American Period

Clearly, the beginning of physical education in the United States involved various physical training systems. These early systems were developed by medical doctors—leaders in the field—who used their background in anatomy and physiology to improve physical training and health for youth and adults. To train teachers in

Table 1.1 Name Changes to the National Association

1885	Association for the Advancement of Physical Education (AAPE)
1886	American Association for the Advancement of Physical Education (AAAPE)
1903	American Physical Education Association (APEA)
1937	American Association for Health and Physical Education AAHPE)
1938	American Association for Health, Physical Education and Recreation (AAHPER)
1974	American Alliance for Health, Physical Education and Recreation
1979	American Alliance for Health, Physical Education, Recreation and Dance (AAHPERD)

the specifics of certain systems of gymnastics, normal or training schools were developed specifically for each system. Finally, leaders in physical education began to see the importance of testing their students to see whether they were improving, and then prescribing corrective exercises if the outcomes were not acceptable. Physical education was becoming less of a training regimen for the masses and more of a way to help improve the health and fitness of individuals.

Early 20th Century: 1900 to 1930

The early 20th century spanned the time from the beginning of the century to 1930. World War I (1914-1918), along with the decreasing physical demands of work for most Americans, had an immense impact on the development of physical education. During this period, it was apparent that a need existed to address the unfit state of America's youth and military, especially after World War I. Experts called for requiring physical training, or physical education, in all school education programs to help enhance youth fitness levels; however, they were not clear about the direction physical education should take. Some physical educators continued to follow traditional German, Swedish, or hybrid systems, while others thought physical education should emphasize military training. In addition, a growing group of physical education programs adopted a sport, games, and dance focus, or a new theme called **new physical education.**

The new physical education paralleled the social educational philosophy of the time. John Dewey's influence on social education, often called progressive education, stressed the importance of social reform by following a child-centered educational approach, allowing children to learn from doing and experiencing life. Helping children learn through sports, games, and play was an important component of progressive education, and by extension, the new physical education.

This new program in physical education focused on more than just training the physical body; it also helped to develop the whole person (mind and body) within the values of education (Freeman 2001). Whereas the old systems educated only the physical, the new physical education educated *through* the physical—developing the spirit, mind, and body through a physical education program (Halsey 1961). Physical education began to be seen as more than just performing gymnastics or calisthenics.

Influential Leaders

The pioneer leaders of the new physical education included Thomas Wood, Clark Hetherington, and Mabel Lee, among others. Although many leaders of this era were prodigies of Delphine Hanna, each made his or her own mark on the continued development of physical education and future leaders of the profession.

Thomas Wood

Thomas Wood, MD, was the root of the new physical education with his program called natural gymnastics. This new form of gymnastics centered on the concept that planned movement not only helped improve strength and endurance, but also enhanced the physical skills useful in play and sports (LaSalle 1951), which contributed to the life, environment, and culture of each person (Van Dalen and Bennett 1971).

Clark Hetherington

Clark Hetherington was a student under Thomas Wood while at Stanford University and became a huge promoter of natural gymnastics. His holistic conception of the new physical education contributed to an understanding of the overall education process. Specifically, he believed physical education should address four areas: (1) *organic*—the development of vital organs through muscular training and high nutrition; (2) *psychomotor*—the enhancement of the neuromuscular system for power and skillful movements; (3) *character*—the development of social and spiritual powers; and (4) *intellectual*—the enhancement of natural incentives to learn (Hetherington 1910). His concepts were the cornerstone for the new physical education and are very similar to the domains of learning in physical education that we accept today (see chapter 2).

Mabel Lee

Although physical activity and sport for women were becoming more socially accepted during this time, many still believed that exercise and physical education were not needed by, nor were they appropriate for, females. While teaching at the University of Nebraska in the late 1920s, Mabel Lee, PhD, was faced with the all-too-common belief that physical education was not only a nonessential and trivial part of education, but also a great nuisance imposed on students (Lee 1978). She was up against such attitudes from the school's health center, area physicians, the local community, and even women themselves. She received daily student pleas and doctors' notes excusing "apple-polishing" female students from participating in physical activity (Lee 1978). Lee relentlessly battled for physical education by using statistics that demonstrated the horribly unfit status of University of Nebraska women. Gradually, with her persistence, she was able to cut down the number of excuse slips and transformed attitudes about the importance of exercise and physical education for females.

> Notes excusing students from physical education class continue to be a problem in physical education today. How might you handle excuse notes when you become a physical education teacher?

Changes and Movements Affecting Physical Education

Other major changes and movements that were occurring during the early 20th century also had an effect on American physical education. Because more states were passing legislation requiring physical education to be included in curricula, more teachers were needed to fill those positions. As a result, more four-year degrees were offered in teacher training schools at various colleges and universities, with physical education credits being counted toward graduation (Leonard and McKenzie 1927). The content in teacher training programs became more consistent as well. Not only were students taught about the various systems, depending on the direc-

Luther Gulick, MD, 1865-1918.

Courtesy of the Library of Congress

tors of those school programs, but they were also taught about age-level development and scientific measurements of posture, motor performance, and cardiorespiratory fitness. All in all, programs were beginning to train teachers in more than just physical training.

During this period, progressive movements in recreation, playgrounds, and health, as well as the huge popularity of sports, also influenced physical education programs. Luther Gulick, MD, was an influential leader in recreational activities and sports. His passion was the enrichment of human life through play (Nash 1960). He was a strong advocate for after-school play and recreation areas for children, as well as after-school athletic leagues, especially for boys and men (Gulick 1920). He believed that both recreation and exercise must be socialized into the public arena to encourage all people to use school and public facilities. His energy and enthusiastic direction helped in the development of recreational pursuits, including camping and outdoor educational programs. He established many organizations such as the Playground Association of America, the Boy Scouts of America, and the Camp Fire Girls, and helped develop physical education within YMCAs (Nash 1960).

Summary of the Early 20th Century

Overall, the early 20th century was a time when traditional systems of gymnastics were tested; sports, games, and dance were added to programs. New systems of physical education were developed, and scientific studies of physical training conducted on men and women were informing the future development and improvement of physical education.

Mid-20th Century: 1930 to 1970

The stock market collapse of 1929, the Great Depression that followed, and the beginning of World War II (1941) mark the early part of this era, and the start of the Cold War (1945) and the civil rights movement (1954) round out the mid-20 century (1930-1960s). The poor economic conditions of the Depression affected physical education programs across the country to some degree. Some programs were cut because physical education was not considered an important subject area. This perception changed somewhat during and after World War II, when once more the nation was faced with the realization that a good portion of America's military personnel and recruits were unfit.

Not only were young men in the armed forces unfit, but also, school-aged children failed to meet even a minimum standard of muscular fitness, especially when compared to European children using the results from the Kraus-Weber tests (Kraus and Hirschland 1953). These simple abdominal, low back, and hamstring tests determined whether children had sufficient strength and flexibility to withstand the daily demands of normal living. As a result of these poor scores, Kraus and Hirschland (1954) urged that physical activities for children be increased and regular intervals of muscle testing be given. Physical education again became the vehicle to help enhance the physical fitness levels of American's youth, thus improving its status and role in school programs.

> Do you think the present goals of physical education are similar to the physical fitness emphases of the mid-20th century?

Disturbing evidence of poor fitness among military personnel and school-aged children prompted President Eisenhower to establish a President's Council on Youth Fitness in 1956. In addition, AAHPER responded and developed the Youth Fitness Tests in 1957, which included pull-ups and modified pull-ups, straight-leg sit-ups, the shuttle run, the 600-yard run/walk, the 50-yard dash, the standing broad jump, and the softball throw for distance. Physical education teachers across the United States administered these tests to assess the physical fitness status of American youth. To date, fitness testing has remained a part of most physical education programs across the country.

The urgency to improve physical fitness lasted only a short while; near the end of this era, children were again found to be in poor physical condition (Halsey 1961). President Kennedy continued to stress the importance of national fitness. This led to the establishment of another fitness testing program by President Lyndon Johnson in 1966, the President's Physical Fitness Award program. Students aged 10 to 17 who earned top-scoring performances in various fitness tests earned a President's Physical Fitness patch. To date, the Fitnessgram (Cooper Institute 2010) and the President's Challenge (www.presidentschallenge.org) are the two most common fitness programs used in schools nationwide (Morrow et al. 2009).

Trends

The latter part of the 1950s and the 1960s saw an increase in leisure time. Sports, lifetime, and recreational activities became more visibly appealing to Americans. Following in Luther Gulick's footsteps, Jay Nash, PhD, became an influential leader in outdoor education and recreation during this time. Many parks, playing fields, bowling alleys, golf courses, and swimming pools were being constructed across the United States. Camps, including summer, youth, day, sport, outdoor, and school camps, became popular as well (Lee 1983).

Physical education programs were also beginning to include more sports, games, and lifetime movement activities, such as dance, swimming, camping and hiking, golf, and bowling. In addition, other activities were included to help improve body mechanics: stunts, games, and gymnastics apparatuses (e.g., trampolines, tumbling mats, uneven bars, high beams). In the 1960s, calisthenics (e.g., jumping jacks and toe-touches) became a common addition to physical education programs to enhance physical fitness, because many believed that lifetime activities did not adequately address students' lack of fitness (Siedentop 2009).

High school students taking part in a rope drill at camp. Safety regulations and exercise practices certainly have changed since 1952!

Fred Morley/Fox Photos/Getty Images

Physical education was initially exposed to another concept during this era, that of **movement education.** Dr. Rosalind Cassidy, EdD, continued the work of Clark Hetherington early on in her career; however, in 1947 she joined the staff at UCLA where she became a leading advocate for movement education and was considered by many to be an expert in the science of movement principles for children and youth (Van Dalen and Bennett 1971). Movement education became popular during the 1960s and 1970s and is still used today by many who teach physical education at the elementary level.

Finally, one more trend was beginning to take shape during this era. A steady increase in physical education research was occurring at colleges and universities across the United States. Charles McCloy, PhD, a recognized research professor in physical education (McCloy 1930), strongly believed that physical education should be advanced through research. This research not only enhanced the status of physical education in higher education, but was also responsible for changing the face of the discipline.

Summary of the Mid-20th Century

On the whole, many movements and trends affected physical education during the mid-20th century (1930-1960s), including sports, dance, and lifetime and recreational activities. An instructional trend was also occurring at universities across the United States. A majority of leaders in the field during this era were receiving advanced degrees in physical education (e.g., PhDs and EdDs) instead of medical degrees. Physical education teaching requirements in colleges and universities throughout the country also became more advanced during this time (Van Dalen and Bennett 1971). In addition, there was a growing desire to help the then-termed handicapped and mentally retarded children in the public schools, although no formal school mandate had yet been declared. Finally, research on physical fitness and movement expanded, significantly affecting the growth of the profession in the decades to follow. Table 1.2 provides a summary of the early leaders who helped develop physical education in the United States.

Late 20th Century: 1970 to 2000

The 1970s to the end of the century was a period of vast growth and change in physical education. During the early 1970s, education across the United States drifted away from required course work and began to give students more freedom to select classes of interest. Although the importance and benefits of physical activity were known, many believed that physical education should not be a required content area of the curriculum (Freeman 2001). By 1980, however, pressure to hold teachers and schools more accountable for content and student learning was taking hold. A reformation back to required courses, accountability, and standards was in process.

Development of National Standards

In response to the growing concern over content standards and accountability, NASPE (National Association for Sport and Physical Education, an association of AAHPERD) created a task force in 1986 to develop a definition of what physically educated students should know and be able to do. This definition centered on five major areas and was used to help create physical education content standards (see figure 1.5 on page 22). In 1995, NASPE published the second edition of *Moving Into the Future: National Standards for Physical Education,* which delineated six standards (see chapter 2) for states and school districts.

Table 1.2 Early Leaders in the History of American Physical Education

Leaders	Main contributions
	GERMAN GYMNASTICS SYSTEM
Dr. Charles Beck (1798-1866)	First known teacher of physical education; taught at Round Hill School in Massachusetts, 1823
Dr. Charles Follen (1796-1840)	Opened first American college gymnasium at Harvard College; opened first American public gymnasium in Boston
Dr. Francis Lieber (1800-1872)	Opened first American swimming school in Boston
	SWEDISH GYMNASTICS SYSTEM
Dr. Hartwig Nissen (1856-1924)	Introduced Swedish gymnastics in 1883; director of physical training in Boston
Nils Posse (1862-1895)	Leader in Swedish gymnastics teacher training
Amy Morris Homan (1848-1933)	Directed Normal School of Gymnastics
	AMERICAN GYMNASTIC SYSTEMS
Catharine Beecher (1800-1878)	Developed calisthenics for girls and women (and boys)
Dio Lewis, MD (1823-1888)	Developed his light system of calisthenics using many handheld implements
Edward Hitchcock, MD (1828-1911)	Emphasized personal hygiene and began anthropometric measurements; first president of AAPE in 1885
Dudley Sargent, MD (1849-1924)	Director of Harvard Summer School; emphasized light gymnastics and personal hygiene; advanced anthropometric measurements for men; used corrective, remedial measures; president of AAPE in 1890 and 1892
Robert Roberts, MD (1849-1920)	Leading YMCA director and leader of physical training
William Anderson, MD (1860-1947)	Initiated first meeting in 1885 that began the national association; taught at teacher training schools of physical education; president of AAPE in 1887
Delphine Hanna, MD (1854-1941)	Developed first college physical education teaching program for credit at Oberlin College; developed anthropometric measurement for women; became first woman to achieve professor rank
Luther Gulick, MD (1865-1918)	Leader in play, recreational activities, and the YMCA; founder of many associations; president of APEA in 1903
Thomas Wood, MD (1865-1951)	Developed natural gymnastics (the new physical education)
R. Tait McKenzie, MD (1867-1938)	Leader of the playground movement; international advocate; surgeon and famous sculptor; president of APEA in 1912
Clark Hetherington (1870-1942)	Promoter of the new physical; established the four initial processes for physical education (organic, psychomotor, character, and intellectual)
Jay Nash, PhD (1886-1965)	Promoter of the new physical education; leader in the playground and recreational movement; president of AAHPE in 1942
Rosalind Cassidy, EdD (1890-1980)	Promoter of the new physical education; initial work on movement education
Charles McCloy, PhD (1886-1959)	Researcher (measurement in motor skills, movement, and fitness); president of AAHPE in 1937
Mabel Lee, PhD (1886-1985)	Advanced physical education and sports for women; president of APEA in 1931
Dorothy Ainsworth, PhD (1894-1976)	International advocate for physical education and sports for girls and women; president of AAHPER in 1950
Eleanor Metheny, PhD (1908-1982)	Leader of movement education

FIGURE 1.5

NASPE's Definition of a Physically Educated Person

HAS learned skills necessary to perform a variety of physical activities;
KNOWS the implications of and the benefits from involvement in physical activities;
DOES participate in physical activity;
IS physically fit;
VALUES physical activity and its contribution to a healthful lifestyle.

NAPSE 1995.

Academic Shift

Departments of physical education at colleges and universities were beginning to change during this time, as was the overall discipline of physical education. Thus far, departments of physical education existed to help train and prepare future physical education teachers (an applied focus). However, because of the magnitude of scientific research from departments of physical education during the 1950s and 1960s, a trend was beginning to emerge. A wealth of research was being published on exercise-related topics as well as other areas such as motor learning and motor development, tests and measurements, and the psychology of sport. Gradually, departments of physical education were becoming more academic in focus and less applied (Henry 1964).

This academic content shift resulted in the development and growth of specialized undergraduate and graduate programs within departments of physical education such as exercise physiology, biomechanics, motor learning, motor control, health, sport psychology and sociology, and sport history (Siedentop 2009). These academic subdisciplines didn't really fit under the traditional term of *physical education*. Consequently, some departments of physical education fractured, or split, and many departments (and related organizations) began changing their names during the 1990s to reflect the more global and academic scope of the field. In addition, these name changes were made to make departments appear more respectable in the eyes of academia and grant-funding entities. *Department of kinesiology, department of exercise and human movement,* and *department of exercise science* are just a few of names of these departments at colleges and universities today as a result of this shift.

In 1974, the American Alliance of Health, Physical Education and Recreation (AAHPER) also changed its name from *American Association* to *American Alliance* to better reflect the emerging academic subdiscipline areas. The restructuring of AAHPER was done to maintain the global, or umbrella, term of *physical education* and reduce the splintering of the developing subdisciplines into their own groups and organizations (Siedentop 2009), with dance being formally added in 1979. Currently, AAHPERD is an alliance of five national associations and publishes a variety of annual and quarterly academic and applied journals (see table 1.3).

Did the name of your department change as a result of the discipline shift during the late 20th century? If so, what effect did it have on program offerings (majors and minors)?

Table 1.3 AAHPERD Associations and Journals

AAHPERD associations	
AAHE	American Association for Health Education
AAPAR	American Association for Physical Activity and Recreation
NAGWS	National Association for Girls and Women in Sport
NASPE	National Association for Sport and Physical Education
NDA	National Dance Association
AAHPERD journals	
AJHE	*American Journal of Health Education*
JOPERD	*Journal of Physical Education, Recreation and Dance*
MPEES	*Measurement in Physical Education and Exercise Science*
RQES	*Research Quarterly for Exercise and Sport*
	Sports Management Education Journal
	Strategies: A Journal for Physical and Sport Educators
IEJHE	*The International Electronic Journal of Health Education*
	The Journal of Coaching Education
WSPAJ	*Women in Sport and Physical Activity Journal*

Development of Instructional Models

Although the content of physical education has remained relatively consistent during the last half century, new teaching approaches and an emphasis on fitness became apparent during the latter part of this period. Actually, many of the models described in the following sections are still being used by physical educators today.

Movement Education

As previously mentioned, movement education had its beginnings in the 1950s under Rosalind Cassidy. It became popular in the 1960s and 1970s under the leadership of Eleanor Metheny, PhD, who taught at the University of Southern California for 29 years and believed that physical education was a tool to help enhance movement through which children could express, explore, develop, and interpret their world (Metheny 1954). Movement education helps elementary-aged children develop and refine fundamental movement patterns, such as running, hopping, skipping, throwing, catching, and kicking by allowing them to practice these skills using various patterns of locomotion (i.e., curved, straight, or zigzag pathways), or by performing skills using varying degrees of force (i.e., soft to hard) or elements of time (i.e., slow to fast). These movement concepts are intertwined with fundamental skills when presented to children.

Humanistic Model

The individualized, or humanistic, model popular during the 1960s and 1970s allowed students to be part of the teaching–learning act (Heitmann and Kneer 1976). Instruction was individualized, allowing each person to develop his or her own uniqueness. Students became more responsible for what and how they learned. This model was not the traditional one-size-fits-all method of teaching; rather, it accommodated each student individually within a class setting. This model reflects the current student-directed teaching style of Mosston and Ashworth (2002), which places the teacher as a guide and the student as the self-educator.

Concepts-Based Model

The focus of the **concepts-based model** is to help students learn about content and the concepts of moving (the "whys") while participating in physical activities. Content from the subdisciplines in physical education (e.g., exercise physiology, biomechanics, motor learning and development, sport psychology, history) are used to help students learn concepts while they participate in a variety of activities (Mohnsen 2003). For example, the concept of force production may be the focus in softball, golf, or tumbling, whereas the concept of energy production could be the focus in physical fitness and conditioning activities. Initially presented in 1981, the *Basic Stuff Series I* and *II* provided teachers with a conceptual approach to teaching physical education (AAHPERD 1981, 1987).

Responsibility Model

During the 1980s, the **responsibility model** was introduced, followed by the more current social and personal responsibility model (Hellison 2003). Don Hellison, PhD, developed this framework to enhance the personal and social skills of students, especially at-risk and troubled students. His model delineates a series of responsibility levels for students to attain, such as learning to respect others by being in control of their own emotions and behavior, demonstrating a willingness to try to practice during class, being able to work independent of the teacher, and being able to help others.

Sport Education Model

The **sport education model** (Siedentop 1994; Siedentop, Hastie, and van der Mars 2004) became popular in the 1990s. The model provides students with an opportunity to experience the multifaceted aspects of sports. Within the model, students develop skills and learn how to play the game while being members of a team. Each group determines its team name and affiliation, and designates team roles such as coach, equipment manager, sport information director, conditioning coach, and other duties found among sport teams. Under the guidance of the teacher, teams develop their own practice plans, scrimmage, and compete in preseason, in-season, and postseason play, followed by an end-of-the-season (unit) celebration.

Modifying the rules or equipment of traditional team sports can help kids develop and hone skills.

Tactical Games Approach

During the latter 1990s, the **tactical games approach**, or teaching games for understanding (Griffin, Mitchell, and Oslin 1997; Werner, Thorpe, and Bunker 1996), became popular. This model focuses on helping students understand the tactics, or strategies, of how to play the game, more so than the physical skills needed for playing the game. Students are exposed to lead-up and modified games that help them understand tactical concepts such as how to get open to receive a pass, creating space as an offensive strategy, and placing an object to obtain a scoring advantage.

Cooperative Approaches

Other models, or approaches, to teaching physical education that came into being during the 1990s included cooperative games and group initiative activities involving problem-solving games and trust-building activities. These activities often accompanied the growing popularity of ropes courses, climbing walls, and outdoor adventure education programs, which have become accepted components of physical education.

Fitness Education Model

Last, but not least, is the **fitness education model**. During the latter 20th century, physical fitness was once again an important national issue as people recognized the need to increase the physical activity levels of children. More specifically, the promotion of cardiorespiratory fitness was identified as a public health objective (Simons-Morton et al. 1987). Although it was important to enhance the cardiorespiratory fitness of children and adolescents, it was becoming more important to promote all aspects of health-related fitness (cardiorespiratory fitness, muscular strength and endurance, flexibility, and body composition) by teaching various physical activities.

The generic fitness education model was developed to focus on improving health-related physical fitness components, along with fitness knowledge (Jewett, Bain, and Ennis 1995). In this model, physical education teachers select activities that will help students develop and improve their personal fitness levels. Some fitness models also integrate performance- or skill-related fitness components (balance, speed, agility, coordination, power), whereas others add health and wellness content.

Traversing walls, where you climb horizontally rather than vertically, helps develop teamwork and problem-solving skills along with strength and coordination.

Physical Fitness and Physical Activity Programs

In addition to the fitness education model, many other fitness-based and physical activity programs were established during this time. By following a concepts-based model, Dr. Charles Corbin developed a fitness–concepts approach called Fitness for Life. The model was based on the importance of not only helping students improve their health-related fitness levels, but also teaching them about the facts of exercise and how to evaluate personal levels of fitness, plan personal exercise programs, and become good fitness and exercise consumers (Corbin 1987). Currently, many schools across the country use Fitness for Life (Corbin and Lindsey 2007).

Another program that was developed near the end of the 20th century was PE4Life, founded in 2000. Phil Lawler's mission was to develop a program that inspired active, healthy living by advancing the development of daily health- and wellness-based physical education programs for all children (www.PE4life.org). He termed his program the new PE, because he recognized that the old sport skills, games, and athletic performance curricula did not address the physical activity needs of all students.

One other program developed during this time, SPARK (Sports, Play, and Active Recreation for Kids; www.sparkpe.org), is a research-based organization focused on combating the low levels of physical activity and fitness of children. Initially, SPARK was an evidenced-based elementary physical education program. In other words, research was used to demonstrate the effectiveness of SPARK. Their programs now include middle and high school, as well as after-school and early childhood programs (McKenzie, Sallis, and Rosengard 2009). Its function is to help improve the physical activity levels, fitness, and health of children by disseminating current information to teachers, school districts, and others who educate students in physical education settings.

Fitness Testing

In addition to the development of various fitness education models and programs, extensive changes in physical fitness testing occurred during the latter half of the 20th century. These changes were initiated in 1977 by a computerized fitness report card developed by Charles Sterling and used in a Texas school system. The Cooper Institute for Aerobic Research (Dallas, Texas) further developed the software program, and by 1991, Fitnessgram emerged (Plowman et al. 2006). Through the sponsorship of the Campbell Soup Company, Fitnessgram was piloted from 1982 to 1984. Physical education teachers used AAHPERD's youth fitness tests (described earlier) as the test battery and recorded scores using the Fitnessgram program. By 1985, Fitnessgram was marketed nationwide. Prudential Insurance took over sponsorship from 1991 to 1997, and in 1999, AAHPERD, in agreement with Human Kinetics, became the publisher for Fitnessgram and its testing manual.

From 1958 to 1974, very little was done to change the norm-referenced fitness tests used by teachers across the country, such as AAHPERD's Youth Fitness Tests and the Presidential Physical Fitness Tests (Plowman et al. 2006). These tests were based on percentiles and norm-referenced standards, and many physical educators did not favor using percentiles to demonstrate whether fitness levels were reached. In addition, the types of fitness tests and awards system were also in question. As a result of the dissatisfaction with the fitness tests, changes began to take place. Based on years of extensive work, in 1987 Fitnessgram developed its own set of criterion-referenced fitness tests, standards, and an awards program called Physical Best, through AAHPERD (Plowman et al. 2006). By 1992 Physical Best broadened the cutoff scores for the various fitness tests to include the currently used healthy fitness zones. Fitness scores that fall within the zones represent a health-enhancing level of fitness. Some of the fitness tests currently found in Fitnessgram (Cooper

Institute 2010) include the mile run, PACER, the 1-mile walk, curl-ups, push-ups, trunk lifts, and the back-saver sit-and-reach (see chapter 9 for more information).

The Presidential Physical Fitness Tests of the 1960s also changed during this time, as did the battery of fitness tests for the President's Challenge (www.presidentschallenge.org). It now includes several levels of physical fitness awards based on norm- and criterion-referenced standards.

Mandates

Several laws passed during this period changed the course of physical education. The growing concerns about accessibility for the handicapped during the 1950s and 1960s led the way to official action during the latter 20th century. Public Law 94-142, or the Education for All Handicapped Children Act (EAHCA), passed in 1975, mandated that free and appropriate public education be available for all handicapped children. Handicapped children were mainstreamed, or placed into regular classrooms that previously did not have disabled children. This mandate created initial challenges, because physical education teachers at that time had no knowledge of or preparation for dealing with students with disabilities in a regular physical education setting.

By 1990 the **Individuals With Disabilities Education Act (IDEA)** changed the terminology to include all people with disabilities instead of just handicapped children, and the law required that students with disabilities be placed in the least restrictive environment. This meant that students were required to be placed in

It is imperative that teachers learn to adapt situations and modify rules to make all PE activities as inclusive as possible. It may take a little creative thinking, but in the end, inclusion is beneficial for everyone.

regular classrooms unless the goals and objectives outlined in their individualized education programs (IEPs) were not being achieved. To date, many physical educators still believe that **PETE** (physical education teacher education) programs do not include enough adapted physical education preparation to adequately prepare teachers to successfully teach within an inclusive gymnasium.

Another law was mandated during the early 1970s that had a tremendous impact on physical education and sports. **Title IX** (a part of the Education Amendments of 1972) mandated equal sport and physical education opportunities for females in all institutions receiving federal aid. Prior to this law, girls and women did not have equal access to such things as sporting equipment, facilities, instruction, and activities. In regards to physical education, this law generally meant that there needed to be equal access to all course offerings, and that physical education classes could not be conducted separately, solely on the basis of sex (i.e., single-sex classes).

Although the intentions of Title IX were encouraging, misinterpretations of the law by many administrators caused a great deal of harm to physical education programs (Lee 1983). For example, many of the previously separate physical education departments for men and women were joined, and more often than not, the newly formed departments were headed by men. In addition, some of the smaller schools that had limited equipment and facility space could not accommodate both men and women together and ended up dropping physical education programs altogether (Lee 1983).

A further misinterpretation by physical education administrators was that all physical education classes now had to combine both girls and boys (i.e., coed classes). According to Title IX, however, students may be separated according to gender in certain situations, including participation in contact sports such as wrestling, boxing, rugby, ice hockey, football, basketball, and other activities involving bodily contact. Students may also be grouped by gender for classes on human sexuality (Blaufarb 1976).

Within a coed class, teachers cannot split the class into boys and girls when teaching noncontact activities; however, students may be grouped by the ability of individual performances. As an example, a teacher can group a class by skill level (i.e., beginner, advanced) as part of a learning task whereby the groups could include any number of boys and girls. Finally, teachers cannot use one standard test of skill or progress for the entire class if it has an adverse effect on members of one sex (Blaufarb 1976). If, for example, a test clearly has an advantage for boys (e.g., tests strength), the teacher would have to either find a different test compatible for both sexes or find a similar test for girls.

One final mandate, which occurred in 1991, has had an enormous impact on physical education. As part of the standards-based education movement of the 1980s, the U.S. federal government became involved and mandated **No Child Left Behind (NCLB)**. This law affected kindergarten through high school grade levels and held schools and teachers more accountable for helping students learn. In part, schools were required to show improvement in test scores in core academic subjects including English, reading, language arts, math, science, foreign languages, civics and government, economics, arts, history, and geography (NCLB 1991). To date, physical education is not part of the core academic subjects of NCLB. Because physical education is not included as a core academic subject, this law, alongside emerging issues and trends, has created challenges for physical education in the new millennium. As school districts struggle to raise academic test scores in the core classes, many physical education programs have been reduced or eliminated to allow more time to teach within the core subject areas.

Summary of the Late 20th Century

The latter half of the 20th century was a period that expanded the discipline of physical education into many subdiscipline areas of study. Along with that transformation came more global, or inclusive, name changes to many departments of physical education, resulting in the collapse of some departments. Name changes also prompted many organizations that had *physical education* in the title to change as well. Many teaching models became prevalent during this time, which provided more variety in presenting physical education content to students. Finally, the three main federal mandates to education of this period had a huge impact on physical education.

Early 21st Century: 2000 to Present

Current issues in physical education have the potential to make history in the decades to come. Although the field may seem to have not changed much in recent years, it faces several challenges in the present era.

Challenges

One challenge to the field is the declining supply of and demand for PETE programs (Boyce and Rikard 2008) in colleges and universities across the United States. These programs offer not only Bachelor of Arts or Bachelor of Science degrees for those who would teach K-12 programs, but also PhDs for those who will eventually become college professors in PETE. A decline in the number of doctoral programs in teacher education institutions means fewer professionals available to fill vacancies in physical education teacher training programs for undergraduate K-12 physical education students (Woods, Goc Karp, and Feltz 2003; Woods, Goc Karp, and Judd 2009). With fewer programs and professors to educate new PETE faculty, who will be qualified to teach physical education at the K-12 level? These issues could become a major problem facing physical education in the decades ahead.

Another trend that poses a challenge for physical education is the increase in online courses (e-learning) in physical education. High school and college-level students can fulfill physical education credits by taking classes on the Internet. In fact, 22 states (43 percent) allow secondary-level physical education credits to be achieved via online courses, and not all of these courses are taught by physical education specialists (NASPE and AHA 2010). One can view online physical education courses as an advantage, especially for those who have scheduling or inclusion difficulties or who find independent learning more valuable (Ransdell et al. 2008). On the other hand, online courses can be perceived as counterproductive to many physical education objectives, including the competent development of physical activity skills (not just becoming physically fit), socializing and cooperating with other students, and actually moving instead of sitting in front of a computer (Buschner 2006). Regardless of the stand one takes on e-learning, online classes are here to stay with ramifications unknown to the future of physical education.

> Do you believe online courses in physical education are an acceptable way to fulfill high school or college physical education requirements?

Demonstrating the worthiness of physical education in the educational world has been a constant struggle throughout history, and continues to be a challenge today. As previously mentioned, not all states mandate physical education for school-aged children, and only five states require physical education at every grade level (NASPE and AHA 2010) . In addition, some states that require K-12 physical education, or require some type of physical education credit for graduation, also allow for exemptions. For example, students can receive physical education credit if they participate in JROTC, interscholastic sports, a marching band, or cheerleading (NASPE and AHA 2010). Such deals are not made in traditional academic subjects, however: Students cannot receive exemptions from math, English, or science by, for example, working as the treasurer of the band club, writing for the school newspaper, or volunteering in a science museum after school. Moreover, not all states require a certified physical education specialist to teach physical education classes. Clearly, physical education still struggles to maintain its value and merit in school education.

Furthermore, the exclusion of physical education from the core academic subjects of NCLB (No Child Left Behind) adds to the sense that it has less value or merit than other subjects. As a result of the pressure to improve academic test scores as part of NCLB, many school administrators believe that more time in the school day must be devoted to the core academic areas. As a result, physical education classes have been reduced or eliminated from curriculum requirements across the United States (NASPE and AHA 2010).

Trends

In the past, the lack of physical fitness of our military and youth has rallied the nation around the importance of fitness and physical education in the schools. Once again, it appears physical education teachers are using a renewed interest in physical fitness to maintain the niche of physical education in American education in the new millennium.

The country's current fitness and physical activity agenda has been the result of the widely recognized obesity epidemic plaguing the United States; more American youth and adults are overweight and obese than in any time in history. The prevalence of overweight and obese youth and adults remains high; roughly 31.9 percent of American children and adolescents are overweight or obese (Ogden, Carroll, and Flegal 2008), and 34 percent of adults aged 20 years and over are obese (Centers for Disease Control and Prevention 2007).

Clearly, obesity is a serious health concern, and many factors have been connected to the huge rise in obesity rates. As a result, increasing the physical activity of all citizens has been on the agenda in all sectors of society, from city planning committees and local governments, health care establishments and fast-food restaurants, to area schools. After-school activity programs, online activities and nutritional Web sites, and many locally sponsored physical activity events have become widely prevalent. Federally funded programs such as Coordinated School Health have also been adopted to help schools create a more health-conscious place for learning.

Technological tools and games to enhance physical activity levels have become a trend during this era. Pedometers are a familiar device used to measure daily physical activity levels based on the number of steps accumulated throughout the day. Many physical education programs incorporate pedometers to help students identify their own physical activity levels. Various forms of heart rate monitors are also being used in physical education programs to help students understand the connection between physical activity intensity levels and heart health. Some monitors allow students to download their heart rate data into a computer software program (e.g., Polar E600), which provides valuable feedback on their intensity levels during class. In addition, physical education teachers use this data to demonstrate program effectiveness to parents and administrators (see chapter 10 for more information on fitness-related technology).

> Could physical activity data collected on pedometers or heart rate monitors be used as evidence to satisfy physical education credit?

Heart rate monitors are now available in many physical education programs to help students more accurately check their heart rate intensities.

Photo courtesy of Jane Shimon

New-generation exergaming activities (active video games) are also finding their way into homes and school programs across the United States to help motivate youth to increase their physical activity levels (Epstein et al. 2007). Dance Dance Revolution, Wii Fit systems, and Game bikes are examples of exergaming programs. Children and adults participating in these gaming activities usually expend around 2 to 7.5 calories per minute at low to moderate intensity levels, depending on the individual and type of activity (Haddock et al. 2008). Because research into exergaming is relatively recent, whether these activities positively affect children's health, and the longevity of continued participation in exergaming activities, are not known (Daley 2009). In addition, whether exergaming will become a gateway for participation in other physical activities or be included into mainstream physical education programs is yet to be seen.

Recent research has demonstrated a positive link between physical fitness and academic scores. In other words, students who are more physically fit tend to have higher academic achievement scores than their unfit peers (California Department of Education 2005; Castelli et al. 2007; Coe et al. 2006; Sallis et al. 1999). Most recently, statewide data collected by the Texas Education Agency, in association with the Cooper Institute, reported that higher levels fitness were associated with better academic performance, better school attendance, and fewer disciplinary problems related to drugs, alcohol, and violence (Cooper Institute 2009). The state of New York is conducting a statewide study to provide further evidence to support the importance of enhancing the fitness levels of youth. This is good news and physical educators are using this information as a catalyst to demonstrate that physical education is an important content area in school curricula and should not be minimized or cut from school programs.

The escalating rise in awareness of the importance of physical activity and fitness has resulted in major changes in many physical education programs across the United States, especially at the secondary level. Some high schools align physical education to a strictly health-related fitness and health system by having students learn about health and nutrition concepts; participate in strength training and conditioning activities using such equipment as treadmills, stair steppers, elliptical machines, and stationary bicycles; and work toward developing personal fitness programs (Freeman 2001). This apparent curriculum shift is slowly removing traditional sports, games, dance, and outdoor and lifetime activities from physical education programs, especially at the high school level. Pedometers and heart rate monitors are beginning to replace basketballs, volleyballs, golf clubs, and tennis rackets. The fitness trend has even made its way to the elementary level: Youth-sized cardiorespiratory exercise machines and strength training equipment are now available for children to use in schools and fitness clubs.

The direction of physical education is being challenged once again at this time (Hawkins 2008). It appears the discipline is coming full circle in history by returning to an emphasis on physical training. (Go to the online resource to complete a worksheet that will help you review the history of teaching physical education.) Questions to consider include: Should physical education be all about enhancing health-related fitness, or is there more to the purpose and value of physical education? What do such implications suggest about our work? Should we challenge these societal trends and determine ways to support or test the current position? These questions are critical to the direction and focus of physical education in the years to follow.

Realistically, there isn't enough time allotted to physical education classes to enhance the fitness levels of our youth, especially when many elementary school children have physical education only once or twice a week, while adolescents may only be required to take physical education one semester in sixth and seventh- grades, or one semester or one year of physical education during their entire time in high school. It is obvious that physical education alone cannot provide the activity and fitness benefits children need. Currently, a National Physical Activity Plan (www.physicalactivityplan.org) is underway to help individual states meet the physical activity and fitness needs of our children.

Summary

The new millennium poses both familiar and new challenges for physical education. Time will tell whether the positive associations between fitness scores and academic achievement currently being reported will alter the scope and perceived value of physical education in school programs. Only time will tell whether there will be enough teacher educators to train future physical education leaders, what impact e-learning will have on physical education, and whether trends in curricular changes toward physical fitness will help students become more physically active as adults and increase their desire to participate in activities for a lifetime.

What do you think your role will be in determining the future of physical education? What do you plan to do?

▶ Discussion Questions

1. How do the concepts of the new physical education during the early 20th century reflect present national physical education standards?
2. How do the struggles of early leaders and the academic value placed on physical education compare with current issues and perceptions of physical education teachers and programs within the overall educational curriculum?
3. What does history tell us about the role of fitness in physical education, and how does that position compare to present-day beliefs? Go online and complete the history worksheet in the online student resource.
4. How have the various instructional models developed in the late 20th century contributed to current physical education programs?
5. How do present-day state, district, and national AAHPERD conferences and conventions relate to the concepts of the Harvard Summer School and early normal schools of the past?
6. How does your state compare to the 2010 Shape of the Nation Report: Status of Physical Education in the USA? How does the Shape of the Nation Report reflect the history of physical education across time? You can access the report at www.aahperd.org/naspe/publications/Shapeofthenation.cfm.

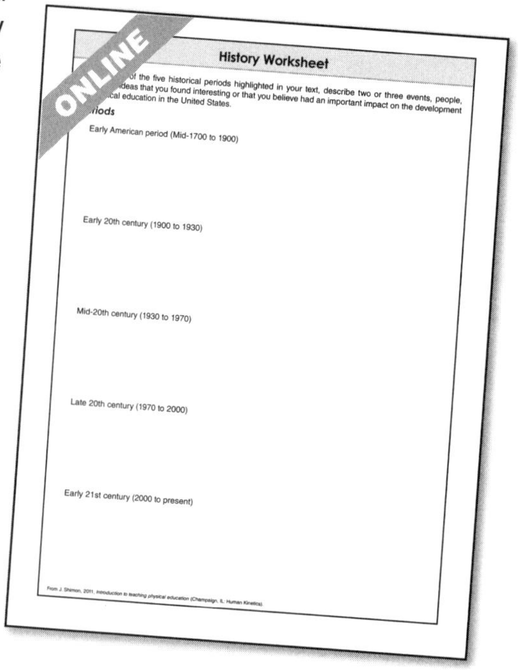

CHAPTER 2

Purpose, Benefits, and Philosophy

CHAPTER OBJECTIVES

After reading this chapter, you will be able to:

- ☐ Define the purpose of physical education through the four domains of learning.
- ☐ Describe NASPE's National Physical Education Standards.
- ☐ Describe the benefits of participating in a quality physical education program.
- ☐ Describe the importance of developing a sound teaching philosophy.
- ☐ Explain how various philosophical views have affected the development of physical education over time.
- ☐ Recognize traditional philosophical foundations and how they relate to teaching physical education.

KEY TERMS

affective domain
cognitive domain
existentialism
idealism
naturalism
physical activity
physical education
pragmatism
psychomotor domain
realism
social domain

Physical education plays a role in the overall educational process by helping children and adolescents develop in a physically active setting. It is the only curricular area in the school program that focuses on the development of skills necessary for lifelong physical activity. This role should not be taken lightly; quality instruction has become increasingly important.

The evidence is clear that physical inactivity is directly related to overweight and obesity issues. And the human price tag is severe: These health-related issues decrease the quality of life, limit functional independence, and shorten the life span. In addition to the human toll, the financial costs of obesity-related illnesses fatten medical bills as well. According to the CDC (2009b), obese individuals spend 42 percent more on health care than those of normal weight, totally $147 billion more in health care costs.

As you begin your quest to become a physical education teacher, it is important to recognize the purpose and value of physical education in the school program and beyond. This understanding will determine your teaching philosophy and the direction you will take as a physical educator.

Purpose of Physical Education

What is the purpose of physical education? Why should physical education be taught in schools? Some respond by saying, "Physical education helps kids get in shape," or, "Physical education assists students in developing a healthy lifestyle." Others reply, "Physical education helps kids learn about teamwork and fair play," or, "Physical education allows kids to have fun!" All of these answers fit into the purpose of physical education; however, there's more to physical education than just allowing kids to be busy, happy, and good (Placek 1983).

Many people use the term *physical activity* to mean physical education. However, physical activity should not be confused with physical education. **Physical activity** involves bodily movements that help increase energy expenditure and health-related fitness levels. Physical activities can range from low- to high-intensity activities to individual, dual, or team-related sports and games. Physical education, on the other hand, is a process of learning that uses physical activities to help develop the whole person, mind and body. Obviously, both physical activities and physical education are important to include in children's lives.

To further clarify the purpose of physical education, we can place it into a learning context, one that consists of categories, or domains, of learning. Bloom (1956) divided learning into three domains: psychomotor, cognitive, and affective. Some educators use these three domains of learning, and others use four. For the purpose of this textbook, the affective domain has been separated into the affective and social domains.

Psychomotor Domain

The **psychomotor domain** is unique to physical education. Addressing the psychomotor domain consists of developing the physical movement (neuromuscular) skills and health- and performance-related fitness skills needed for playing games and sports and being physically active. Movement skills such as skipping, throwing, dodging, balance, and coordination, as well as fitness skills including cardiorespiratory endurance, are all in the psychomotor domain. These components of the psychomotor domain are not used by people only during their school years; adults need these skills for various occupations and to help them remain physically active throughout their lives. Because the psychomotor domain is unique to physical education, it is important that you make sure your students become skillful and fit movers.

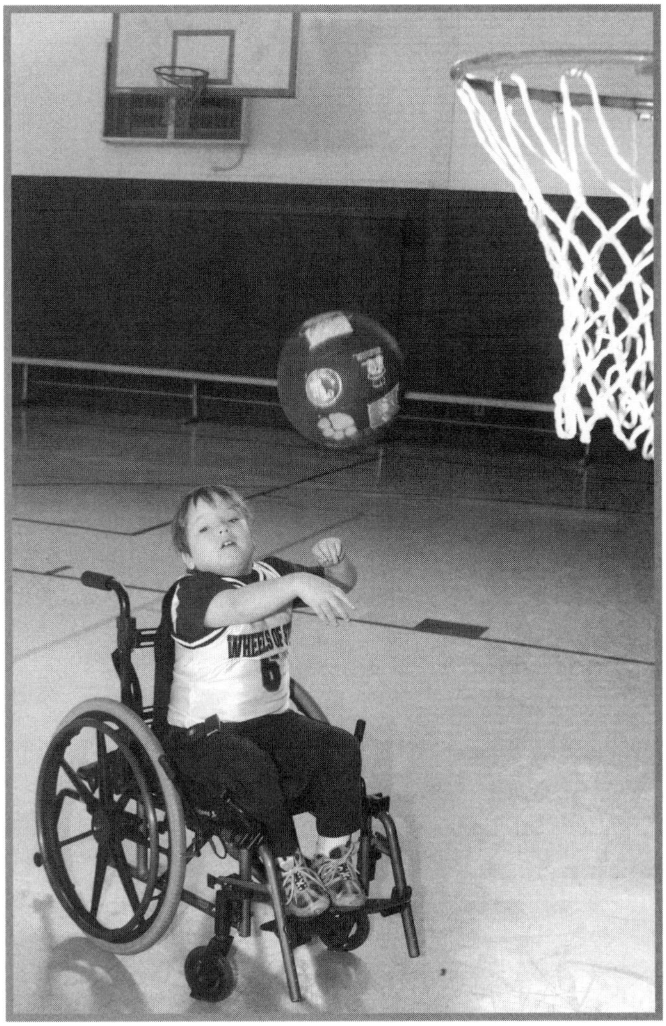

Skill development is an important component of the psychomotor domain.

Cognitive Domain

The **cognitive domain** addresses the thinking, or knowledge-based, components of physical education. Another purpose of physical education is to help students become PE literate. In other words, you must help students develop an understanding of the activities in which they participate; they should understand, for example, the concepts of balance and support, various game rules and tactics, the FITT principle (frequency, intensity, time, and type of exercise or activity), and the importance of developing and implementing their own activity or fitness programs.

Affective and Social Domains

In addition to addressing the psychomotor and cognitive domains, you will also need to help students develop positive attitude toward physical activities, along with the ability to work collaboratively and responsibly with others. The **affective domain** of learning addresses the attitudes and feelings students have about being active, and their confidence levels. Helping students appreciate and enjoy moving, playing, and working toward better fitness outcomes is another purpose of physical education. If you give students opportunities to experience success in fun and meaningful ways as they learn and develop movement skills, hopefully they will continue to find enjoyment in being physically active adults.

Finally, the **social domain** involves helping students develop appropriate social skills. What better way to develop teamwork, fair play, responsibility, and getting along with others than through participation in sports, games, and physical activities taught in physical education?

The purpose of physical education is more than just keeping students active in physical activities. Physical education is about physically educating students in movement, concepts, and physical activity skills. It is about helping them gain confidence in their abilities and allowing them to enjoy moving and being active independently or within groups.

National Physical Education Standards

The National Association for Sport and Physical Education (NASPE) includes the domains of learning within its purpose statement for physical education: "The goal of physical education is to develop physically educated individuals who have the knowledge, skills, and confidence to enjoy a lifetime of healthy physical activity" (NASPE, 2004). The word *lifetime* demonstrates an emphasis on more than just

Using teamwork, a social domain component, these students aim to keep the ball from touching the ground with only the ropes.

getting children and adolescents active and fit today; we must also prepare them to be physically active in the future. That's why teaching lifetime physical activities, skills, and concepts is an important part of physical education.

NASPE has developed six National Standards for Physical Education (2004), which include the four domains of learning previously described. The goal of the national standards is to help students lead physically active lives as students and as adults. In addition, the national standards provide a guideline for individual states to use when developing or revising their own standards. The standards describe the skills, abilities, and dispositions (attitudes) students need to lead physically active lives. Each standard is broken down into grade ranges (K-2; 3-5; 6-8; 9-12) so teachers can identify what students at each level should know and be able to do. Table 2.1 illustrates just one example of an outcome students should be able to do for each of the NASPE standards within each grade range.

How do your state physical education standards reflect the National Physical Education Standards?

Benefits of Physical Education

Now that the purpose of physical education has been described, what about its benefits? What are the advantages, gains, or rewards to students who participate in a quality physical education program? These questions can be answered using the four domains of learning as our guide.

Psychomotor Benefits

The psychomotor benefits students obtain from physical education are plentiful. First, as a result of physical education, students can develop a strong foundation of

Table 2.1 Example of Learning Outcomes Based on NASPE Standards

Grades K-2	3-5	6-8	9-12
Standard 1: Demonstrates competency in motor skills and movement patterns to perform a variety of physical activities			
Skips, hops, gallops, slides, etc., using mature form	Balances with control on a variety of objects	Uses correct knots for belaying while rock climbing	Selects and uses the correct club for an approach shot in golf
Standard 2: Demonstrates understanding of movement concepts, principles, strategies, and tactics as they apply to learning and performance of physical activities			
Explains the purpose of a warm-up	Describes how heart rate monitors physical activity intensity	Explains game tactics involved in playing tennis doubles	Plans a personal conditioning program
Standard 3: Participates regularly in physical activity			
Engages in a variety of activities during leisure time	Maintains a physical activity log	Accumulates a specified number of steps during the day	Monitors and adjusts activity to meet personal physical activity needs
Standard 4: Achieves and maintains a health-enhancing level of physical fitness			
Moves transversely along a rock wall	Participates in activities that require muscular strength	Maintains heart rate in target heart rate zone for 20 minutes	Assesses personal health-related fitness status
Standard 5: Exhibits responsible personal and social behavior that respects self and others in physical activity settings			
Uses equipment and space safely and properly	Cooperates by taking turns and sharing equipment	Plays within the rules of the game or activity	Participates successfully in a cooperative and diverse learning group
Standard 6: Values physical activity for health, enjoyment, challenge, self-expression, and/or social interaction			
Willingly tries new movement skills	Identifies positive feelings with participation in physical activities	Recognizes positive opportunities for social and group interaction	Creates self rewards for achieving personal fitness activity goals

Standard 1 is reprinted from NASPE 2004.

fundamental movement skills that establish the groundwork for the more specialized skills needed for participating in physical activities, games, and sports. Skills such as running, jumping, twisting, throwing, catching, kicking, climbing, and dodging are examples of fundamental movements. There is evidence to support the statement that children who establish competent movement skills are more likely to be active adolescents and adults (Okely, Booth, and Patterson 2001).

Second, the physical benefits of being active are widely known. Consider the list of benefits in figure 2.1 on page 40. The Centers for Disease Control and Prevention (CDC 2009a) has indicated that to obtain the benefits of physical activity, children need to participate in 60 minutes of physical activity daily. Most of this activity should be in the form of aerobic activities at moderate intensity levels. Moderate-intensity levels include activities that make one breathe harder than normal or an intensity rating of 5 or 6 on a scale of 1 to 10. Plenty of activities students perform in physical education class take place at moderate intensity levels. In addition, the CDC recommends that three days out of the week should include aerobic activities of vigorous intensity, activities that require one to breathe much harder than normal (i.e., a rating of 7 or 8 on a scale of 10). Activities such as team handball, speedball, circuit training, and ultimate provide

Go online to complete a case study about the purpose and benefits of physical education.

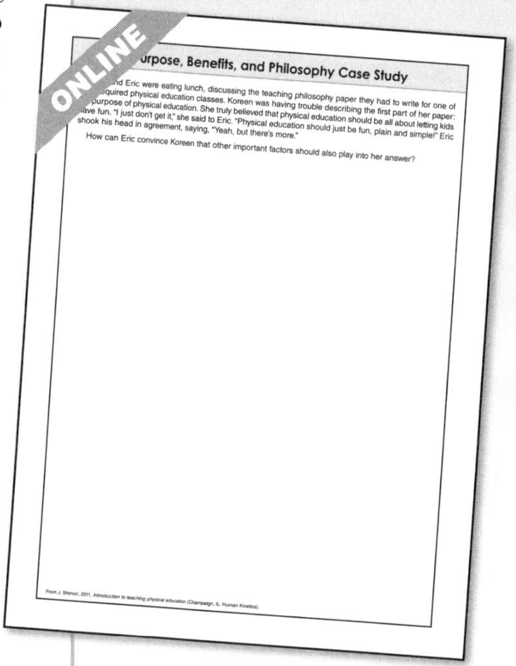

ONLINE
...urpose, Benefits, and Philosophy Case Study
How can Eric convince Koreen that other important factors should also play into her answer?

This student is working on his climbing skills by navigating spots on the floor. Challenging him to see how fast he can climb will help increase the intensity of this exercise.

Photo courtesy of Corinne Morgan

opportunities for students to participate at a higher level of intensity. Additionally, three days a week should also include muscle-strengthening and bone-strengthening activities (e.g., jump rope, running, resistance training) as part of the recommended 60 minutes of daily physical activity (see figure 2.2)

We know the psychomotor benefits of physical activity and understand the importance of raising the health-related fitness levels of children. We also know that intensity levels are important to emphasize to maximize those benefits (Ortega et al. 2008). It's no surprise, however, that many students do not like to work at higher levels of effort, such as running laps around the gym or track. It's hard and uncomfortable for students to participate in vigorous activities when they are not in condition to do so. In fact, their heart rates and perceived rates of intensity (exertion) already may be at high levels when participating in low- to moderate-level activities. Therefore, you must be mindful of the various fitness levels of your students and work with them to improve. One size does not fit all when it comes to activity and fitness enhancement.

Cognitive Benefits

Students become PE literate by learning about physical education and fitness content, but they are most likely receiving a hidden cognitive benefit as well. During the past 25 to 30 years, an increasing number of studies have addressed the connection between physical activity and academic achievement. Various studies have shown that participating in physical

FIGURE 2.1

Physical Benefits of Being Physically Active

- Controls weight by expending calories consumed each day
- Reduces the risk of cardiovascular disease by lowering blood pressure and improving cholesterol levels
- Reduces the risk of type 2 diabetes
- Reduces the risk of some cancers, including breast and colon cancers
- Strengthens bones and muscles
- Improves mental health and mood, especially with aerobic exercise
- Increases chances of living longer

From CDC 2009.

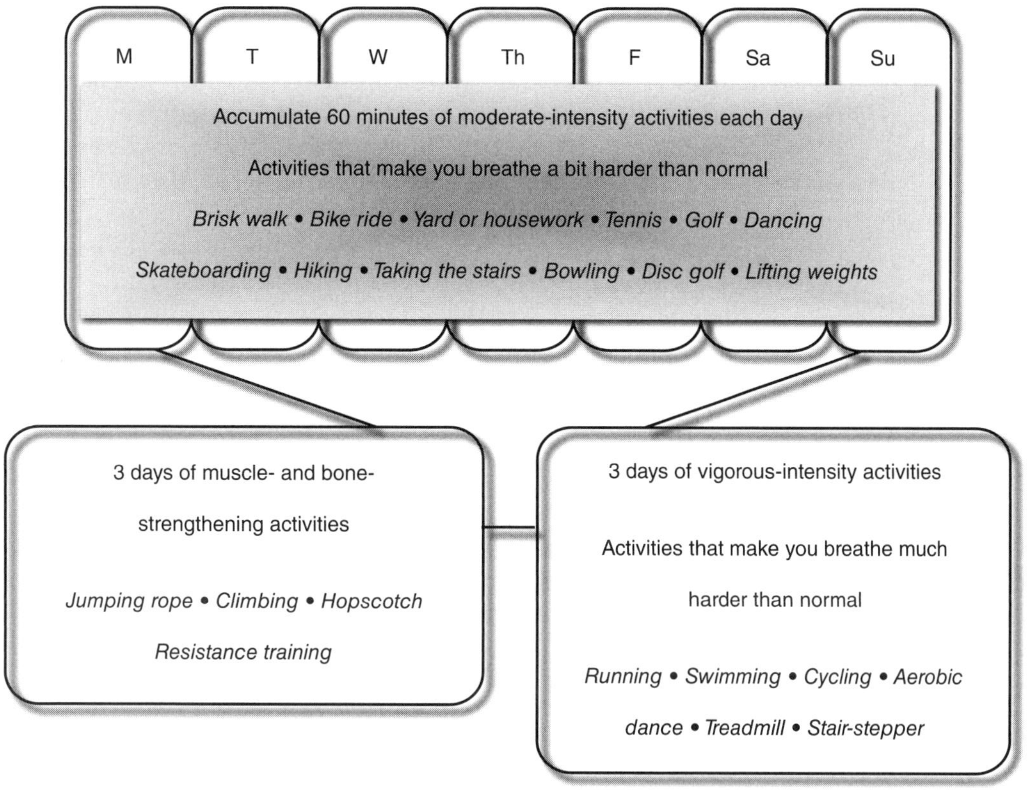

FIGURE 2.2 Sample physical activity plan.

activities can increase blood flow to the brain, resulting in improvements to mental alertness and intellectual functioning for both youth and adults (Colcombe and Kramer 2003; Hiliman et al. 2009; Sibley and Etnier 2003). As stated in chapter 1, research studies also have shown a positive relationship between higher fitness levels and academic scores, as well as improvements in school attendance and behavior. Several states are conducting similar studies to determine the role physical education and physical activity have on students' academic achievement scores. Thus far, the news is good. The evidence has shown that requiring physical education classes or increasing time for physical education has not interfered with students' improvement in other subjects (Sallis et al. 1999; Shephard 1997).

Affective and Social Benefits

Do you feel better being physically active? Does your mood improve, or do you find yourself less tired or stressed out than before? It is commonly supported in the literature that participating in physical activities can have a positive psychological effect on the well-being of children, adolescents, and adults. Physical activity can be a great pick-me-up! Regular physical activity can help improve self-esteem and confidence in performing skills, and reduce the signs and symptoms of stress, anxiety, and depression.

Sometimes, however, physical education classes can be stressful or negative experiences, especially for students who are less skilled. It is important that you present lessons and activities in meaningful and relevant ways to all class members (Sabo et al. 2004) to enhance their enjoyment and the positive affective benefits physical education can offer.

What physical education activities have you participated in that could be classified as moderately or vigorously intense? What types of physical education activities can combine both aerobic and strength training into one activity?

Physical education also offers a unique setting in which to foster positive interactions among students. Through quality, structured activities and games, physical education can help students develop appropriate game play behaviors, such as treating equipment and players with respect, playing fairly with regard to rules and etiquette, and demonstrating good sporting behaviors. In addition, allowing students to interact within groups or teams helps to strengthen problem-solving and reasoning skills. All of the social benefits from physical education are skills students can use throughout life, whether playing on a recreational softball team or in a bowling league, or interacting with coworkers on the job.

Physical education has the potential to make significant contributions to the overall education and development of children and adolescents in many ways (Bailey 2006). All the benefits previously described truly depend on quality instruction and physical education programs. Just because the nature of physical education allows students to be active and play does not mean they will automatically gain the benefits associated with physical activity. It is up to you to plan and implement sound lessons based on developmentally appropriate practices that allow for successful and positive experiences.

Most physical education programs do not provide a full 60 minutes of recommended moderate- to vigorous-intensity daily physical activity. As a result, students must complete some of their daily physical activity outside of school. Hopefully, students who have developed confidence in their skills, gained a good understanding of the concepts, and found value and enjoyment from being active in physical education will find the time to be physically active outside of school as well.

Learning to work cooperatively to complete a task is a skill that will benefit students throughout life.

Philosophy of Physical Education

Many physical education teachers in the United States follow curriculum content standards and outcomes. You may wonder, then, why a physical education philosophy is important if you will be teaching to the standards. A personal teaching philosophy helps shape your values and areas of emphasis. What is *really* important to you about physical education? What value does it hold for you? Philosophy is the pursuit of fundamental truths and wisdom that will provide a clearer focus and understanding of what you do (Kretchmar 2005).

Philosophy is usually derived from two areas: values and science (Zeigler 1964). Values involve speculation, or what you believe has meaning and value (axiology). Your speculative side is usually guided by your present values of what is right or wrong, good or bad, or even beautiful or unattractive.

Professional Profile: Adrian Flores

Photo courtesy of Don Disney

BACKGROUND INFORMATION

I have a bachelor's degree in science (kinesiology as a major with a minor in education) from the University of Texas at El Paso. My current position is at Aoy Elementary, where I am a physical education teacher for grades K-5. My past positions include freshmen basketball coach, assistant coach for varsity football, and a health fitness specialist for the district. In the past, I was the Teacher of the Year (campus level) and was nominated by the Texas Association for Health, Physical Education, Recreation and Dance (TAHPERD) for the State Physical Education Teacher of the Year.

Why did you decide to become a physical education teacher?

My decision to become a PE teacher was based on my love of working with children and sports. My dad, a former coach himself, inspired me to pass on my love of sports to others, especially children.

What do you like most about your job?

The best part about my job is working with the students and helping them become successful academically and physically. Developing lifelong learners and inspiring my students to achieve their goals are what make teaching fun.

What is the most challenging part of your job?

Sometimes the perception of PE is that it's playtime for students and not a real class where kids learn. Trying to change the stereotype of physical education is a challenge. Today's PE includes lessons that focus on keeping the students active and integrates core subjects into many of the activities.

How have you continued to grow professionally?

As a professional, I am open to new ideas that will improve my teaching so that I can have a positive effect on my students' learning. I make it a point to attend professional development seminars that are offered locally or out of town. Communicating and networking with other coaches are key factors that have affected my professional career.

What advice would you give a college student who wants to become a PE teacher?

Teaching is dynamic, and you need to be willing to change and learn. As a teacher, you need to be willing to change because kids change each year. During your teaching career, be prepared to make changes in your day-to-day activities instead of getting too comfortable with your routine. What I call the "new PE" involves searching for new ideas, integrating the core subjects, avoiding elimination games (such as dodgeball and tag games where kids are sitting), and minimizing students' time standing in lines so that all students are actively engaged.

Your values may be derived, in part, from what you believe about reality (metaphysics), such as evolution or creationism, religion, higher orders, or harmony within the universe. Part of your philosophy is also determined by what is critical—in other words, the attainment of knowledge (epistemology) and what seems logical or makes sense (logic). Often you determine what makes sense based on your past experiences and what has worked for you or not. Your philosophy also is informed by what you know, the importance of that information, and how you learned it. The process of how you learned throughout the years will play a part in your professional teaching philosophy (see figure 2.3).

Your philosophy is more than just your thoughts and opinions, however. Your professional principles of physical education will become a source of direction that will determine the aims and values of your thoughts and actions. Thus, your beliefs will mirror what you do (Cowell and France 1963). For example, if you full-heartedly

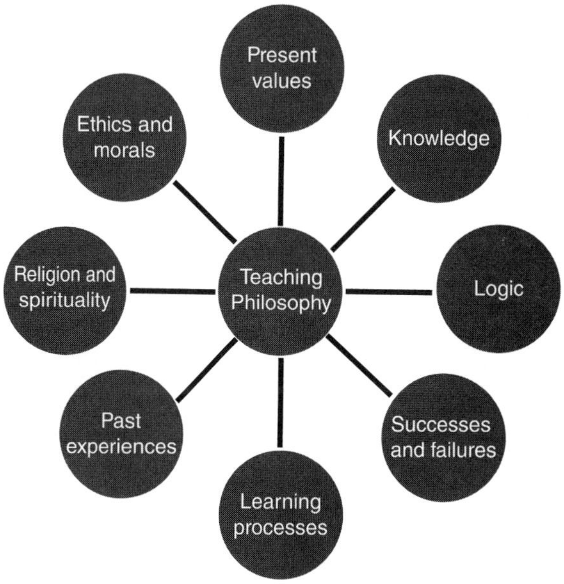

FIGURE 2.3 Many factors influence your teaching philosophy.

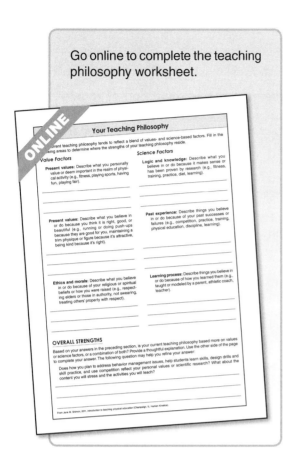

Go online to complete the teaching philosophy worksheet.

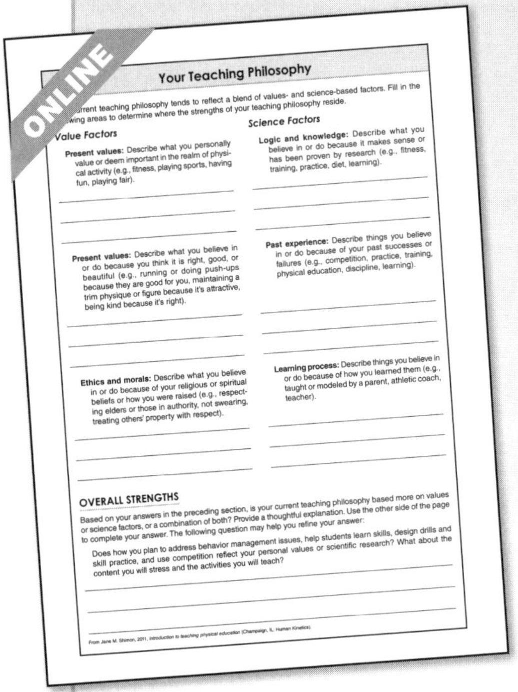
ONLINE

Your Teaching Philosophy

...rrent teaching philosophy tends to reflect a blend of values- and science-based factors. Fill in the ...wing areas to determine where the strengths of your teaching philosophy reside.

Value Factors

Present values: Describe what you personally value or deem important in the realm of physical activity (e.g., fitness, playing sports, having fun, playing fair).

Present values: Describe what you believe in or do because you think it is right, good, or beautiful (e.g., running or doing push-ups because they are good for you, maintaining a trim physique or figure because it's attractive, being kind because it's right).

Ethics and morals: Describe what you believe in or do because of your religious or spiritual beliefs or how you were raised (e.g., respecting elders or those in authority, not swearing, treating others' property with respect).

Science Factors

Logic and knowledge: Describe what you believe in or do because it makes sense or has been proven by research (e.g., fitness, training, practice, diet, learning).

Past experience: Describe things you believe in or do because of your past successes or failures (e.g., competition, practice, training, physical education, discipline, learning).

Learning process: Describe things you believe in or do because of how you learned them (e.g., taught or modeled by a parent, athletic coach, teacher).

OVERALL STRENGTHS

Based on your answers in the preceding section, is your current teaching philosophy based more on values or science factors, or a combination of both? Provide a thoughtful explanation. Use the other side of the page to complete your answer. The following question may help you refine your answer:

Does how you plan to address behavior management issues, help students learn skills, design drills and skill practice, and use competition reflect your personal values or scientific research? What about the content you will stress and the activities you will teach?

From Jane M. Shimon, 2011, *Introduction to teaching physical education* (Champaign, IL: Human Kinetics).

believe that being a skillful mover will help students become physically active adults, the majority of your physical education content will involve learning, practicing, and applying skills to various activities. If you truly value fitness and health, your program will be geared toward helping students reach higher fitness levels. If your belief is that students need to ultimately get along with others and work cooperatively to solve problems, then your program will consist mainly of group work and shared learning situations. In addition, developing a philosophy will help you articulate the meaning of physical education, the purpose and role physical education plays in the overall scheme of education, and the value and worth of learning physical education content (Davis 1963b).

Philosophies Connected to the History of Physical Education

You know that your professional philosophy reflects what you believe is most important; however, it also has to be logical, sensible, and linked to the historical philosophies of physical education (Siedentop 2009). Some of the past social and educational philosophies of physical education were presented in chapter 1. Past leaders based their programs and ideals on the philosophies of the time. For example, the German and Swedish gymnastics systems were both built on a nationalist philosophy, one that provided a unified sense of being and purpose to a nation. World Wars I and II ignited a desire to improve the physical fitness and health status of youth and adults. The importance of physical training and fitness reflected the philosophy of physical education at the time.

During the development of the United States, there was also a popular belief that physical fitness and competitive sports were important ways to develop the moral, mental, and religious qualities of men (Mechikoff and Estes 1993). This philosophy was called muscular Christianity. In a sense, the work of Robert Roberts and the YMCA helped to spread this type of character education across the country and had a great impact on the development of physical education and sport programs.

Thomas Wood developed the new physical education as a result of the progressive education movement of John Dewey. As you recall, his philosophy was based on a child-centered and natural educational approach, which was influenced by the attitude of social reform of the time. Within this philosophy, physical education was seen as an important way to allow students to play and participate in sports and games to achieve positive social goals.

Another example of how philosophy guided physical education in the past involved play and recreation. Luther Gulick's main passion was the importance of play. His philosophy of play was part of the movement that helped increase the development of playgrounds and recreational pursuits, which led to the inclusion of lifetime sports and activity offerings in physical education. Many physical educators believed that play and lifetime pursuits, along with positive social interactions, should be the primary focus of physical education.

Also mentioned in chapter 1 was movement education. This philosophy gained acceptance as a method to help children develop movement skills to their fullest potential (Metheny 1954). In fact, many educators today still follow some aspects of this philosophy when teaching elementary physical education.

The social unrest of the 1960s spawned by the Vietnam War and the human rights movement resulted in a humanistic teaching philosophy that gave students more freedom in their own learning. Instruction was centered on enhancing each individual's distinctive learning needs and interests, instead of the traditional one-size-fits-all method of teaching.

Finally, the wellness and fitness movements of the 1980s up to the present day are built on the philosophy that personal attention to improving one's overall health and wellness is the key to human fulfillment. This philosophy informs many current physical education programs.

One philosophical view not touched on in chapter 1 is constructivism, a philosophy developed from the progressive education theories of John Dewey and Jean Piaget. Those espousing this philosophy believe that students learn through the exploration of previous knowledge. Therefore, concepts are more important than isolated facts. The teacher is the guide to help students discuss what they currently know by asking questions that appeal to their interests. Students participate in experiences that help them construct their own understanding and knowledge. This philosophy centers on helping students think for themselves as they try to make sense of the world in which they live.

Helping students improve skills and confidence is an important part of physical education.

Traditional Philosophical Positions

Because you are just starting out in your quest to become a physical educator, you may benefit from considering traditional philosophies to help you determine your own. Traditional philosophies include idealism, realism, pragmatism, naturalism, and existentialism. As you read through the general descriptions of these traditional philosophies, ask yourself where you stand, what you value, and what you believe. Remember, a professional philosophy provides direction; it keeps you true and honest about your beliefs toward teaching physical education.

Idealism

Idealism is based on knowledge; it is subject- or content-centered. Idealism is a product of the Greek philosopher Plato. Ideas generated about truth are gathered from what science has shown to be true. Knowledge helps develop the mind and provides people with the ability to reason.

Physical education teachers who follow an idealistic philosophy believe it is important to select the content and subject matter students will learn (Davis 1963a). For example, the teacher will make sure students understand why it is important to perform skills correctly or why exercise is important. Thus, this philosophy emphasizes knowledge and the understanding of information, making physical activity a secondary focus.

Playground equipment helps children develop movement skills and enhances body awareness.

© Thomas Perkins

Physical educators espousing idealism also value the whole person, which means that they want their students to do well. This doesn't mean that teachers want their students to win as many awards as possible; rather, it means that they are also concerned with fostering character development (moral and spiritual values) and helping students play fairly, make ethical and moral choices, and be good sports. Therefore, it is important for the idealist to select activities that help students shape themselves into the best people they can be.

Because teachers who follow this philosophy are foremost concerned with content, testing students is important. However, they also favor helping students achieve quality character, which is assessed using more subjective, or personal, measures, such as journal writing.

Realism

Realism is based on the evidence that demonstrates something works. Aristotle, a Greek philosopher, believed that if something could be proven and made sense, then it was true; it was real. Realists use planned and proven courses of instruction that are orderly and methodical. Testing is conducted to determine the results of the process.

During instruction, physical education teachers who emphasize a realistic philosophy usually explain and demonstrate the parts of a skill, have students focus on those parts of the skill, and eventually lead them to practice the whole skill. By practicing skills in an organized fashion, students learn the meaning of the content. Teachers are interested in the process of learning, which provides direction and meaning to student effort and motivation (Holbrook 1963). Overall, as students practice within a guided structure, they build competence in their skills, which allows them to make better skill adjustments. Finally, teachers test students using objective measures to determine whether the program and instruction work, which ultimately confirms that what they are doing is worthwhile.

Pragmatism

Pragmatism is an American philosophy based on experience as the source of truth. John Dewey's ideas of progressive education were based on a pragmatic philosophy: Learn by doing. Experience is the first tenet of pragmatism (Burke 1963), because it is through experience that we develop our ideals and truths. If our experience is successful, a truth is developed based on that experience. Because emphasis is on the student, the pragmatist also believes that to reach personal well-being in all phases of life, one must be able to develop effective social skills and efficacy (Burke 1963).

Physical education teachers often take this learn-by-doing philosophy literally to mean "just let students play." This notion is a huge misconception of pragmatism. Yes, activity and play are very important to this philosophy, but social and democratic interactions are also essential. Therefore, selecting a variety of games and team sport activities that support socialization (e.g., working together to solve problems, following rules, playing fair) is important to those who hold this philosophy.

Teachers who follow a pragmatic approach become guides, or aides, in helping students learn *how* to think rather than *what* to think. They allow groups to work cooperatively to solve problems that coincide with taking part in team activities. Therefore, experience and truth are arrived at through successful problem-solving activities (Freeman 2001).

As for testing and assessment, it is not surprising to guess that gathering objective test scores is not important for the pragmatist. Such a teacher focuses more on subjective measures that address cooperative group work and experiences that contribute to solving problems. The sport education model and tactical games approach mentioned in chapter 1 follow a pragmatic approach to learning.

Naturalism

Naturalism is based on the premise that children are ready to learn based on their own individual development (nature); therefore, truth encompasses what the mind and body experience while exploring the environment, especially during play (Cowell and France 1963). Naturalism is based on the philosophy of Jean-Jacques Rousseau, as well as the more current views of John Dewey and the concepts behind the natural gymnastics of Thomas Wood. A naturalist designs activities that help meet the developmental needs of each student. Accordingly, teachers follow students' growth and development patterns as well as interests to best facilitate the learning

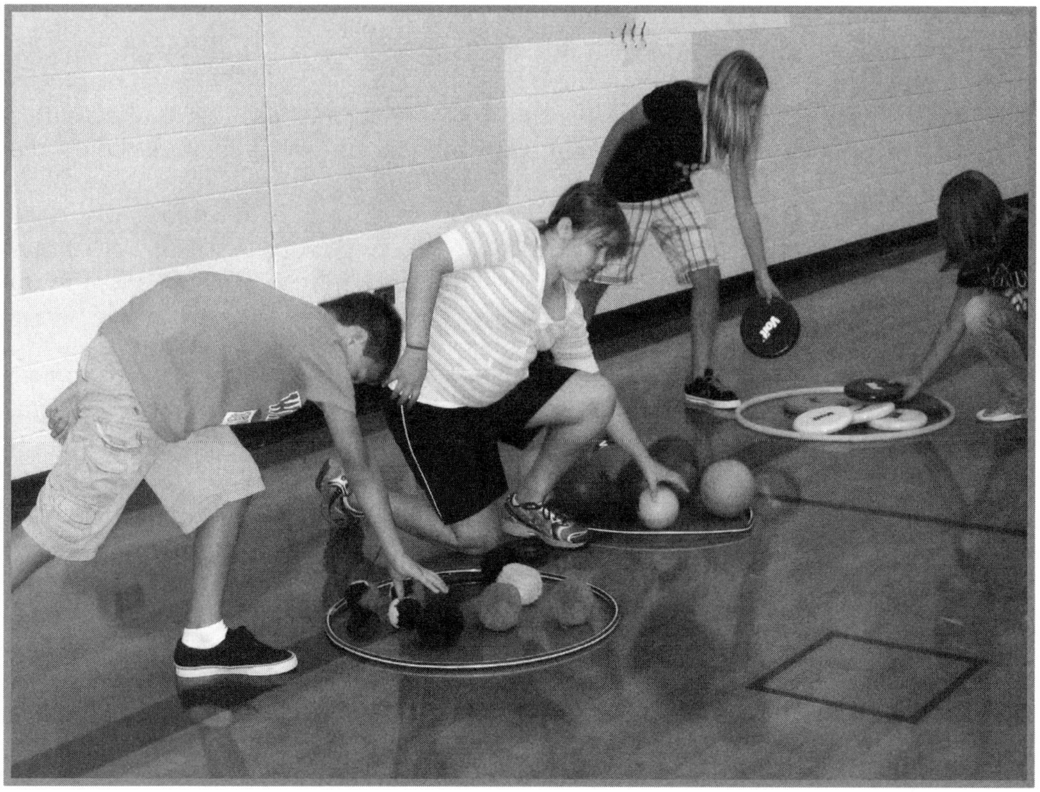

Naturalist teachers will often provide students with a variety of equipment choices, such as different types and sizes of balls, to play with, explore, and accommodate their skill and developmental level.

Photo courtesy of Jane Shimon

process through activity. Naturalists are the guardians, the planters, the guides in helping each student adjust and learn through his or her environment (Cowell and France 1963).

Although teachers who follow a naturalist philosophy plan and organize lesson content and activities according to the developmental levels of students in the class, they take a more supervisory role in the gymnasium. For example, they give students plenty of opportunity to play and explore movements within their own working spaces by allowing them to select the type of equipment and to use it within their developmental readiness levels. In other words, they help students see how to learn, but nature does the teaching (Freeman 2001).

Naturalist teachers emphasize individual development over social development and responsibility. Although competition is not generally advised, games and sports are used to help students learn about themselves. Similar to pragmatics, naturalists do not rely on objective testing and tend to assess students on individual improvement.

Existentialism

Existentialism is a philosophy based on the notion that truth or learning falls on the shoulders of each individual. Based on the philosophy of Jean-Paul Sartre, which came about in the early 1900s, existentialism revolves solely around an individualist process of learning about oneself, regardless of whether the person fits into society (Freeman 2001). An existentialist allows students to choose activities they want to learn and do. The existentialist believes that the choices students make and the consequences of those choices develop personal responsibility and ultimately determine what is real, what is true.

Teachers who follow an existentialist approach stimulate students to come to know themselves and acknowledge their existence (Davis 1963). Because emphasis is on the individual, teachers initially offer a variety of individual or dual activities from which students can select. Little or no lesson planning or prep work is required because all of the learning is up to the students; therefore, there are no real goals or objectives for teaching within this philosophy, other than helping students make choices and holding them accountable for those choices. Testing and assessments are not significant. You might guess that an existentialistic philosophy is not common in most physical education programs.

More than likely, you have found that you are partial to an assorted list of ideas from several of the known philosophies (Zeigler 1964). That's OK. You don't need to be a complete pragmatist or realist; however, it is important that your beliefs match what you practice and teach. Your philosophy must support what you do. So, the question is, What is really important to you about physical education? What value does it hold for you? Is an understanding of physical education content knowledge most critical for students to acquire, or is learning sports, fitness, and activity skills through planned progressions essential? Are you the one who will provide students with the information and knowledge, or is it better for you to be a guide in allowing students to come up with answers themselves? Is functioning appropriately within a social group most important, or is being able to make personal choices and accepting responsibility for those choices best? Is it imperative for you to develop planned and careful learning experiences, or is it better for students to be spontaneous and experience learning on their own? Do you think it's important to test students on what they have learned, or to use more subjective types of measurements? What is your physical education philosophy at this stage in your career? Use table 2.2 as an overview to help you determine your initial professional philosophy.

Table 2.2 Familiar Philosophies Applied to Physical Education

	Idealism	Realism	Pragmatism	Naturalism	Existentialism	Humanism	Constructivism
Main concept	The mind and knowledge; understanding self and character development	Objectives, outcomes, and evidence; what is real	Experience; learn by doing; develop social responsibility	Individual readiness to learn; natural development	Self-awareness and self-responsibility	Develop personal talents and total potential; self-actualization	Students learn how to learn; learning is built on what is already known
Curriculum and content	Information is more important than activities; creative, problem-solving, and fitness activities are used	Value placed on teaching sports, games, and fitness skills and technique	Team games and sports; variety is valued	Play and self-directed activities allow students to explore movements	Individual, dual, and fitness activities are part of choice of activities	Cooperative games over competitive games; enjoyment is important	Learning concepts of games and fitness is important
Teaching methods	Teacher is the source of knowledge and facts; selects and delivers information; leads discussion	Teacher is in charge; orderly lessons; step-by-step progressions, drills, and practice	Teacher guides students in how to think; helps students cooperatively solve problems within groups	Teacher guides experiences designed according to the developmental level of students	Teacher helps students develop responsibility through choices and consequences	Teacher individualizes instruction for each student and facilitates the learning process	Teacher is the knowledge expert; prompts students to ask questions; guides students to finding answers
Evaluation	Objective and subjective (personal) assessments are used	Objective tests and measurements are important (product)	Uses more subjective, self, and group assessments	Subjective measures, self-assessments	Self-assessments	Process is more important than product	Process is just as important as product; objective and subjective measures are used

Summary

Physical education has a unique role in the school program, because it is the only content area that allows students to develop movement and fitness skills. Physical education also plays an important role in helping develop the cognitive, affective, and social domains of learning within the school program. Physical education also creates an opportunity for students to benefit from being physically active during the school day. The many benefits of participating in daily physical education are amplified when you teach within a quality program and follow sound teaching practices. Quality programs and good teaching methods can be traced to a solid teaching philosophy, which helps provide focus and direction for both you and your students.

Discussion Questions

1. What are the four domains of learning as they pertain to physical education?
2. Which domain(s) of learning is/are most important? Do you think the emphasis of each domain changes as students move from elementary to secondary schools? Explain your answer.
3. Why should physical education be included in the school's overall curriculum?
4. How does physical activity differ from physical education?
5. What traditional philosophies are apparent in some of the physical education teachers you know?

CHAPTER 3

Duties and Challenges

CHAPTER OBJECTIVES

After reading this chapter, you will be able to:

- ☐ Recognize the many duties and roles physical education teachers may assume.
- ☐ Discuss all the factors that encompass being a positive role model.
- ☐ Describe liability and the importance of ensuring a safe learning environment.
- ☐ Discuss how the teacher–coach role conflict may negatively affect instruction and physical education programs.
- ☐ Identify other potential issues that affect instruction and physical education programs.
- ☐ Recognize how poor instruction leads to accountability issues in physical education.

KEY TERMS

accountability
assumption of risk
foreseeability
liability
malfeasance
misfeasance
negligence
nonfeasance
role model
teacher–coach role conflict
time-on-task

A teaching career in physical education involves more than teaching children in a gymnasium. Physical education teachers have many teaching as well as nonteaching duties they are assigned to perform throughout the year. In addition, teachers are frequently faced with various issues that affect their teaching environment, such as limited equipment or gym space, large class sizes, or unfavorable perceptions of physical education by their colleagues and community. Physical education teachers also may face the unique challenges that occur when assuming a dual role of both teacher and coach.

Teaching Duties

Many people think that the duty of a physical education teacher is to simply "roll out the ball," supervise games, and allow students to play and have fun. Although allowing students to play and have fun is important, you are preparing to become a quality physical education teacher, not a recreation director or playground supervisor. Your teaching duties will include developing and teaching effective lessons that provide appropriate development and learning opportunities for all students and that follow national, district, or state standards. The following section outlines the teaching duties you will face as a physical education teacher.

Lesson Planning and Instruction

Obviously, your main duty as a physical education teacher is to teach. However, quite a bit of preparation and planning time is required prior to actually teaching the lessons. Usually, teachers receive a planning period (prep period) during the school day to help with the planning process. The time spent getting ready to teach lessons may involve creating new lesson plans or revising previous plans. You might have to create a special handout or task sheet for students to use, develop station posters for students to view, or construct overhead transparencies or PowerPoint slides to use during a lesson. You also may have to gather and organize the equipment needed for upcoming lessons. In addition, prep time gives you time to develop assessment criteria, construct tests, and grade assignments. As you can see, your duties involve a lot more than just teaching students.

Positive Role Modeling

Another teaching duty you will assume is that of being a **role model,** a person who models healthy attitudes, behaviors, and values. If you do not think of being a role model as a teaching duty, you may wish to reconsider. Your attitudes, values, and behaviors will be viewed by those around you every time you step into the gym or work with students. Students are quite aware of what is going on during class, especially with their teacher. For example, your students will notice quite quickly if you have a positive or negative attitude toward teaching. Students can also sense whether you are prepared. They will notice your skill level and knowledge of the content, and will be in tune to your image, including your body build, clothing, and fitness level. Teachers exhibiting the following send a very clear, negative message to their students:

- Not appearing to care about students or teaching
- "Winging it," and not being prepared
- Not knowing how to perform a certain skill or having a limited understanding of concepts, rules, or game strategies

Maintaining a neat, healthy, and professional appearance demonstrates that you take pride in yourself and are living the principles that you teach.

- Teaching in a grubby T-shirt, worn-out jeans, or flip-flops
- Being overweight, obese, or out of shape

What you model, whether positive or negative, will make a huge impact on your students and the school community (Maggard 1984; Spencer 1998). Modeling behaviors that promote physical activity and fitness is important (Cardinal 2001), as is modeling behaviors that demonstrate teaching competency, display professional responsibility and respect, and reveal enthusiasm and a caring and warm disposition (character). Being a positive physical education teacher role model *is* an important teaching duty.

Safety and Liability

One last teaching duty you will assume is that of ensuring safety and recognizing factors that affect liability. **Liability** is a legal responsibility that can be enforced by a court of law. Because physical education (and athletics) carries a higher risk for injury than other activities, and because we live in a litigious society, you must be diligent about providing a safe learning environment for your students. You need to be aware of the fact that you could be held liable if a student sustains some type of harm (Dougherty 2010).

All teachers are considered to be acting in loco parentis ("in the place of the parent"), meaning that the care they provide students during the school day is similar to that of a responsible parent. If teachers do not provide a standard of care that is consistent with an accepted or established standard of conduct, students may sustain injuries and negligence may be cited. **Negligence** is a type of tort, or legal wrong, that results in physical injury or damage to a person's reputation or property (see figure 3.1 on page 54). In physical education classes, negligence is the most common tort and is often the result of injury due to nonfeasance or misfeasance.

FIGURE 3.1

Examples of Tort

- **Negligence:** Failure to act in a reasonable and prudent manner.
- **Defamation:** Harm to reputation by spoken (slander) or written (libel) words.
- **Assault:** Threat to inflict harm on someone.
- **Battery:** Unlawful use of physical force on someone.

Nonfeasance, or an act of omission, is the failure to do something that should have been done. If a teacher either leaves a classroom unsupervised and a student is injured, or fails to teach students how to do a forward roll correctly and someone gets hurt, that teacher is guilty of nonfeasance. Another example is allowing students to play a game outside near sprinkler heads and hoses, which results in a student tripping over a hose and getting injured. In these cases, the teacher failed to supervise, teach correctly, and remove obvious hazards from the playing area.

Another type of negligence is called **misfeasance,** or an act of commission, whereby a teacher's actions are incorrect. Physical educators can be found guilty of misfeasance if they were, for example, to teach a skill incorrectly, resulting in an injury, or not allow for enough space for children to participate safely. For instance, relay races are a common activity in physical education classes. If a teacher designates a stopping area that is too close to a wall, students could become injured because of the limited space in which to slow down after finishing their leg of the relay. Although space is provided, it could be determined to be inadequate or wrong and misfeasance affirmed.

Malfeasance is the third type of negligence. Although uncommon in physical education, malfeasance is when harm or injury results from doing something illegal. Punishing a student with physical force (corporal punishment) would be an example.

Can you think of examples of nonfeasance, misfeasance, and malfeasance that can occur during physical education classes?

To determine that a teacher was negligent, the court must prove that the teacher did not follow a standard of care. To prove negligence, the courts must demonstrate all four of the following factors:

1. The teacher had a legal *duty* to perform or act in a certain way.
2. The teacher *breached that duty*, usually by an act of misfeasance or nonfeasance.
3. There was *actual harm* to the student.
4. The teacher's negligence directly resulted in the injury, termed *proximate cause.*

Let's say a physical education teacher left her seventh-grade class for a short time to do some last-minute work in her office. She left her students alone while they played games of three-on-three basketball. During her absence, one of the modified games got out of hand and a few of the students got into a shoving and pushing match that resulted in two of them getting hurt. One boy fractured his clavicle after falling on his side, and the other sustained an injury to his right eye. Parents of the injured boys decided to sue the teacher for negligence. How does this scenario match up to the four factors of negligence?

1. *Did the teacher have a duty?* Yes, the teacher had a duty to supervise her students.
2. *Did the teacher breach her duty to supervise?* Yes, the teacher left the gym, even if it was for a short time. Teachers should never leave their classes unsupervised.
3. *Was injury involved?* Yes, two students sustained physical injury.
4. *Was proximate cause evident?* Yes, given that the teacher left the gym, she was not able to directly supervise the basketball games and, therefore, was not able to prevent the overly aggressive rough-housing and injuries that occurred as a result of her absence.

The teacher in this simplified scenario would most likely be found negligent due to an act of nonfeasance because she failed to supervise her class. A standard of care for all physical education teachers is to provide proper supervision during lessons and in the locker room.

Some might say that those seventh-grade boys assumed some risk of injury when they began to play rough. This type of defense is called **assumption of risk**, or a person's understanding and acceptance that participation in a voluntary activity involves risk of injury. Although this defense is used in the sporting world, it does not work in physical education. First, physical education class is not a voluntary activity, unlike after-school sports; it is part of the school's curriculum. Second, an assumption of risk defense is never upheld in court for children because of their age. Finally, assumption of risk does not free teachers (and coaches) from litigation if using poor standards of care.

Ensure that playing fields are safe for students to practice and play. Remove inappropriate or unnecessary objects that could hinder the task or game.

Teachers more frequently use a defense called comparative negligence, in which a portion or percentage of the damage or blame is assigned to the injured (plaintiff) and the accused (defendant). The bottom line is that you must make sure—every day—that you are following prudent and safe practices and securing a safe environment for your students.

One of the easiest ways to maintain a safe environment is to practice foreseeability. **Foreseeability** is the ability to recognize potential danger and immediately follow up with an appropriate action or behavior. In other words, if you see something that could be a potential safety problem, fix it. For example, if you were to see sprinkler heads and hoses in your playing area, you should recognize the potential for someone to trip over them and become injured. Foreseeing the potentially harmful situation would help you to take appropriate action: You could either remove the sprinklers and hoses or find a different area in which to conduct your class. If equipment is scattered on the floor during a lesson in the gym, have students pick up the equipment and put it away instead of having them play around it and risking injury. If you see a few students provoking each other with abusive words, intervene to prevent a fight or psychological harm. By paying attention to your surroundings and taking the appropriate actions, you can prevent problems and protect yourself from litigation.

Most often, negligence in activity-related lawsuits involve issues of supervision, instruction (selection and conduct of the activity), and environmental conditions including facilities and equipment. Other areas of litigation are first aid and transportation.

Supervision

Improper supervision is one of the main litigation areas for physical educators (Merriman 1993). As previously stated, all teachers have a responsibility to supervise and remain with their classes at all times. Supervision in physical education consists of the following duties:

- Do not leave the class. Send responsible students for help if an emergency arises.
- Enforce, reinforce, and post safety class and school rules.
- Keep students and the class in constant view; generally, observe from the periphery.
- Monitor the weather.
  - Move the class indoors if high heat and humidity exist.
  - Move the class indoors if a thunderstorm appears imminent. If you hear thunder in the distance, keep in mind that lightning has struck from as far away as 10 miles (16 km). So, a good rule of thumb to follow is, "If you hear it, clear it; if you see it, flee it" (Walsh et al. 2000).
- Provide safe spotting and specific supervision of high-risk activities (e.g., archery, gymnastics, tumbling, collision sports, wall and rock climbing).
- Supervise locker rooms. This can become an issue when some students dress quickly and head to the gym or activity area, while others are still in the locker room dressing. It is difficult to supervise two areas at once.

Instruction

Improper instruction is another common litigation area in physical education; it is the most basic responsibility of physical educators (Adams 1993). Instruction can range from the scope and sequence of your written lesson plan (written legal evidence) to what you do and say in the gymnasium. The following are examples of safety principles to follow when involved in instructional situations:

- Adjust or modify activities as appropriate for students with health and other limitations.
- Demonstrate competence with the content.
- Group students according to size, skills, or experience when contact is involved.
- Keep activities within the skill levels of students.
- Provide accurate technique demonstrations and explanations.
- Provide sufficient and safe space for practice and games.
- Teach appropriate sequences of activities; progress from simple to complex.
- Use and instruct students in the proper use of equipment and safety devices (eye protection, pads, etc.).
- Warn students of possible danger.

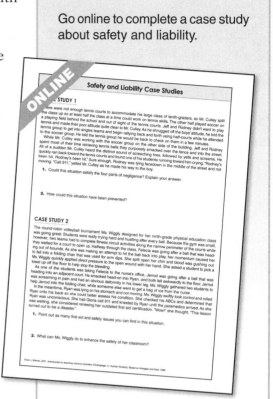

Go online to complete a case study about safety and liability.

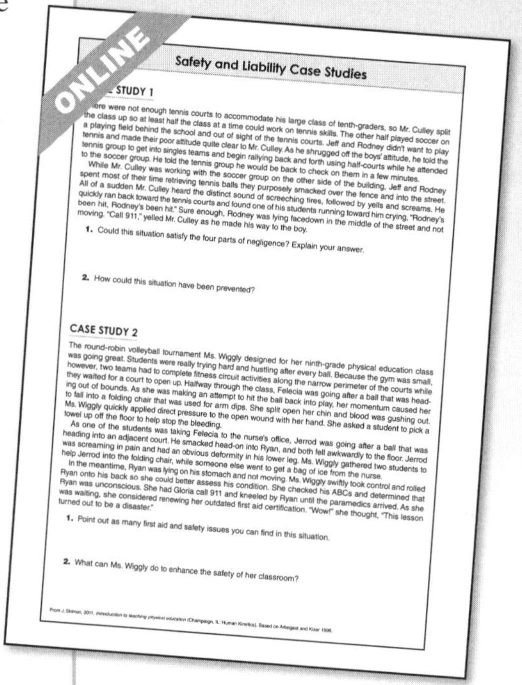
ONLINE

Safety and Liability Case Studies

STUDY 1

ere were not enough tennis courts to accommodate his large class of tenth-graders, so Mr. Culley split
the class up so at least half the class at a time could work on tennis skills. The other half played soccer on
a playing field behind the school and out of sight of the tennis courts. Jeff and Rodney didn't want to play
tennis and made their poor attitude quite clear to Mr. Culley. As he shrugged off the boys' attitude, he told the
tennis group to get into singles teams and begin rallying back and forth using half-courts while he attended
to the soccer group. He told the tennis group he would be back to check on them in a few minutes.
While Mr. Culley was working with the soccer group on the other side of the building, Jeff and Rodney
spent most of their time retrieving tennis balls they purposely smacked over the fence and into the street.
All of a sudden Mr. Culley heard the distinct sound of screeching tires, followed by yells and screams. He
quickly ran back toward the tennis courts and found one of his students running toward him crying, "Rodney's
been hit, Rodney's been hit." Sure enough, Rodney was lying facedown in the middle of the street and not
moving. "Call 911," yelled Mr. Culley as he made his way to the boy.

1. Could this situation satisfy the four parts of negligence? Explain your answer.

2. How could this situation have been prevented?

CASE STUDY 2

The round-robin volleyball tournament Ms. Wiggly designed for her ninth-grade physical education class
was going great. Students were really trying hard and hustling after every ball. Because the gym was small,
however, two teams had to complete fitness circuit activities along the narrow perimeter of the courts while
they waited for a court to open up. Halfway through the class, Felecia was going after a ball that was heading out of bounds. As she was making an attempt to hit the ball back into play, her momentum caused her
to fall into a folding chair that was used for arm dips. She split open her chin and blood was gushing out.
Ms. Wiggly quickly applied direct pressure to the open wound with her hand. She asked a student to pick a
towel up off the floor to help stop the bleeding.
As one of the students was taking Felecia to the nurse's office, Jerrod was going after a ball that was
heading into an adjacent court. He smacked head-on into Ryan, and both fell awkwardly to the floor. Jerrod
was screaming in pain and had an obvious deformity in his lower leg. Ms. Wiggly gathered two students to
help Jerrod into the folding chair, while someone else went to get a bag of ice from the nurse.
In the meantime, Ryan was lying on his stomach and not moving. Ms. Wiggly swiftly took control and rolled
Ryan onto his back so she could better assess his condition. She checked his ABCs and determined that
Ryan was unconscious. She had Gloria call 911 and kneeled by Ryan until the paramedics arrived. As she
was waiting, she considered renewing her outdated first aid certification. "Wow!" she thought, "This lesson
turned out to be a disaster."

1. Point out as many first aid and safety issues you can find in this situation.

2. What can Ms. Wiggly do to enhance the safety of her classroom?

From J. Shimon, 2011, *Introduction to teaching physical education* (Champaign, IL: Human Kinetics). Based on Arbogast and Kizer 1996.

Facilities and Equipment (Environmental Conditions)

You are responsible for making sure the facilities and playing areas are safe and free of potential hazards such as dusty or wet gym floors, potholes, rocks, glass, and so on. If hazards exist and no other area can be used during class, make sure to report the danger to an administrator and clearly mark and close off that area to students. In addition, remove equipment that may attract unwanted attention and pose a dangerous situation for students (attractive nuisances). Gymnastics spring boards stored in the corner of a gymnasium and nonsecured climbing ropes suspended from the ceiling are examples of attractive nuisances. The following are other duties that provide for the safe use of facilities and equipment:

- Maintain records of equipment repairs and new purchases.
- Periodically conduct safety checks of all facilities, grounds, and equipment.
- Use properly maintained and appropriate equipment for the intended activity.

First Aid and Emergency Procedures

It stands to reason that all physical educators should hold current first aid and CPR certifications. If a medical situation arises, it is your duty to provide proper basic first aid and emergency care within your training capabilities. You can also send students to the school nurse or a certified athletic trainer if one is present at the school. The following are other first aid and emergency protocols:

- *Do not* hand out *any* type of medication to students, not even aspirin or Tylenol.
- Establish an emergency plan within the physical education department. Determine who does what (i.e., who stays with the injured person, who calls for help, who secures additional first aid equipment, and who flags down emergency response personnel).
- Fill out an injury report form for all accidents and injuries, and file them with the school nurse.
- Keep a stocked first aid kit readily available, not locked away in a storeroom closet.
- Know how to handle hazardous materials (e.g., bodily fluids).
- Know the medical conditions of your students and honor medical excuses.

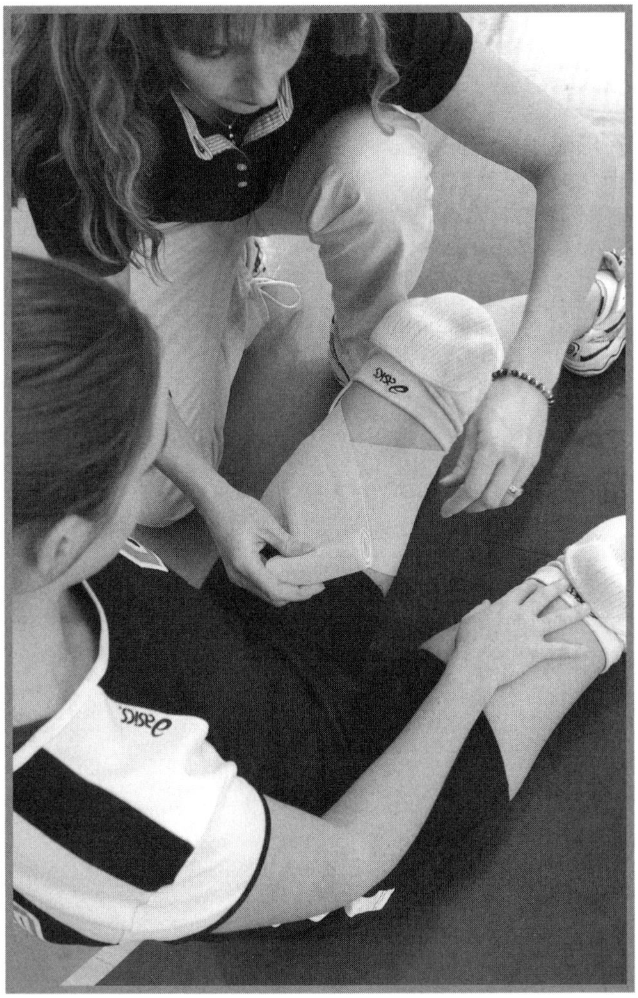

Physical education teachers must be prepared to administer first aid. Keep a first aid kit nearby at all times.

Transportation and Field Trips

Physical education classes are sometimes held off-campus, for instance, at a local bowling alley, skating rink, or golf course. Before scheduling a field trip, make sure the event has been approved through the school administration. It is essential to gain consent from parents through the use of written consent forms. No student should be allowed to attend a field trip without proper parental approval. In addition, schools may request parents to sign participation agreement forms that indicate an agreement to participate with an understanding of the specific inherent dangers of the activity, and outline safety procedures that will be used to prevent harm (Dougherty 2010). A participation agreement form does not, however, release teachers from liability during a field trip. Finally, arrange for a school bus; do not transport students in your own car or allow students to drive their own cars.

Overall, physical education teachers who conduct themselves in a prudent manner, use common sense, and practice foreseeability while teaching will maintain safe teaching and learning environments. Some physical education teachers and coaches also purchase personal liability insurance, just in case they are sued. The American Alliance for Health, Physical Education, Recreation and Dance (AAHPERD) offers liability insurance to its members. Some school districts provide teachers and coaches with protection against financial loss as a result of school-related litigation.

Nonteaching Duties

In your role as a physical education teacher you may be asked or required to perform tasks that do not involve instruction. These nonteaching duties may be part of a union contract or just assumed duties of the school. For example, at the elementary level you might be assigned bus, lunch, or recess duty, and at the secondary level you may have hall or study hall duties. Part of the school day may involve writing up a student referral for inappropriate behavior or contacting a parent about the status of his or her child. School days may include a variety of meetings with students, parents, or focus groups to discuss students' progress. There may be weekly core meetings with other classroom teachers, or with a team of professionals to develop and review individualized education programs (IEP) for students with special needs. Addressing students with special needs or those on special plans will more than likely required a lot of daily or weekly written assessments and reports as well. The amount of paperwork required of teachers is usually a surprise for most student and first-year physical education teachers.

Do schools in your area have school-based liability policies for their teachers and coaches? What are the specific safety rules and policies of these schools?

Coaching is another nonteaching duty many physical education teachers assume. Many are hired because of their additional coaching experience or willingness to coach. If you are interested in coaching as well as teaching, it may be beneficial to gain coaching experience now, as an undergraduate student. Often, local schools seek out eager and competent college students to coach their sport teams. These coaching opportunities could be a wonderful addition to your resume.

There are many other nonteaching duties physical education teachers may assume during the school year. Teachers often serve on various school committees, such as curriculum planning committees or equipment and facilities committees, and are usually expected to attend teacher in-service days or workshops as part of professional development. In fact, many states require teachers to obtain additional professional development credits each year to maintain their teaching licensure. These credits can also be acquired by attending educational conventions, conferences, or meetings.

Physical education teachers may elect to dedicate their time to professional commitments, which could include becoming involved in state, district, or national associations or staying current with professional journals or books. Some physical educators prepare special presentations for parent–teacher conferences, organize annual spring-fling events for students, or host Jump Rope or Hoops-for Heart events, sponsored by the American Heart Association. A portion of the money raised from these events goes to the hosting school and to the state's AHPERD association.

Professional commitment may also take the form of advocating for children's health needs and physical education by developing or maintaining a physical education Web site for the school, contributing regular news items to the school bulletin, organizing student tournaments and activities during lunchtime, or developing a fitness

Taking on the role of coach can be a major part of your continuing education and help you round out your teaching experience.

What professional development requirements do teachers in your district have to meet to maintain their teaching licenses or credentials?

and wellness program for students, faculty, and staff. The National Association for Sport and Physical Education (NASPE) has a variety of useful online products and materials available for physical education teachers to use for advocacy efforts.

There is obviously a lot more involved in teaching physical education than meets the eye. Table 3.1 lists some of the teaching and nonteaching duties you may be expected to perform as a physical educator. How do these compare to the duties expected of physical educators in your town or city?

Issues and Concerns

Teaching physical education is a wonderful career choice. As with any career choice, however, it is important to be aware of the problems and issues involved with that choice. As mentioned in chapter 1, global issues affecting physical education include the potential shortage of teacher preparation programs, e-learning, and the No Child Left Behind legislation. This section covers more specific issues related to the **teacher–coach role conflict**, the instructional environment, and accountability.

Teacher–Coach Role Conflict

Many physical education teaching positions include coaching responsibilities. It is not uncommon for the teacher-coach to work 10 to 15 hours per day during the sport season, not including weekend hours. Performing teaching and coaching jobs equally well is often difficult, and at times the stressful demands of those roles can challenge one's commitment to both jobs. As a result of this dual responsibility, coaching usually becomes the dominant role, even though teaching is the full-time position.

Why do countless numbers of teacher-coaches end up committing more of their time, attention, and energy to coaching than to teaching? One explanation is that

Table 3.1 Duties of a Physical Education Teacher

Teaching duties	Nonteaching duties
Assess students. Act as a positive role model. Contact parents and guardians. Create class materials. Develop tests and assignments. Grade papers and tests. Plan lessons. Maintain a safe environment. Maintain and order equipment. Meet with and advise students. Attend teacher, group, and core meetings. Write up referrals and reports.	Advocate for physical education • Create news flyers (bulletins, PE Web site). • Present at parent–teacher night. • Be involved with the school, parents, and the community . • Host Jump or Hoops for Heart events. • Involve the community. Attend in-service workshops and conferences. Be involved at the local, state, regional, and national levels. Perform bus, hall, lunch, and study hall duties. Coach. Do committee work. Run before- and after-school programs and lunchtime tourneys. Develop staff and faculty fitness and wellness programs. Stay current with the professional literature.

Professional Profile: *Niki Bray*

Photo courtesy of Niki Bray

BACKGROUND INFORMATION

I am the athletic director at Central High School in Memphis, the department chair of physical education, and the head coach of the girls' basketball team. I have a bachelor's of science degree in K-12 physical education and health. I have a master's degree in K-12 administration and school supervision. I am the 2010-2011 secondary chair for the Tennessee Association for Health, Physical Education, Recreation and Dance (TAHPERD). I am a 2010-2011 Teacher of the Year nominee.

Why did you decide to become a physical education teacher? How did that lead to your positions as coach and athletic director?

I wanted to become a teacher from a very young age. I've never wanted to be anything else. I was a year-round athlete playing every sport I could sign up for. In high school, I knew I wanted to coach after I finished playing college basketball. After coaching a few years, I decided I wanted to make a difference for all sports in my school and decided to accept a position as athletic director.

What do you like most about your job?

The thing I like most about my job is working with the kids. I love helping students develop physically, mentally, and socially. It is most rewarding to see your students develop into young men and women and to know that you had a hand in helping them reach their goals. I love helping nonathletes become confident and competent physically active young people.

What is the most challenging part of your job?

The most challenging part of my job is time management and balance. I love being a coach, a teacher, a teacher leader, and an athletic director. However, each position requires a lot of time and dedication. Because I want to do well in each position and I am driven to work hard, finding a balance is a challenge and making time for myself and my family can be difficult.

How have you continued to grow professionally?

One of the greatest ways that I have grown is in my desire to play a bigger role. I not only make sure that I help my students, my classes, and my school become better, but I also try to participate in projects with universities, my district, my local and state associations, and national associations to help improve the education for students statewide as well as nationally.

What advice would you give a college student who wants to become a PE teacher, coach, or athletic director?

Being a teacher, coach, or athletic director is a lot of work and requires that you care more about others than most people think you should. It requires you to have high standards for integrity, character, and honesty because you are a major influence in the lives of children.

many teacher-coaches value athletics over teaching. Unlike most teaching positions, coaching can be a glamorous and prestigious job. Sport and athletics are an important part of American culture. The significance placed on sports can be seen from professional athletics to local community pee-wee teams. Coaches are usually prominent and valued figures in the community and school, especially when they are successful. As such, coaching becomes a form of identity for the teacher-coach (Sage 1987).

Part of the conflict also stems from the fact that most teacher-coaches believe that to keep their jobs (coaching), they need to win, so they must commit more time to coaching than to teaching. Ironically, teacher-coaches are seldom fired for their teaching inadequacies (Millslagle and Morley 2004).

It's safe to suggest that many teacher-coaches enjoy coaching over teaching. That's not to say that they do not enjoy teaching; however, the many contextual differences between the two can make coaching more pleasing. First, coaches have fewer athletes to coach than students to teach (consider that physical education classes can have in excess of 50 students per teacher). It becomes increasingly difficult and frustrating to maintain a quality education program when teaching large class sizes. Second, coaches work with student-athletes who are usually more physically skilled, whereas the secondary-level physical education teacher instructs students with an extensive range of ability levels, from those with poor movement skills to those who are exceptionally skilled for their age. A lot of work and effort are required to create an effective and satisfying learning environment to accommodate all ability levels. Third, coaches commonly work with student-athletes who want to play; their attitudes and motivation to practice and improve are often inspiring. On the other hand, physical education teachers have to work with many students who do not like physical education or disrespect the teacher, especially at the secondary level. Constantly dealing with apathetic or ill-mannered students who do not want to be in class can become wearisome (see table 3.2).

Although not as common, the teacher–coach conflict can also work in reverse. Sometimes the teacher-coach determines that the stipend for coaching is not worth all the extra effort and time demands. As a result, the quality of coaching may suffer while more time and energy are directed toward good teaching. The teacher-coach may even resign from coaching responsibilities.

Being aware of the teacher–coach role conflict can help you be more mindful of the dual roles you may face as a physical education teacher. Your attentiveness to this conflict will help you approach both roles in a balanced way and commit strongly to teaching physical education as well as coaching (Ryan 2008).

Instructional Environment

The teaching and learning environment may pose another set of issues you could face as a physical education teacher. Teaching where there are good facilities, plenty of space and quality equipment, and manageable class sizes is ideal. However, that is not always the case. At the elementary level, physical education specialists sometimes have to conduct physical education classes in a cafeteria. The space is usually small, with lunch tables or other pieces of furniture stacked against walls. Because multipurpose rooms and elementary gymnasiums are used for many other

Table 3.2 Factors Affecting the Teacher–Coach Role Conflict

Factor	PE teacher	Coach
Class size vs. team size	Classes often large and hard to manage.	Team size often manageable; assistant coaches often included.
Teaching facilities vs. athletic facilities	Teaching facilities may be small, limited, or in poor condition; athletic facilities may be prohibited from use.	Athletic facilities often well maintained.
Teaching equipment vs. athletic equipment	Equipment often limited, old, or in poor condition; athletic equipment may be prohibited from use.	Equipment often new or in good condition; plentiful.
Student vs. athlete attitude and motivation	Students may have poor attitudes and low motivational levels.	Athletes generally demonstrate positive attitudes and high motivation.
Student vs. athlete skill ability	Huge range of ability levels to teach.	Skill levels are of higher caliber.
Teacher vs. coach identity and status	May have school recognition.	May have school, community, and statewide recognition.
Teacher vs. coach intrinsic and extrinsic rewards	Usually no extrinsic rewards; student success may be intrinsically rewarding.	Games and matches won; conference, district, and state titles; praise from parents and the community; newspaper and radio appearances; coach and player awards.
Overall teacher vs. coach enjoyment and positive experiences	Negative	Positive

functions, physical education is often excluded from the space to accommodate other school events, such as band and choir concerts, school photographs, and assemblies. If elementary physical education specialists cannot hold their classes in the gymnasium and cannot go outside because of poor weather, where do they teach their classes? Sometimes children do not receive physical education that day or week, and sometimes the physical education teacher has to conduct creative activities in a regular classroom or hallway. Although these scenarios may sound extreme, many elementary physical education specialists face them.

Facility issues can also be a problem at the secondary level. Many older schools have only one gym, which can become a serious issue when two or three physical education classes have to share that space at the same time. Poor facilities, such as broken-down tennis courts, gymnasiums with dismal lighting, and rock- or glass-infested softball fields or playing areas also pose problems. These situations do not present a productive environment for teaching or learning.

Further, schools that are overcrowded or have limited budgets to purchase new or additional equipment are a concern for physical education teachers. If class sizes are too large for one teacher to accommodate successfully, and if equipment is limited, students are usually waiting in long lines for a turn to use a piece of equipment, limiting their opportunities to improve.

Overcrowded classes with poor facilities and equipment are taxing on students as well as teachers. These conditions can contribute to additional stress, misbehavior, and potentially dangerous situations. Unfortunately, these factors are especially evident in larger urban settings, areas of great ethnic diversity, and lower socioeconomic regions, where many teachers begin their careers (Clements 2009). New teachers often do not have the skills or experience to understand and relate to students whose cultures, languages, attitudes, and socioeconomic issues differ from their own. If you obtain your first teaching position in an urban setting and do not feel confident about teaching the diverse students in your charge, seek advice from experienced urban physical education teachers (Clements 2009).

Remember, the preceding issues are problems you *could* face. Many elementary and secondary schools have wonderful facilities, ample equipment, and manageable class sizes that make teaching physical education a joy.

Go online to complete a case study about accountability and the teacher–coach conflict.

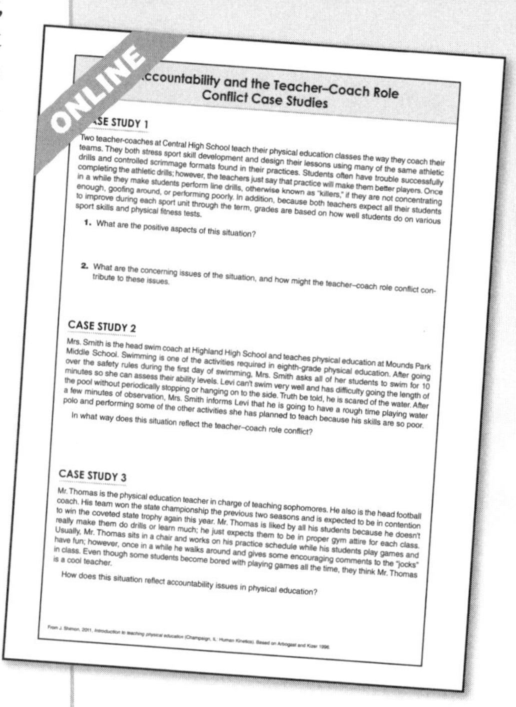

Accountability

One last essential issue involves the lack of **accountability** in physical education. Being accountable means that teachers and schools are responsible for providing quality instruction and sound curricula. Regrettably, programs across the United States that do not offer quality physical education, and physical education teachers who do not follow best teaching practices, detract from the excellent programs and instruction that serve students well.

A wide range of accountability issues exist in physical education. Some of the essential problems, including programs that do not address standards or objectives, poor grading, and ineffective teaching practices, are listed in figure 3.2 on page 64. A few of those issues need further attention. Let's start with issues related to grading and assessment.

FIGURE 3.2

Teacher Behaviors That Demonstrate Lack of Accountability

Curriculum Issues

- Does not follow or meet any local, state, or national standards.
- Has no direction or focus; no goals or objectives.
- Instruction results in no meaningful student outcomes.

Grading and Assessment Issues

- Grades only on participation, dress, and/or effort.
- Does not assess student learning.
- Cannot demonstrate that program objectives and standards have been met.

Teaching Practice Issues

- Allows team captains to pick students in front of the class.
- Uses exercise as punishment.
- Encourages solo performances that lead to embarrassment.
- Does not teach (e.g., follows the three Rs: take *roll*, *roll* out the ball, *read* the newspaper).
- Uses inappropriate games (elimination, poor time-on-task, no objective, embarrassment, unsafe).

Grading and Assessment

If you were hired tomorrow to teach physical education at a secondary-level school, how would you grade your students? Would you base a percentage of the grade on skill performance? Written tests? Fitness? Assignments? Participation? Dress? Effort? One of the issues affecting secondary physical education is that many teachers do not hold their students accountable for learning; therefore, they do not assess or grade them on anything other than participating in class and wearing appropriate attire. In other words, receiving an A in physical education means that students excel at dressing appropriately and participating during class. If math teachers, for example, followed similar practices, an A in math would suggest that students were outstanding at bringing paper and pencil to class and working on math problems.

Although some believe that assessing or grading according to skill level is unfair, skill development is central to physical education and included in the National Physical Education Standards. Yes, it is not fair to grade students on their skills if they have not been given enough time to practice and improve, especially if skill performance is based on the *product,* or outcome, (e.g., number of serves made over the net); however, it is fair to grade students on the *process* of skill performance or the components of skill technique, such as whether they can step consistently with the opposite foot when throwing a ball.

The main point here is that physical education is a subject area in the school's overall program, and student outcomes should be assessed and graded as they are in every other subject area. Being accountable for assessing or grading physical education objectives is one way to uphold the value and importance of physical education. More information on grading and assessments can be found in chapter 9.

Go online to do a quick case study about accountability.

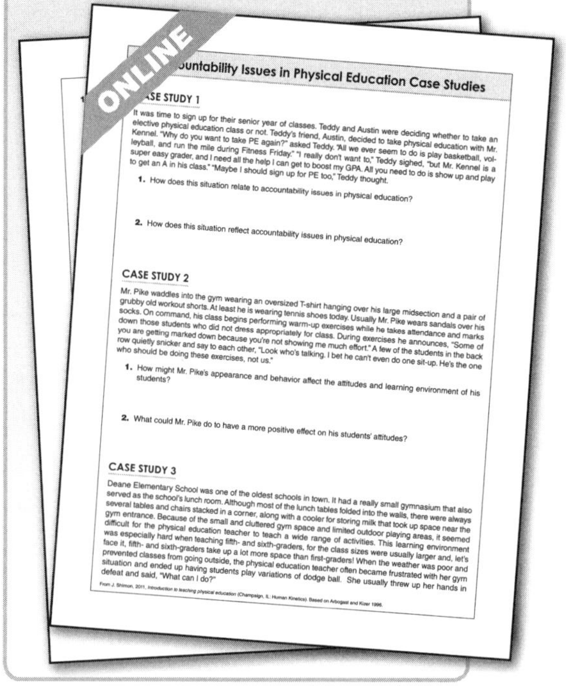
ONLINE

...untability Issues in Physical Education Case Studies

...SE STUDY 1

It was time to sign up for their senior year of classes. Teddy and Austin were deciding whether to take an
elective physical education class or not. Teddy's friend, Austin, decided to take physical education with Mr.
Kennel. "Why do you want to take PE again?" asked Teddy. "All we ever seem to do is play basketball, volleyball, and run the mile during Fitness Friday." "I really don't want to," Teddy sighed, "but Mr. Kennel is a
super easy grader, and I need all the help I can get to boost my GPA. All you need to do is show up and play
to get an A in his class." "Maybe I should sign up for PE too," Teddy thought.

1. How does this situation relate to accountability issues in physical education?

2. How does this situation reflect accountability issues in physical education?

CASE STUDY 2

Mr. Pike waddles into the gym wearing an oversized T-shirt hanging over his large midsection and a pair of
grubby old workout shorts. At least he is wearing tennis shoes today. Usually Mr. Pike wears sandals over his
socks. On command, his class begins performing warm-up exercises while he takes attendance and marks
down those students who did not dress appropriately for class. During exercises he announces, "Some of
you are getting marked down because you're not showing me much effort." A few of the students in the back
row quietly snicker and say to each other, "Look who's talking. I bet he can't even do one sit-up. He's the one
who should be doing these exercises, not us."

1. How might Mr. Pike's appearance and behavior affect the attitudes and learning environment of his students?

2. What could Mr. Pike do to have a more positive effect on his students' attitudes?

CASE STUDY 3

Deane Elementary School was one of the oldest schools in town. It had a really small gymnasium that also
served as the school's lunch room. Although most of the lunch tables folded into the walls, there were always
several tables and chairs stacked in a corner, along with a cooler for storing milk that took up space near the
gym entrance. Because of the small and cluttered gym space and limited outdoor playing areas, it seemed
difficult for the physical education teacher to teach a wide range of activities. This learning environment
was especially hard when teaching fifth- and sixth-graders, for the class sizes were usually larger and, let's
face it, fifth- and sixth-graders take up a lot more space than first-graders! When the weather was poor and
prevented classes from going outside, the physical education teacher often became frustrated with her gym
situation and ended up having students play variations of dodge ball. She usually threw up her hands in
defeat and said, "What can I do?"

From J. Shimon, 2011, *Introduction to teaching physical education* (Champaign, IL: Human Kinetics). Based on Arbogast and Kizer 1996.

Instruction

One accountability issue that drastically affects physical education is poor teaching practices. You may have experienced a physical education teacher who did not follow good teaching practices. For instance, it is not an acceptable practice to allow captains to pick teams in front of the class, yet some teachers still use this grouping technique. For obvious reasons, the least popular or least skilled students are almost always picked last. This poor teaching practice does nothing to foster student self-esteem and confidence.

Another significant poor teaching issue revolves around physical education teachers who don't put much effort into their teaching duties. Unfortunately, many believe that the only thing physical education teachers do every day is supervise game play. Why does this perception exist? It's the result of teachers throughout time who have not followed best teaching practices, who conform to the three Rs of teaching: take *roll*, *roll* out the ball, and *read* the newspaper (i.e., basically, do nothing) while students play games. In essence, those who follow the three Rs mar the profession and cheat students out of experiencing a quality physical education program.

One final poor teaching practice to address is the use of inappropriate games and learning tasks. Because games are used quite extensively in physical education to help students apply skills, strategies, and concepts, game selection is an important consideration. You can find games from numerous sources including textbooks, journals, conferences, and Web sites; however, not all games are good games. Consequently, buyer beware! What should you look for to recognize a bad game or learning task? The following are the components of inappropriate games (Williams 1992):

1. *Games that eliminate students from play.* Elimination removes students from attaining further experience and practice opportunities. Students who are eliminated first are often those who need additional practice the most.
2. *Games that use poor time-on-task strategies.* Using poor **time-on-task** activities or games limits the amount of time students have to practice or play. Poor time-on-task examples include (a) waiting too long for a turn or an opportunity to play, (b) waiting too long to use a piece of equipment, (c) using large-sided teams or groups that limit the number of ball touches or practice opportunities, and (d) using complicated rules and time-consuming instructions that take time away from active play and learning.

Can you think of games or activities you have played during physical education classes that could be classified as inappropriate, or bad, games?

Small-sided games are an effective way to maximize time-on-task.

3. *Games that don't teach toward an objective.* There should always be a purpose or reason for using a game during class. If the game has no objective, it serves no purpose.
4. *Games that cause embarrassment.* Embarrassment can lower self-esteem and confidence and decrease the likelihood that students will enjoy physical education and look forward to being physically active in the future.
5. *Unsafe games.* Some games have a higher potential for unnecessary injury based on the game itself or the equipment used.

Some inappropriate games that have been voted into the *Physical Education Hall of Shame* (Williams 1992, 1994) are duck duck goose, kickball, relays, Simon says, line soccer, and the infamous game of dodgeball. You may wonder why these games are labeled inappropriate. For example, although the game of duck duck goose is a fun circle game commonly played by young children, it has poor time-on-task qualities. Only two children at a time are involved in the activity, and there is a chance that some students will never get picked. In addition, the game lacks a clear purpose.

Do you believe that the games listed here, or other games considered inappropriate, could be modified to turn them into appropriate, or good, games, or should they not be used in physical education at all? When selecting games or activities to include in your lessons, make sure they are considered appropriate.

- Provides plenty of time-on-task.
- Does not use elimination.
- Does not embarrass students.
- Teaches toward an objective.
- Is safe.

Summary

As a physical education teacher, you will have many teaching and nonteaching duties. In addition to teaching students in the gym, you will be required to maintain a safe learning environment, meet yearly state teaching licensure requirements, and make a professional commitment to advocate for physical education and be a positive role model for the profession.

Accountability issues continue to plague physical education with bad press and less-than-favorable attitudes toward physical education. Poor teaching practices, along with ineffective programs, have contributed to the mediocre views of the discipline. In the current climate of budgetary shortfalls, physical education programs that fail to establish accountability for quality instruction and fail to meet district, state, or national standards face being cut from school programs. As a profession, we cannot continue to offer poor programs or follow inadequate teaching practices. It is up to you to live up to your physical education training, and not only do what you are currently being trained to do, but also live up to your expectations of yourself as a quality physical education teacher (Helion 2009).

▶ Discussion Questions

1. What factors contribute to being a positive role model in physical education?
2. What situations that occur in the gymnasium or on the field could lead to nonfeasance and misfeasance?
3. How can the teacher–coach role conflict contribute to accountability issues in physical education?
4. What games played in physical education contain components of bad games? How could you modify them to make them good games?

PART II

TEACHING PHYSICAL EDUCATION

There are those who believe teaching is a piece of cake; how hard can it be, really? Actually, effective teaching within a quality physical education program involves a lot more than making sure students are playing games and having fun. Not only does quality teaching rely on the scientific evidence gained from pedagogical investigations, but also, physical education teachers draw from research conducted in a variety of subdisciplines such as motor learning, growth and development, and the psychology of sports and physical activity. In addition to the science side of teaching, effective teaching also involves applying effective tactics with students and delivering lessons in unique ways, which is often referred to as the art of teaching.

Overall, the message is clear: If one of your goals is to become a great physical education teacher, you will need to learn, understand, and develop a solid foundation of teaching skills that will contribute to student learning and successful teaching. The three chapters in this section will help you on your way.

CHAPTER 4

Organization and Instruction

CHAPTER OBJECTIVES

After reading this chapter, you will be able to:

- ☐ Describe how to effectively and efficiently manage noninstructional tasks during a lesson.
- ☐ Portray assorted instructional tasks performed by physical education teachers.
- ☐ Explain the components that comprise effective demonstrations.
- ☐ Discuss how extensions and applications are used to enhance learning and motivation.
- ☐ Use various practice considerations to augment skill progression.
- ☐ Describe teaching styles that can be used to support student learning.

KEY TERMS

application activities
augmented feedback
closed-skill practice
command style
corrective, specific feedback
distributed practice
divergent style
extensions
general, positive feedback
guided discovery style
informative feedback
instructional tasks
knowledge of performance
knowledge of results
lead-up games
massed practice
modified games
noninstructional tasks
open-skill practice
part skill practice
practice style
reciprocal, or peer, style
self-check style
teaching cues
teaching styles
whole skill practice

How do you organize, manage, and teach a class of 20 first-graders or 35 middle school students? In other words, how will you get their attention and organize them into groups? What factors will you consider when demonstrating a skill or when planning for skill development and practice? What type of teaching style will you use? This chapter answers these questions by providing essential strategies and concepts for classroom organization and teaching physical education.

Noninstructional Tasks

Classroom organization consists of tasks such as getting students' attention, taking attendance, grouping students, and handing out and collecting equipment. All of these common **noninstructional tasks** take time away from the main lesson, yet are important parts of the lesson. Therefore, your goal is to develop a normal routine for accomplishing organizational tasks quickly and efficiently so students can spend most of their lesson time in instruction and activity (Oslin 1996).

It is up to you to develop your own set of effective classroom organizational strategies to use when you teach. The following sections offer a variety of options to choose from during upcoming teaching opportunities.

Appropriate Attire

Changing into appropriate physical education attire is usually a routine at the secondary level. Although students often dislike changing for physical education class, they need to understand that wearing physical education uniforms or activity clothing and tennis shoes is important for safety as well as personal hygiene reasons. They also need to know what protocol to follow if they forget to bring a change of clothes or shoes to class. Many physical education teachers have clean, used clothing (e.g., t-shirts, shorts, sweat pants) available for students to borrow if they forget to bring a change of clothes, whereas other teachers deduct participation points if students are not in appropriate clothing for class. Although not as common, some teachers, even at the elementary level, have a collection of used tennis shoes for students to wear if they forget their shoes. The shoes are sanitized with a disinfectant spray after each use.

> Would you allow students to participate in physical education without appropriate attire and tennis shoes? What are the pros and cons of such a decision?

Taking Attendance

You will need a routine that allows you to take class roll quickly. Although elementary physical education teachers normally do not take attendance for each class (it's the classroom teacher's duty), some designate a sitting area (home base) in the gym for each student. These areas may be line markings, numbers, or colored dots painted on the floor. This simple organizational strategy allows teachers to quickly gather children into a workable area for instruction, which is particularly useful when teaching at the elementary level.

At the secondary level, recording attendance is required and normally occurs at the beginning of class. Because taking attendance takes time away from the main lesson, teachers use a variety of techniques for completing this task quickly. Many arrange students alphabetically in squad lines. This allows them to quickly determine who is absent. It's also a great way for teachers to learn students' names. Some teachers assign squad leaders to report who is absent in each line, whereas others

Painting floor markings on an elementary school's gym floor will help organize students.
Photo courtesy of Jane Shimon

take attendance during a warm-up routine. Finally, in schools that require all teachers to submit their class attendance at the start of each period, physical education teachers take attendance before sending students to the locker rooms to change for class.

What are other ways physical education teachers can take attendance quickly and efficiently at the elementary and secondary levels?

The classroom organizational tasks that follow are preceded by scenarios to orient you to the progression of getting students ready for instruction.

Stop Signals

Scenario: Students are scattered throughout the gym. How will you get their attention to begin class?

One of the first organizational components you need to establish is an effective stop signal. A stop signal is something you say or do during class to quickly get students' attention. Students know it is time to stop and pay attention when they hear the signal. A stop signal needs to be distinct and loud enough for everyone to hear, especially when the gym is filled with the sounds of bouncing balls, laughter, and physical activity.

Perhaps the most common stop signal used in physical education is the whistle. One or two quick bursts of a whistle is an effective way to gain students' attention. The whistle is particularly helpful outdoors when students are scattered across playing fields or indoors when the gym is full of noise. Some people can naturally form their own whistle, with or without the use of their fingers; however, using

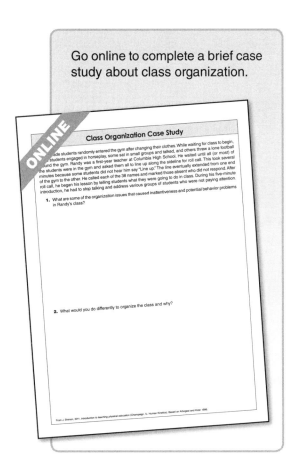

Go online to complete a brief case study about class organization.

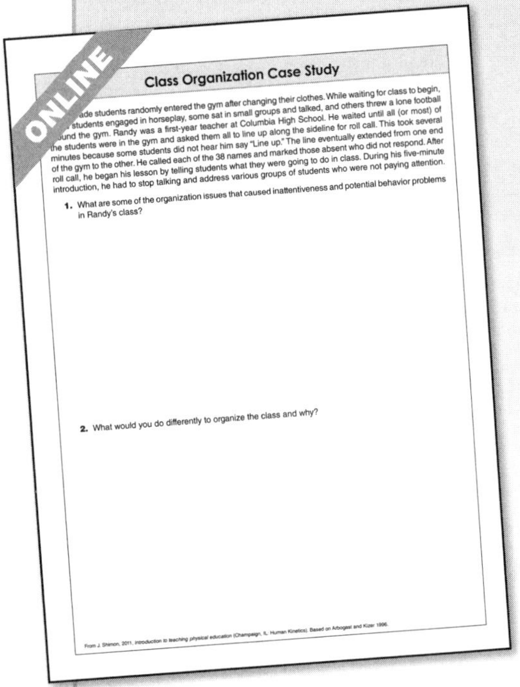
ONLINE

Class Organization Case Study

...ade students randomly entered the gym after changing their clothes. While waiting for class to begin, ... students engaged in horseplay, some sat in small groups and talked, and others threw a lone football ...und the gym. Randy was a first-year teacher at Columbia High School. He waited until all (or most) of the students were in the gym and asked them all to line up along the sideline for roll call. This took several minutes because some students did not hear him say "Line up." The line eventually extended from one end of the gym to the other. He called each of the 38 names and marked those absent who did not respond. After roll call, he began his lesson by telling students what they were going to do in class. During his five-minute introduction, he had to stop talking and address various groups of students who were not paying attention.

1. What are some of the organization issues that caused inattentiveness and potential behavior problems in Randy's class?

2. What would you do differently to organize the class and why?

fingers to create a loud whistle is inadvisable. Remember, a *lot* of germs inhabit the gym, survive on physical education equipment, and end up on your fingers!

Some physical education teachers do not like to use the whistle as a stop signal, so they use their voice. Even a strong, loud voice, though, may not be the most effective stop signal. If students do not hear the signal, the teacher has to take time away from the lesson to stop the class. Also, using a loud voice or shouting throughout the day may lead to vocal injuries (Trout and McColl 2007). To help alleviate the chance of vocal trauma, some teachers use a cordless microphone that transmits their voice to a speaker system in the gym. This is an effective and healthy way to use the voice as a stop signal during class, especially when working with a large class in a noisy gym.

Some teachers use music; when the music is on, students are active, and when the music is turned off, they know to stop and listen for directions. Music is a great stop signal for both elementary and secondary students, and it's especially helpful when the teacher can control the music by remote control from anywhere in the gym. Many elementary physical education specialists say the word *freeze* as a stop signal; others ring bells, beat drums, blow train whistles or horns, or clap their hands in a rhythm. Some teachers hold up their hand, indicating children to stop, and others get students' attention by saying something like, "If you can hear me, clap once." The teacher may have to say this several times until all students are playing attention.

Whatever stop signal you decide to use, it must be something students will quickly recognize as a message to stop and listen. Take time during your undergraduate teacher training to experiment with various stop signals to determine which ones are best for you and are most effective with the students you teach.

Teacher Positioning and Class Formation

Scenario: Students are scattered throughout the gym as you are ready to begin class. You shut off the music as your stop signal and quickly direct students to the center of the gym for instruction. How will you organize the class prior to providing instruction or giving directions?

One of the biggest mistakes beginning physical education teachers make is standing in the middle of the class when speaking to students. If you are positioned in the middle, a number of students will be behind you, out of sight. Students may not be able to hear or see what you are saying or doing, and more important, you cannot see what those out-of-sight students are doing. They could be distracting the rest of the class or not paying attention to instructions. Therefore, the fundamental rule to follow when presenting material to a class is to always position yourself in front of your students.

There are many class formations you can use to keep all students in view while giving instructions (see figure 4.1). Students can be arranged by squads or gathered into a semicircle. Students can also be instructed to line up along one line; however, this arrangement may not be the most effective choice if the class is large, because numerous students at each end of the line will not be able hear you. Additionally,

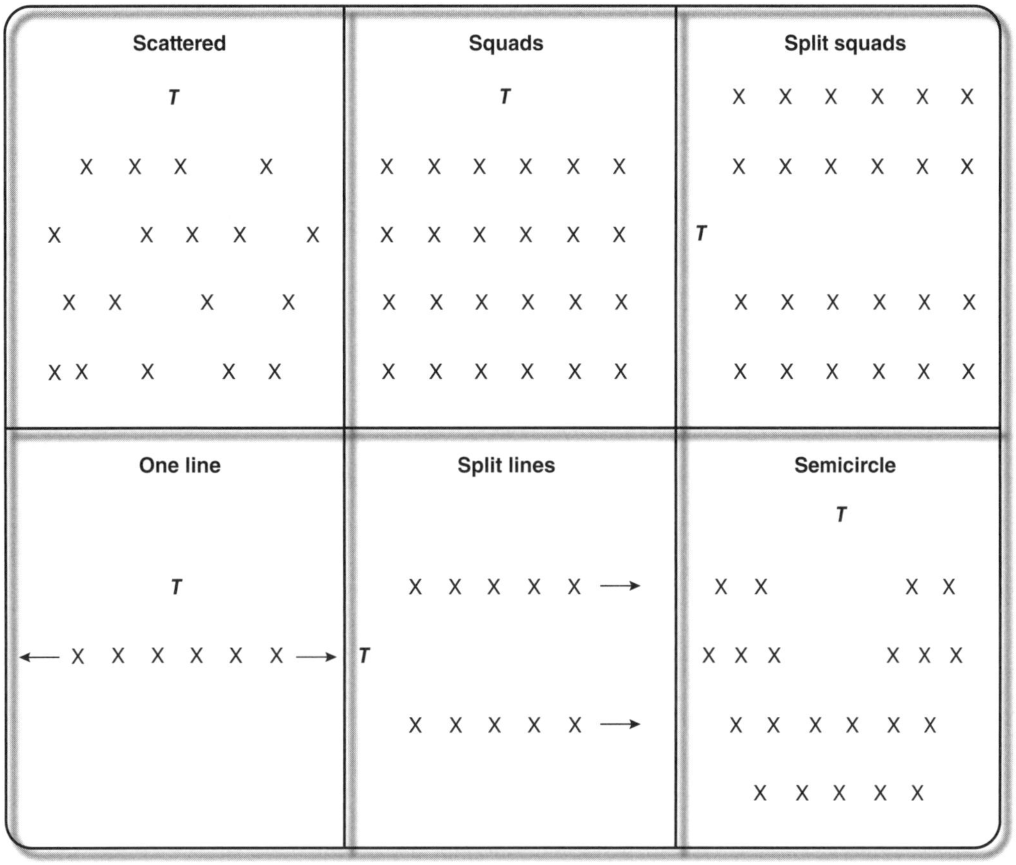

FIGURE 4.1 Various class formations can afford teachers a view of all students.

students are more prone to distractions or to cause disruptions if they are situated at the ends, and they will not know what you have announced. For that reason, use long-line arrangements with discretion.

After gathering students into some type of formation, you have other student organizational issues to consider. First, will students sit or stand during instruction or directions? It is often beneficial for beginning teachers to direct students to sit down, even at the secondary level. This gives you more class control, diminishes student talking and distracting behaviors, and allows you to maintain good eye contact with students, in particular those who are sitting farther away.

Second, you need to pay attention to other distractions occurring at the time. For instance, if class is being held outdoors and the sun is shining, students should not be looking into the sun while listening to instructions. If there is another class in the teaching area, traffic noise from a busy road, or other distractions nearby, students should face away from the distraction. Otherwise, they will tend to focus on the distraction and not on you.

If students have equipment in their hands while seated and listening to instructions, they will fidget with it. In fact, they often pay more attention to their equipment than to the teacher! To alleviate this distraction, ask students to put equipment at their feet or off to one side (no touching) while they are listening. You also can direct students to leave their equipment at the court or a spot on the floor before gathering around for further instruction. Whatever strategy you use, make sure students keep their equipment still or follow a no-touch rule when you are talking.

A teacher has a view of all her students when positioned just outside the circle.

Grouping Students

Scenario: Students are scattered throughout the gym as you are ready to begin class. You shut off the music as your stop signal and quickly direct students to sit down in a semicircle in the center of the gym for instruction. After your instruction, you are ready to place students into groups for skill practice or game play. How will you quickly organize the class into groups?

Most likely, one of your answers to the previous question is to have students count off (e.g., 1 through 6) to determine their groups. Although counting off by numbers does work, it is often not as effective as other methods. This strategy usually takes up too much time, some students may not honor their assigned number (change groups), a few students may jockey for a better position in line to make sure they end up with the same number as their friends, or students may forget their numbers, which is often the case with younger children. Following are other effective grouping options to consider.

Preassigned Groups

Using preassigned groups is a quick and effective method for determining practice groups or teams. You can arrange groups prior to class based on squads, ability levels, knowledge of the activity, or friends. You can also arrange students to work with those outside their normal circle of friends. Group listings can be posted on the gym wall to make the process go even faster when the time comes for students to get into groups.

Student Choice

Allowing students to select their own groups usually enhances motivation because they can work with their friends. When permitting students to select their own partner or group, ask them to get into groups of two or three, or groups of four or five instead of stipulating only even-numbered groups. For example, you might say something like, "I need you all to get into groups of two or three and begin working." Providing an option for odd-numbered groups makes it easier for students who did not find a partner or an even-numbered group to join. In addition, to make this process go quickly, give students a time limit to get into their groups. For example, you might say, "You all have five seconds to get into groups of two or three and begin working."

Objects (Luck of the Draw)

You can randomly hand out objects to students as they warm up or enter the gym. Items such as cards (showing numbers, symbols, shapes, or pictures) or various colored wrist bands, jerseys, or pinnies can be used. Those with similar cards or colored attire constitute students' designated groups for that task. This method also allows you to quickly change groups during the lesson. The following are just a few of the grouping possibilities you can use with a deck of cards: 9s, 10s, jacks, queens, kings, and aces (24 cards and 24 students):

- Six groups of four: four of a kind (e.g., four jacks, four queens)
- Eight groups of three: three of different suits (hearts, diamonds, clubs, or spades)
- Partners: two of a kind (two from the same suit, two from a different suit)

Random Characteristics

You can use a variety of student characteristics for grouping purposes (e.g., color of hair or clothing, month of birth, number of siblings, zodiac sign). As an example, you can have students find a group of two or three who have the same birth month or the same number of siblings. You can also use the class roster to group students based on the letter of their first or last names. The roster method allows you to prescreen the groups.

Team Captains

As stated in chapter 3, having team captains pick students out in front of the class is not an appropriate grouping method. The following are alternative methods for allowing students to pick their own teams:

- Captains can select their teams privately with the teacher while the rest of the class is involved in an activity.
- Captains can pick names out of a hat.
- Captains can pick names alphabetically.

Overall, whatever grouping methods you use, make sure they are quick and effective and match the objectives of the lesson (Lynn and Ratliffe 1999). Also, keep groups small so that students have more opportunity to be involved. Finally, it is helpful to vary grouping strategies. Following the same grouping protocol day after day will become boring and monotonous for most students.

Equipment Distribution and Collection

Scenario: Students are scattered throughout the gym as you are ready to begin class. You shut off the music as your stop signal and quickly direct students to sit down in a semicircle in the center of the gym for instruction. After instruction is complete and your students know what they are going to do, you ask them to quickly find others with the same birth month, and get into groups of two or three, then get their equipment. How will you safely and effectively issue equipment to students?

This cooperative group was formed based on the students' birthdays.

Determining how to quickly distribute (and collect) equipment safely is the final consideration you will need to make before sending students on their way to practice or play. Allowing students to get their equipment all at once is not a safe practice. It usually results in a mad rush and pile-up at the equipment bin, especially at the elementary level. Students can get hurt, or end up waiting in long lines, wasting class time. Here are some options for both equipment distribution and collection:

- Rock-paper-scissors in a group
- Squad leaders for each group
- Girls first, then boys; boys first, then girls
- Tallest or shortest person in a group
- Groups that are sitting quietly
- Various colored clothing

It is imperative that you establish a classroom organization routine that is quick and efficient (see figure 4.2). Remember, the less time you spend on classroom organizational tasks, the more time your students will have to learn and be active. As a recap, the classroom organization scenario that has been unfolding in the preceding sections is finally complete:

Students are scattered throughout the gym as you are ready to begin class. You shut off the music as your *stop signal* and quickly direct students to *sit down* in a *semicircle* in the center of the gym. After instruction is complete and your students know what they are going to do, you ask them to quickly find others who have the *same birth month* and get into *groups of two or three.* You request the *tallest member of each group to gather the needed equipment*, while the rest of the group finds a practice area. You turn the music back on as students begin working in their groups.

Instructional Tasks

It is now time to examine those components of the lesson that deal with instruction, otherwise known as learning task presentations. **Instructional tasks**, such as providing demonstrations and explanations, using teaching cues, and giving feedback, contribute to student learning.

FIGURE 4.2

Classroom Organizational Strategies

- Use an effective stop signal.
- Position yourself in front of all students when providing instruction.
- Have students seated.
- Face students away from distractions (e.g., sun, noise, other classes).
- Have students keep equipment still or follow no-touch rule.
- Use a variety of effective grouping strategies:
    - Prearranged groups
    - Student choice
    - Group identifiers
    - Use quick and safe equipment distribution and collection methods.

Demonstrations and Teaching Cues

Two common ways students learn are by observing and listening. For that reason, demonstrations are an important instructional method for physical education teachers, especially when teaching beginning learners. The following section addresses the five essential concepts you should consider when giving demonstrations.

1. Show It

Physical education teachers often assume that students know how to perform a skill; however, many early learners may not know how to perform the skill, or even what it looks like. Therefore, you need to accurately demonstrate the entire skill (show it) so students can get a general idea. It is important that you show it several times, just in case a few students were not paying attention; a one-time demonstration is not enough. You should also show the skill from various angles, and if the skill can be performed right- or left-handed, demonstrate it for left-handed students as well.

There are many ways to demonstrate a skill. You can show it yourself as the expert model, invite a guest from the community to be a demonstrator, have students view a video clip, ask a student in class to demonstrate, or use a student learner model. A student learner model is a student who demonstrates how to learn a skill in front of the class. The rest of the class observes the student learning the skill through directions and feedback from the teacher (Darden 1997). Keep in mind that, at times, you may want your students to explore or learn movements on their own; when this is the case, do not begin with a skill demonstration.

2. Tell It

Physical education teachers often tend to overload students with excessive information during skill demonstrations (Belka 2002). Although the information may be important, it is too much for students to process and remember at one time, and the lengthy demonstration takes up too much instruction time. For example, let's say a physical education teacher is demonstrating how to do a two-handed set shot in basketball. The teacher demonstrates and explains the following skill elements to the class during the demonstration:

When introducing a new task, provide students with a visual demonstration and an explanation of the task.

"Keep your shooting foot slightly in front of the other foot, slightly bend your knees, and face the basket. Your shooting hand is behind the ball, and your wrist is cocked; your other hand rests alongside the ball. Remember to keep your eyes focused on the basket. Now, as you bring the ball up in front of your body, make sure the shooting hand is facing the basket. Transfer your weight slightly forward as you straighten your legs, spring up, and pump your shooting arm straight up and out. Your nonshooting hand guides the ball. Aim the ball to the hoop. As the ball leaves your hand, release your nonshooting hand off to the side and flick the wrist and fingers of your shooting hand. This will give the ball backspin. Make sure your legs are straight and lift up on your toes."

How many skill elements did the teacher describe? Although the information is accurate, it's too much for anyone to pay attention to, understand, and remember all at once.

While demonstrating a skill to students, keep it simple by explaining only one or two elements at a time (Magill 2007; Schmidt and Wrisberg 2008). Students at all age levels can focus on and remember only one or two pieces of information at a time. Consequently, your job will be to cipher through all the information you know about a skill and select only the most important elements to teach.

This task can be accomplished by using the funnel format (see figure 4.3). Each step within the funnel takes you closer to a condensed list of skill elements to demonstrate to your students. For instance, how could you take the previous comprehensive description of the two-handed set shot and narrow the focus so you do not overload the class with information? What would be the most important skill elements of the set shot you would eventually want students to learn, and what would be the one or two skill elements you would have students focus on first during the initial demonstration?

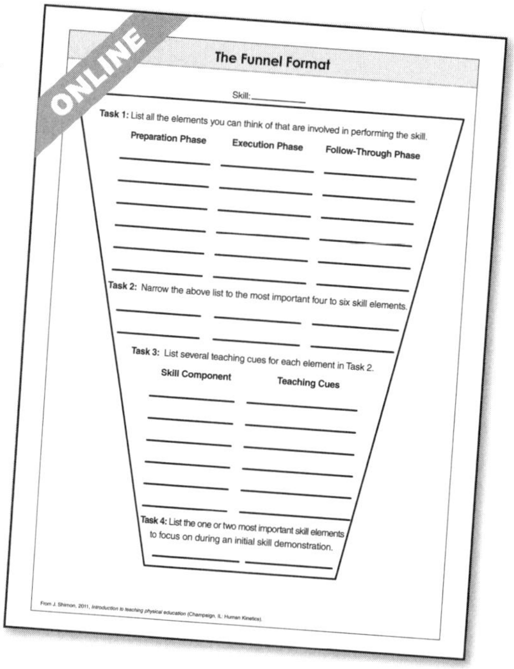
ONLINE

The Funnel Format

Skill: ________

Task 1: List all the elements you can think of that are involved in performing the skill.

Preparation Phase	Execution Phase	Follow-Through Phase

Task 2: Narrow the above list to the most important four to six skill elements.

Task 3: List several teaching cues for each element in Task 2.

Skill Component	Teaching Cues

Task 4: List the one or two most important skill elements to focus on during an initial skill demonstration.

Based on the funnel format example (figure 4.3), you would first focus students' attention on cocking the wrist under the ball and following through. The other important skill elements listed in the funnel format (bending the knees, keeping the eyes on the target, and extending the arm up and out) would be addressed later in the lesson or during subsequent lessons. (You can access the funnel format template by going to the online resource.)

3. Give Teaching Cues

Physical education teachers use verbal teaching cues during demonstrations to describe relevant movements or actions in a meaningful way (Rink 2010). **Teaching cues** are short, catchy words or phrases, acronyms, or even sequences to follow that calls students' attention to key components of a skill (Fronske 2001). For example, some teachers use the phrase *form a triangle* or *look through the window* when describing the hand formation for setting a volleyball. The acronym BEEF is commonly used to describe the four fundamental skill elements in

Skill: *Two-handed set shot*

TASK 1: List all the skill elements that are involved in performing the skill.

Preparation Phase	Execution Phase	Follow-Through Phase
Bend knees	*Shooting hand faces basket*	*Legs are straight*
Ball in front	*Transfer weight forward*	*Lift up on toes*
Face the basket	*Extend arm up and out*	*Flick wrist and fingers*
Shooting hand under ball	*Straighten legs*	*Pull side hand off*
Other hand on side	*Side hand guides ball*	*Release with backspin*
Cock wrist and bend elbow	*Focus eyes on basket*	

TASK 2: Narrow the above list to the 4-6 most important skill elements.

1. Bend knees 2. Cock wrist 3. Keep eyes on basket
4. Extend up and out 5. Flick wrist and fingers

TASK 3: List the teaching cues for each element in Task 2.

Skill Element	Teaching Cues
Bend knees:	*crouch down; little squat*
Cock wrist:	*service tray; hand under ball*
Eyes on basket:	*focus on basket; eyes up*
Extend up and out:	*push up and out; spring up*
Flick wrist and fingers:	*make a swan neck; reach in a jar*

TASK 4: List the 1 or 2 most important skill elements to focus on in the initial demonstration.

Cock wrist
Flick wrist and fingers

FIGURE 4.3 The funnel format helps narrow the focus to the most important skill elements.

a basketball set shot (Balance, Elbow bend, Eyes on target, and Follow-through). A cue sequence that students verbally repeat, such as, *step, together, step, hop* could be used to help them remember a dance step, or the cue *pull and breathe, kick and glide* could be used to help students learn the breast stroke rhythm.

Whatever cues you use, make sure that you constantly direct students' attention to the most appropriate ones (Schmidt and Wrisberg 2008). In addition, you can use several cues for the same skill element in the hope that one of the cues will connect with and make sense to students. For example, you could use the cues *make a swan's neck* or *reach in the jar* when demonstrating the follow-through portion of the set shot. Can you think of other teaching cues you could use for the five skill elements listed in the funnel format in figure 4.3 on page 81?

Teaching cues are important for the following reasons:

- They help students remember how to perform a skill element.
- They limit words and compress information during a demonstration.
- They help students focus on (direct their attention to) a specific element of a skill.
- They help teachers strengthen correct performance when using feedback (Fronske 2001).

4. Provide the Whys

Some students learn and remember skill elements or teaching cues when they can think through the process or the performance (Rink 2010). Therefore, it is always helpful to add a quick justification or explain why a skill is done a certain way. You can also ask students to come up with reasons instead of spoon-feeding them the answers. For instance, you might ask students why it is important to cock the wrist under the ball before shooting it to the basket instead of telling them the answer.

5. Check for Understanding

Finally, how will you know whether your students have comprehended your demonstration, instructions, or directions? Don't assume they get it after giving a demonstration or directions, because if they don't get it, you'll have to spend extra time gathering them back into a class formation to go over the material again. A common check-for-understanding mistake many teachers make is to ask, "Does anyone have any questions?" Physical education teachers rarely get a response from anyone when a question is phrased generally, even if students are unclear of what they are supposed to do. It is wise, therefore, to phrase questions with specific answers in mind. Checking for understanding with a purpose can be done in a number of ways, including the following (Rauschenbach 1994):

- *Shadowing.* You ask students to physically show how to do a certain part of a skill. For instance, after teaching the two-handed set shot, you might say, "Show me how to perform the follow-through part of a set shot" or "Show me how to place your hand under the ball before shooting it." You will be able to quickly tell whether students understood the demonstration, or whether further explanation is needed before they practice the skill.

- *Vocal responding.* You ask the class to respond in unison to a question. For example, you might say, "Give me thumbs-up or thumbs-down if I'm doing the two-handed set shot correctly or incorrectly." Or, you might say, "Tell me what you are supposed to do once I say *go*." The responses will let you know whether more clarification is needed.

■ *Reiteration (echo).* You ask students to find someone next to them and describe or explain what was presented. For example, you might say, "Find someone on your right and explain BEEF." This allows you to watch and listen to responses, and also allows students an opportunity to rephrase the response in their own words.

■ *Question alert:* You present a question to the class and ask students to raise their hands to answer. Once a student provides an answer, restate it so all students can benefit from the reply. Make sure to pick different students to answer questions, because the same students may always be the ones to raise their hands.

Demonstrations are also helpful when showing students how to execute a task (drill) or activity. Can you imagine what would happen if you only explained to a class of seventh-graders a three-person weave in basketball without the use of a demonstration? Physical education teachers often use student volunteers to demonstrate a learning task as they explain how to do it. This method allows everyone to see and hear how it is done, thus minimizing confusion when they are allowed to break into practice groups or play games. Remember, explaining how to do the drill or task is not enough; you also need to *show and tell it!*

Go online to complete a brief case study about demonstrations.

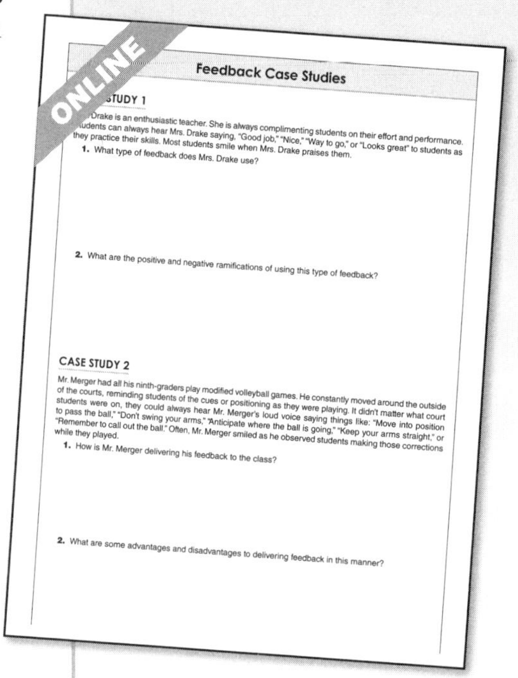

Feedback Case Studies

STUDY 1

Drake is an enthusiastic teacher. She is always complimenting students on their effort and performance. udents can always hear Mrs. Drake saying, "Good job," "Nice," "Way to go," or "Looks great" to students as they practice their skills. Most students smile when Mrs. Drake praises them.

1. What type of feedback does Mrs. Drake use?

2. What are the positive and negative ramifications of using this type of feedback?

CASE STUDY 2

Mr. Merger had all his ninth-graders play modified volleyball games. He constantly moved around the outside of the courts, reminding students of the cues or positioning as they were playing. It didn't matter what court students were on, they could always hear Mr. Merger's loud voice saying things like: "Move into position to pass the ball," "Don't swing your arms," "Anticipate where the ball is going," "Keep your arms straight," or "Remember to call out the ball." Often, Mr. Merger smiled as he observed students making those corrections while they played.

1. How is Mr. Merger delivering his feedback to the class?

2. What are some advantages and disadvantages to delivering feedback in this manner?

Check for understanding by asking specific questions and watching closely as the students perform the skill, as this teacher does by having his students show the correct way to address the ball.

Les Woodrum

Feedback

The final instructional component involves the use of feedback. Providing feedback to students while they practice or play is a critical part of each lesson. Feedback not only helps motivate and reinforce practice attempts, but also helps students consistently improve their performance. There is an abundance of motor learning literature on feedback; the following provides the most essential information you need to know as a beginning physical education teacher.

The most common type of feedback physical education teachers use is **augmented feedback**, otherwise known as external, or extrinsic, feedback. Students receive information (feedback) about their performance outcome through an external source. This source is most often the teacher; however, augmented feedback could also come from analyzing a video of their performance, a peer critique, a stopwatch, the end product of a task (e.g., whether a serve makes it over the net, or an arrow hits the target), or the action of a ball (e.g., backspin on a set shot, topspin on a volleyball serve). Students learn skills more quickly or perform them better at higher levels when they receive augmented feedback during practice (Magill 2007). Therefore, you should use augmented feedback during your lessons.

There are two types of augmented feedback: knowledge of results (KR) and knowledge of performance (KP). **Knowledge of results** is the information students receive as soon as they finish a practice attempt. For example, students know right away whether they made a basket or hit the target in archery. They know how many sit-ups they did in a minute or whether they achieved a backspin on a set shot. This type of external feedback is based on the results, or outcome, of their performance. As a result of the feedback, students may be able to correct the performance if the outcome was not what was anticipated, or they may be motivated to get the same results on the next practice attempt if the outcome was good.

Knowledge of performance is feedback students receive about their movement performance, usually in the form of a verbal comment from the teacher. The following section addresses various types of feedback you can provide students about their technique.

General, Positive Feedback

General, positive feedback is, perhaps, the easiest to use. Phrases such as "Good job," "Way to go," "Keep it up," and "Looks good" are all examples of general, positive feedback that teachers give to students while they are practicing. This type of feedback is a great motivator and helps encourage students to keep working. On the other hand, positive feedback does not help student improve their performance, because nothing specific about the performance is provided. If the teacher uses only positive feedback ("Good job, Julie"), more than likely Julie has no idea what she is doing "good." Is her follow-through good? Is her hand under the ball correctly? She doesn't know.

Corrective, Specific Feedback

Physical education teachers use **corrective, specific feedback** to help correct specific movement errors. For example, if using the teaching cues for the set shot described earlier, you might say: "John, make sure you are following through with your shot—reach in that jar"; "Remember to push up and out to the basket, Mindy"; "Eyes focused on the basket, Brad." Corrective feedback specifically indicates what part of the skill the student needs to correct and focus on during the next practice attempts.

Informative, Evaluative, or Instructional Feedback

Also called evaluative or instructional feedback, **informative feedback** informs students of what they are doing well, which reinforces correct form on future rep-

Corrective feedback should be specific and constructive.

© Human Kinetics/Less Woodrum

etitions. Comments such as, "Joe, I like the way you reach in that jar," and "Your hand is under the ball, Josh" are examples of informative feedback. Keep in mind that even though providing informative feedback to students is helpful, corrective feedback (error information) is more effective for facilitating skill performance (Magill 2007).

Feedback Tips

Physical education teachers often combine two types of feedback. For example, the feel-good feature of general, positive feedback can be combined with informative feedback, as in: "Looks good, Julie, I like the way you reach in that jar," or, "Your hand is under the ball, Josh. Great job!" Combining positive feedback with corrective feedback might sound something like this: "John, make sure you're following through with your shot—reach in that jar. Keep up the good work." Combining corrective or informative feedback with positive feedback is a way to encourage students to continue practicing after receiving more specific feedback.

Corrective feedback and informative feedback are especially helpful when students are first learning how to perform a skill. When they begin performing the skill satisfactorily, less feedback is needed (Schmidt and Wrisberg 2008). Gradually reducing feedback is important, because performances can regress if students become dependent on your feedback (Magill 2007). Finally, instead of giving students verbal feedback, you can ask them a question to help them evaluate their own performances. Questions such as, "What do you need to do to get better backspin on the ball, Jerry?" or "Why do you think the ball traveled off to the right of the basket, Veronica?" can stimulate students' understanding of the skill.

Feedback Delivery

How you provide feedback to students while they are practicing skills or playing games is also an important consideration. Although providing individual feedback to each student in class for every learning task may be ideal, it is not realistic given the limited lesson time and class size. The following are some methods for giving effective feedback:

- *Entire class.* If you see a majority of students doing part of a skill incorrectly, you can quickly stop the entire class and provide corrective feedback to everyone at once. This is an effective way to provide feedback, especially with large classes.
- *Groups.* You may find that groups of students perform different skill errors compared to other groups. As a result, when providing feedback to small groups as a whole, you can quickly accommodate those unique errors frequently occurring in each group.
- *Individuals.* As you monitor the practice area, you can provide feedback to individual students who require extra help. Because offering individual feedback takes time, be mindful of the rest of the class. Some students may go off task or become bored if they remain at one task too long. You need to constantly adjust or change skill tasks while attending to individual students.
- *Talking to ears.* As you monitor the practice area, you can verbally prompt or remind students using teaching cues. This prompting reaches the ears of whoever is in the vicinity and reinforces correct skill movements.
- *Monitoring the periphery.* As you walk around and give feedback to students, keep your back to the wall or perimeter of the practice area as much as possible. This position allows you to keep the class in view in the gymnasium or outdoors.

Often you'll need to project your voice to give feedback to a group of students.

Content Progressions and Practice Strategies

After demonstrating how to perform a certain skill, the next logical step is to have students practice that skill on their own or in groups. After demonstrating the set shot, would you have students practice a set shot drill for the entire lesson? Do you think students would be motivated to continue practicing the same drill after a long period of time? Do you think students would learn how to successfully execute the skill and apply it in a game? If you answered no to these questions, you are correct. The skill progression and practice concepts outlined in this section will help you facilitate skill learning by enhancing opportunities for success, encouraging the value of learning through use of progressions and practice, and fostering motivational levels to improve.

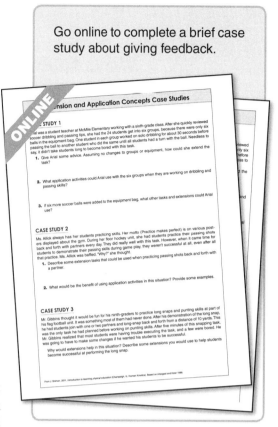

Go online to complete a brief case study about giving feedback.

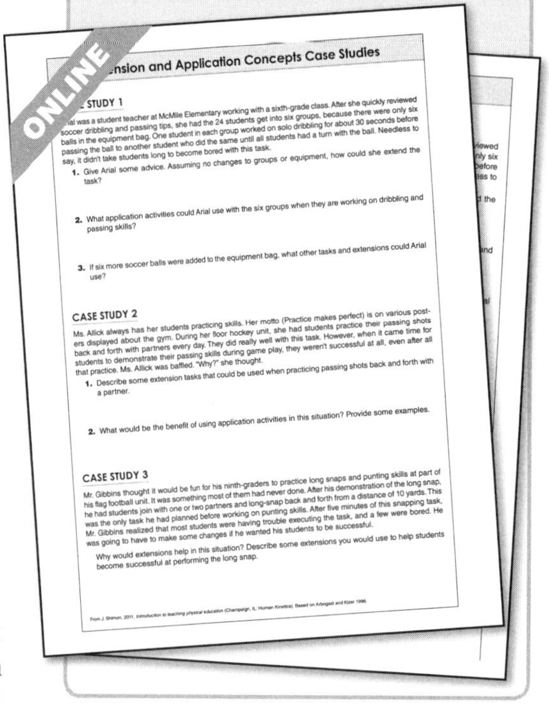

ONLINE

...nsion and Application Concepts Case Studies

... STUDY 1

...al was a student teacher at McMile Elementary working with a sixth-grade class. After she quickly reviewed soccer dribbling and passing tips, she had the 24 students get into six groups, because there were only six balls in the equipment bag. One student in each group worked on solo dribbling for about 30 seconds before passing the ball to another student who did the same until all students had a turn with the ball. Needless to say, it didn't take students long to become bored with this task.

1. Give Arial some advice. Assuming no changes to groups or equipment, how could she extend the task?
2. What application activities could Arial use with the six groups when they are working on dribbling and passing skills?
3. If six more soccer balls were added to the equipment bag, what other tasks and extensions could Arial use?

CASE STUDY 2

Ms. Allick always has her students practicing skills. Her motto (Practice makes perfect) is on various posters displayed about the gym. During her floor hockey unit, she had students practice their passing shots back and forth with partners every day. They did really well with this task. However, when it came time for students to demonstrate their passing skills during game play, they weren't successful at all, even after all that practice. Ms. Allick was baffled. "Why?" she thought.

1. Describe some extension tasks that could be used when practicing passing shots back and forth with a partner.
2. What would be the benefit of using application activities in this situation? Provide some examples.

CASE STUDY 3

Mr. Gibbins thought it would be fun for his ninth-graders to practice long snaps and punting skills at part of his flag football unit. It was something most of them had never done. After his demonstration of the long snap, he had students join with one or two partners and long-snap back and forth from a distance of 10 yards. This was the only task he had planned before working on punting skills. After five minutes of this snapping task, Mr. Gibbins realized that most students were having trouble executing the task, and a few were bored. He was going to have to make some changes if he wanted his students to be successful.

Why would extensions help in this situation? Describe some extensions you would use to help students become successful at performing the long snap.

From J. Shimon, 2011, *Introduction to teaching physical education* (Champaign, IL: Human Kinetics). Based on Arbogast and Kizer 1996.

Extensions

Extensions are tasks you add to drills or games to increase difficulty or complexity, or just to add variation to the task (Rink 2010). For example, let's assume that your first set shot drill in basketball involves students taking shots from various points around the key. What extension could you add to that task? In other words, how could you modify the task, while still ensuring that students practice the set shot in a realistic and functional situation? You could *modify the space* by having students take one step back, you could *modify the skill* by having students take two or three dribbles before performing a set shot, or you could *modify the number of students* in the drill by adding a partner who passes the ball to the person taking the shot. These functional extensions move students toward developing their set shot form (Oslin and Mitchell 1998). Adding extensions to drills and games helps students develop skills in a variety of practice conditions and game formats, accommodates students with diverse skill abilities, and keeps practice and game play lesson segments fresh and exciting. Figure 4.4 (page 88) outlines numerous ways to extend learning tasks.

Before presenting extensions and challenges, make sure they are at the proper level of difficulty for your students. Tasks that are too difficult do not improve performance (Mitchell 2009). Extensions for the set shot could look something like the following:

Task 1: Students work individually on set shots from points around the key.

Extension: Students move back one step from the key and practice set shots.

Extension: Students dribble up to a spot around the key, stop, and take a set shot.

Extension: Students find a partner or two and quickly set up for a shot after receiving a pass.

What extensions can you develop for the following tasks: (1) Students are in pairs serving volleyballs back and forth; (2) students are dribbling their own soccer balls down the court or field.

FIGURE 4.4

Ways to Extend a Drill, Activity, or Game

Modify the Equipment

Smaller/larger targets
Lower/higher heights
Shorter/longer handles
Lighter/heavier objects
Smaller/larger objects

Modify the Intent

Focus on skill technique
Focus on an outcome

Modify the Space

Decrease/increase the area
Decrease/increase the distance

Modify the Students

Change partners or groups
Change numbers in a group
Work solo, then add a partner

Modify the Skill

Practice parts or the whole
Students moving or stationary
Objects moving or stationary

Modify the Playing Conditions

Shadow a defender
Add an active defender
Change the number of defenders

Application Activities

Application activities are used during the learning of a skill to give students opportunities to use the skill in ways that further develop it (Mitchell 2009; Rink 2010). Application activities can allow students to assess their own performances. For example, after you have allowed students to practice their set shots using a variety of extension tasks, you can ask them to see how many times they can accurately execute a set shot in 30 seconds while shooting around the key. This encourages them to test their performance in a slightly more competitive setting. Application activities that challenge students to test their progress (e.g., *How many times can you…? How far can you…? How quickly can you…?*) are fun and motivating ways for students to apply and develop their skills (Rink 2010).

Application activities can also include gamelike settings, such as lead-up and modified games.

Lead-Up Games

Lead-up games (skill games) allow students to practice skills in situations far different from actual games. Usually, these games have little emphasis on rules, team strategies, or positions, yet they allow students to practice skills in more gamelike settings. The following are examples of lead-up games:

- PIG and HORSE in basketball use set shot skills.
- Keep-away games (e.g., two-on-two; three-on-three) use a variety of skills, including throwing, passing, catching, kicking, moving to get open, and dodging.
- Pepper uses batting and fielding skills in softball and passing and hitting skills in volleyball.
- Alley Rally, or Service Court Rally, in tennis uses forehand and backhand skills.

- Sharks and Minnows uses underwater swimming skills.
- Relay races can use various skills; however, students should be competent and confident in controlling their skills before being exposed to fast and competitive activities such as relay races (Rink 2010).

What are other examples of lead-up games you are aware of or have played?

Modified Games

Modified games are a more advanced form of application activity. Modified games are just that—modified versions of the real game. You can modify games not only to help students apply their skills in fun, gamelike settings, but also to introduce game rules, tactics, positions, and team strategies in a less stressful environment (Rink 2010).

Using small-sided games is one way to modify the real game. For instance, instead of playing a real game of five-on-five basketball, half-court games of two-on-two or three-on-three give students more practice opportunities (more ball touches) than regular-sized games and keep them actively involved in the game. Plus, small-sided games usually result in more successful performances because of the decreased complexity of the game (Griffin, Mitchell, and Oslin 1997; Petersen and Cruz 2000).

Games can also be modified by changing scoring rules, such as requiring passes to three different team members before attempting to score, or by making the playing area smaller. For example, you can have two games occurring on one badminton, tennis, or volleyball court by cutting the court in half. A soccer field can be turned into a four-game field by using the width of the playing area instead of the official field.

To place the use of applications in perspective, application activities have been added to the extensions previously described for the set shot:

Task 1: Students work individually on set shots taken from points around the key.

Extension: Students move back one step from the key and practice set shots.

Extension: Students dribble up to a spot around the key, stop, and take a set shot.

Extension: Students find a partner or two and quickly set up for a shot after receiving a pass.

Application: Students see how many set shots they can take from around the key in 30 seconds.

Application: Students find a partner or two and play a game of HORSE. Two attempts to make the challenge shot are allowed.

Go online to complete a brief case study about extensions and applications.

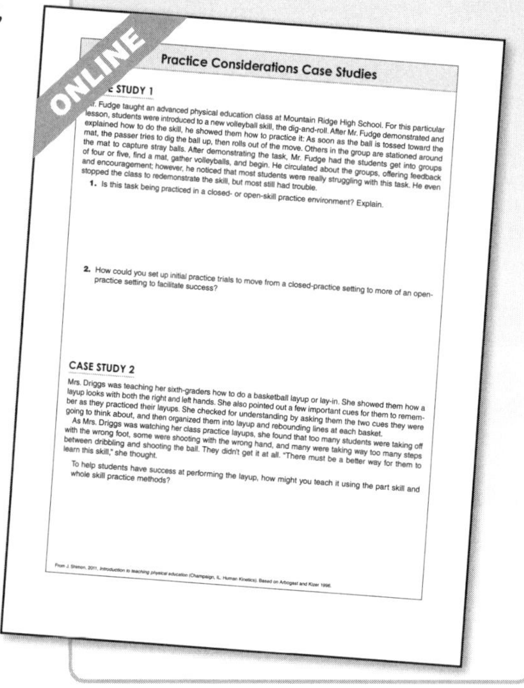
ONLINE

Practice Considerations Case Studies

CASE STUDY 1

Mr. Fudge taught an advanced physical education class at Mountain Ridge High School. For this particular lesson, students were introduced to a new volleyball skill, the dig-and-roll. After Mr. Fudge demonstrated and explained how to do the skill, he showed them how to practice it: As soon as the ball is tossed toward the mat, the passer tries to dig the ball up, then rolls out of the move. Others in the group are stationed around the mat to capture stray balls. After demonstrating the task, Mr. Fudge had the students get into groups of four or five, find a mat, gather volleyballs, and begin. He circulated about the groups, offering feedback and encouragement; however, he noticed that most students were really struggling with this task. He even stopped the class to redemonstrate the skill, but most still had trouble.

1. Is this task being practiced in a closed- or open-skill practice environment? Explain.

2. How could you set up initial practice trials to move from a closed-practice setting to more of an open-practice setting to facilitate success?

CASE STUDY 2

Mrs. Driggs was teaching her sixth-graders how to do a basketball layup or lay-in. She showed them how a layup looks with both the right and left hands. She also pointed out a few important cues for them to remember as they practiced their layups. She checked for understanding by asking them the two cues they were going to think about, and then organized them into layup and rebounding lines at each basket.

As Mrs. Driggs was watching her class practice layups, she found that too many students were taking off with the wrong foot, some were shooting with the wrong hand, and many were taking way too many steps between dribbling and shooting the ball. They didn't get it at all. "There must be a better way for them to learn this skill," she thought.

To help students have success at performing the layup, how might you teach it using the part skill and whole skill practice methods?

From J. Shimon, 2011, *Introduction to teaching physical education* (Champaign, IL: Human Kinetics). Based on Arbogast and Kizer 1996.

Closed- and Open-Skill Practice

Closed- and open-skill practice settings are other options to consider when developing lesson content. It is often helpful to give beginning-level students time to practice the skill by themselves in a stable setting; this gives them time to think through the skill and repeat it at their own pace (Magill 2007; Schmidt and Wrisberg 2008). This is an example of a closed-skill practice setting. **Closed-skill practice** is when a skill is performed repeatedly in a setting that is stable and predictable; keeping the environment the same helps students develop consistency in their performance.

In a closed-skill practice setting, students don't have to worry about judging the trajectory or speed of an objective, they don't have to move to meet an object, nor do they have to deal with defenders or other students in their space. Instead, they can concentrate on their movements and practice the skill over and over without having to think of anything other than the skill itself. A basketball free throw, a volleyball serve, and an archery shot are examples of closed–skills.

On the other hand, an **open-skill practice** setting involves an environment that is constantly changing; it is unpredictable and unstable. It requires students to perform or adapt their movements in response to the dynamic properties of the environment (Schmidt and Wrisberg 2008). In dynamic, or changing, environments, students have to make quick decisions prior to executing skills. They might have to judge the speed of a ball, the angle of an approaching defender, or their own speed. Performing a volleyball spike or a layup in basketball, defending a player, and hitting a groundstroke during a tennis rally are examples of open skills (see figure 4.5).

Although it is helpful for students to learn a variety of skills initially in closed-skill practice settings, eventually they need to move toward practicing in more of an open-skill format. For instance, although it is beneficial to practice their set shot form in a closed-skill environment, ultimately they will need to learn how to shoot a set shot after getting open to receive a pass, or when dribbling into an open area. To do so, they need to practice the set shot in a more dynamic and gamelike setting.

Many activities can be moved along a continuum of closed- and open-skill practice. Depending on your students' skill levels or the type of activity, you may design initial practice situations as closed-skill and then progress to activities that are more open-skill. For example, you may have students practice tasks in which either the students or the objects are in motion and then progress to activities that require both students and objects to be moving. You can then further complicate the task by manipulating the environment: adding defenders or players, or changing equipment or playing surfaces (Gentile 2000). Table 4.1 outlines examples of how to progress from closed- to open-skill practice.

FIGURE 4.5

Example Activities of Closed- and Open-Skill Practice

Closed Skills	*Open Skills*
Archery target practice	Batting a pitched ball
Batting off a tee	Catching a thrown ball
Free-throw/foul shot	Dribbling around cones
Golf tee shot	Fielding a batted ball
Gymnastics stunts	Offensive/defensive moves
Platform diving	Punting a football
Shot put and discus throw	Tennis groundstrokes
Volleyball serve	Volleyball spike
Walking along an empty sidewalk	Walking along a busy sidewalk

Table 4.1 Progressions Within a Closed- and Open-Skill Practice Continuum

	Closed-skill practice	Moving toward full open-skill practice		Open-skill practice	
	Student and object are stationary.	Student is stationary; object is in motion	Student is moving; object is stationary.	Student and object are in motion.	Modify the environment.
Kicking a ball	Stand in place while kicking a stationary ball.	Stand in place while kicking a moving ball.	Move to kick a stationary ball.	Move to kick a moving ball.	Kick to an open space between fielders.
Fielding a ball	Practice how to field a stationary ball.	Stand in place while fielding a moving ball.	Move to field a stationary ball.	Move to field a thrown or batted ball.	Throw base runners out.
Forehand tennis stroke	Practice how to do a forehand stroke without a ball.	Stand in place and bounce/hit the ball; stand in place while hitting a tossed ball.	Move into position to hit a ball suspended from a rope.	Move to hit a tossed or returned ball.	Hit down the line or crosscourt away from an opponent.

Whole Versus Part Skill Practice

> Many skills can be practiced in both closed and open settings. How can a volleyball spike be practiced in a closed setting as well as an open setting? What other open-type skills can be practiced in both settings?

When planning for content development, you will also have to consider whether to have students practice the entire skill all at once (**whole skill practice**), or parts of the skill separately before trying to perform the entire skill (**part skill practice**). Although it is generally recommended to use the whole skill approach as much as possible, it is helpful to consider the complexity and organizational makeup of the skill (Magill 2007) before making the final decision.

The complexity of the skill refers to the number of parts, or components, needed for performing it. Usually, skills that have fewer parts can be taught through the whole approach, such as shooting an arrow or performing a free throw. Skills that have many complex parts (e.g., the tennis serve) may best be taught in parts.

The organization of the skill (i.e., the relationship that exists among the skill parts) must also be considered. If the timing, rhythm, or speed of the skill requires that all the parts work together as one chain of events, the skill should be taught as a whole. For instance, the jump shot in basketball relies on the timing of the jump and the flow of the shot; consequently, the jump shot is a higher organizational skill and should be taught as a whole. If, on the other hand, a skill has many parts that are more independent of each other, the parts could be practiced separately (see table 4.2 on page 92). As an example, the spike in volleyball consists of the approach, the jump, and the hit. Although all the parts comprise the spike, each can be practiced separately without affecting the whole skill. This is an example of a lower organizational skill. The breast stroke is another example of a lower organizational skill. The kick (an independent part) can be practiced separately before adding the pull and the rhythm of the stroke.

When teaching a skill in parts, some teachers find it beneficial to use a progressive approach (Magill 2007). In other words, they have students practice the first two parts of a skill separately and then together. A third part of the skill is practiced separately and then added to the first two parts. Eventually, all the parts are practiced together to form the whole skill. Teaching a line dance is an example of this approach. The first eight-step sequence is taught first, followed by the next eight-step

Table 4.2 Considerations for Whole Versus Part Skill Practice

	Skill complexity	Skill organization
Whole practice	Low—fewer skill parts	Higher dependence on skill parts
Part practice	High—many complex skill parts	Lower dependence on skill parts

sequence. Then the combined 16-step sequence is practiced. Subsequent step sequences are taught and added to the previous steps until students can perform the entire dance. A volleyball spike can also be taught using this progressive approach.

Massed Versus Distributed Practice Schedule

One final practice consideration concerns spacing, or scheduling, the time students spend practicing a skill. If you were teaching a basketball unit, do you think it would be better to have students practice the set shot exclusively for an entire lesson before teaching them another skill (massed practice), or to have them practice the set shot along with other basketball skills for shorter periods of time over the course of many lessons (distributed)? **Massed practice** schedules consist of lots of skill repetition condensed into fewer lessons (e.g., day 1: dribbling; day 2: passing; day 3: set shots), whereas **distributed practice** schedules offer students shorter bouts of practice time extended over more lessons (e.g., day 1: dribbling and passing; day 2: dribbling, passing, and set shots; day 3: dribbling, passing, set shots, and layups) (Magill 2007). Overall, massed and distributed practice provides the same amount of time in which to practice skills; they just differ in the way time is allotted to practice those skills.

Generally, units and lessons that distribute shorter and frequent skill practice over time usually have greater potential to enhance student performance and learning than do those that mass skill practice into a short amount of time (Magill 2007; Rink 2010). In addition, students are less likely to become bored or tired or to lose interest when shorter bouts of practice are scheduled over the course of each lesson. In view of that, when planning lessons for a unit of instruction, schedule short periods of skill practice each day to help students learn and develop their skills. Within this schedule format, skill progressions using closed- and open-skill practice concepts, extensions, and applications can be especially helpful. Go online to complete a brief case study about practice considerations.

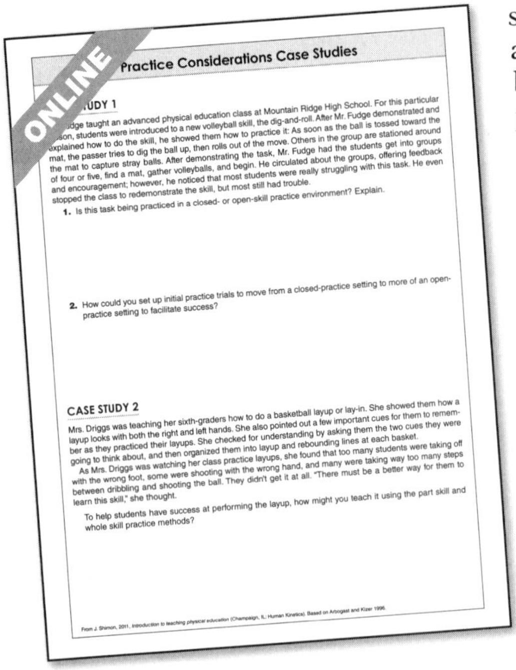
ONLINE

Practice Considerations Case Studies

UDY 1

dge taught an advanced physical education class at Mountain Ridge High School. For this particular son, students were introduced to a new volleyball skill, the dig-and-roll. After Mr. Fudge demonstrated and explained how to do the skill, he showed them how to practice it: As soon as the ball is tossed toward the mat, the passer tries to dig the ball up, then rolls out of the move. Others in the group are stationed around the mat to capture stray balls. After demonstrating the task, Mr. Fudge had the students get into groups of four or five, find a mat, gather volleyballs, and begin. He circulated about the groups, offering feedback and encouragement; however, he noticed that most students were really struggling with this task. He even stopped the class to redemonstrate the skill, but most still had trouble.

1. Is this task being practiced in a closed- or open-skill practice environment? Explain.

2. How could you set up initial practice trials to move from a closed-practice setting to more of an open-practice setting to facilitate success?

CASE STUDY 2

Mrs. Driggs was teaching her sixth-graders how to do a basketball layup or lay-in. She showed them how a layup looks with both the right and left hands. She also pointed out a few important cues for them to remember as they practiced their layups. She checked for understanding by asking them the two cues they were going to think about, and then organized them into layup and rebounding lines at each basket.

As Mrs. Driggs was watching her class practice layups, she found that too many students were taking off with the wrong foot, some were shooting with the wrong hand, and many were taking way too many steps between dribbling and shooting the ball. They didn't get it at all. "There must be a better way for them to learn this skill," she thought.

To help students have success at performing the layup, how might you teach it using the part skill and whole skill practice methods?

From J. Shimon, 2011, *Introduction to teaching physical education* (Champaign, IL: Human Kinetics). Based on Arbogast and Kizer 1996.

Teaching Styles

The final piece of instructional information you need to be familiar with involves the various ways to teach lessons, called **teaching styles.** Using various teaching styles within a lesson can motivate students to participate and learn, develop critical thinking and problem-solving skills, and work cooperatively. Teaching styles can be direct (teacher centered) or indirect (student centered), depending on various classroom factors (see table 4.3).

When teachers require more class control to teach specific techniques or potentially high-risk activities, such as archery, rock climbing, or various tumbling skills, they usually use a teacher-centered approach. On the other hand, when they want students

Table 4.3 Considerations for Using Direct or Indirect Teaching Styles

	Direct, or teacher-centered	Indirect, or student-centered
Students	Beginner learners dependent on the teacher to learn; large class sizes.	May or may not be beginners; mature enough to work independently.
Teacher	Requires more structure or classroom control.	Accepts less structure or classroom control.
Time	Time is limited for preparation, instruction, or delivering content.	May require more time for class preparation, actual class time, or both.
Content	Focus is on performing specific skills, techniques, rules, or safety.	Focus is on individual learning strategies, cognition, creative input, problem solving, or critical thinking.

to explore movements, determine solutions to a problem, or become more creative in their learning, teachers might opt for more student-centered styles of teaching.

Physical education teachers often use several teaching styles in one lesson. They may start with more teacher-centered styles and end with student-centered strategies. This section outlines the essential information you need to know about various teaching styles. For a more thorough look at teaching styles for physical education teachers, refer to the text by Mosston and Ashworth, *Teaching Physical Education* (2002).

Teacher-Centered Styles

Physical education teachers often default to the teaching style that is most familiar and comfortable to them, usually one that their own teachers or athletic coaches used. This style is often referred to as a direct, or command, style of teaching. The **command style** of teaching is the most teacher-centered style, meaning that the teacher is in command of all aspects of the lesson. The teacher tells students what to do, how do to it, when to do it, and where to do it. In other words, students all do the same task, in the same way, at the same time, and in a designated location.

The command teaching style follows the instructional tasks outlined earlier in the chapter. For example, the teacher demonstrates how to do the skill or task, explains how and where the task will be practiced, and, on the teacher's command, students can begin. This style is useful when teaching certain skills that call for precision or accuracy or when safety is a concern. Perhaps most important, the command style offers a sense of control in the classroom, a critical consideration for beginning teachers.

You will most likely rely on the command style of teaching as you begin your career, move to a new school, or start a new semester. Once you have established your classroom management and have gained a better understanding of your students, you can begin to use other teaching styles. Although the direct, or command, style of teaching is the most frequently used by physical education teachers, it is quite rigid and neither allows for individual differences in performance or learning, nor encourages cognitive or creative efforts.

If you want to maintain a sense of control during a lesson, yet would like students to have an opportunity to make some choices as they practice their skills, you can use one of a number of teaching styles that accommodate both teacher and student. One such style is called the **practice style** of teaching. Within this style, you have control over the skills students practice and usually control the time spent practicing those skills. Students, on the other hand, have a choice of how and when they practice those skills.

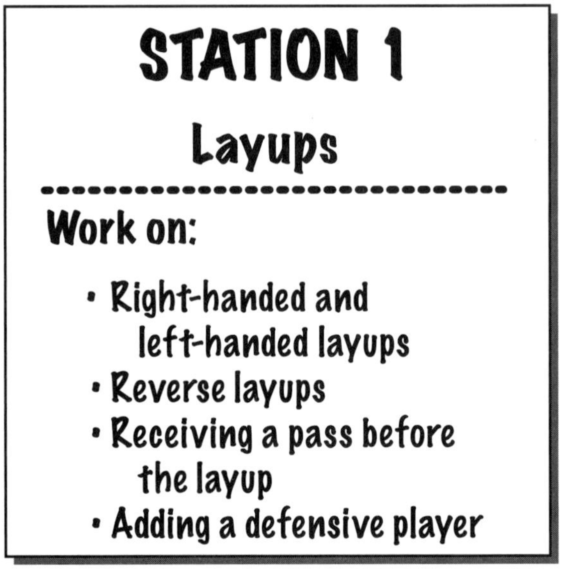

FIGURE 4.6 Example of a station poster with several tasks listed for students to perform.

The practice style often involves a station, or circuit, format. For example, during a basketball lesson, station 1 could be designated as the layup station, which could include the following tasks: right-handed and left-handed layups, reverse layups, adding a defender, and receiving a pass before the layup (see figure 4.6). Students at this station all have the same tasks to work on; however, they can choose which tasks they want to do, the order in which they do them, or both. When time is up and they rotate to the next station, they have a new set of skills and tasks to select from (see figure 4.7).

The practice style can also be applied to student groups. You can assign groups of students to an area (e.g., a basketball hoop) where they work on assigned tasks, such as various layup activities. After a period of practice time, you can stop the entire class and assign students a new set of tasks to select from (e.g., set shot tasks) or have them move on to something else, such as a lead-up or modified game. The following are some suggestions for when you are using a practice teaching style:

- *Create posters* or information cards that include several tasks for students to select from, in addition to directions, pictures, or diagrams if needed.
- *Visually designate station areas.* If you are using stations, tape station posters on walls, or place them on cone caddies (see figure 4.8) so students know where to go on each station rotation.
- *Determine an appropriate time limit.* Students could get tired if the time frame is too long, or bored if there are not enough tasks for them to do within group work or at each station.
- *Play recorded music* while students are practicing their tasks. Turn down the volume or shut off the music as a signal to stop and rotate to the next station.

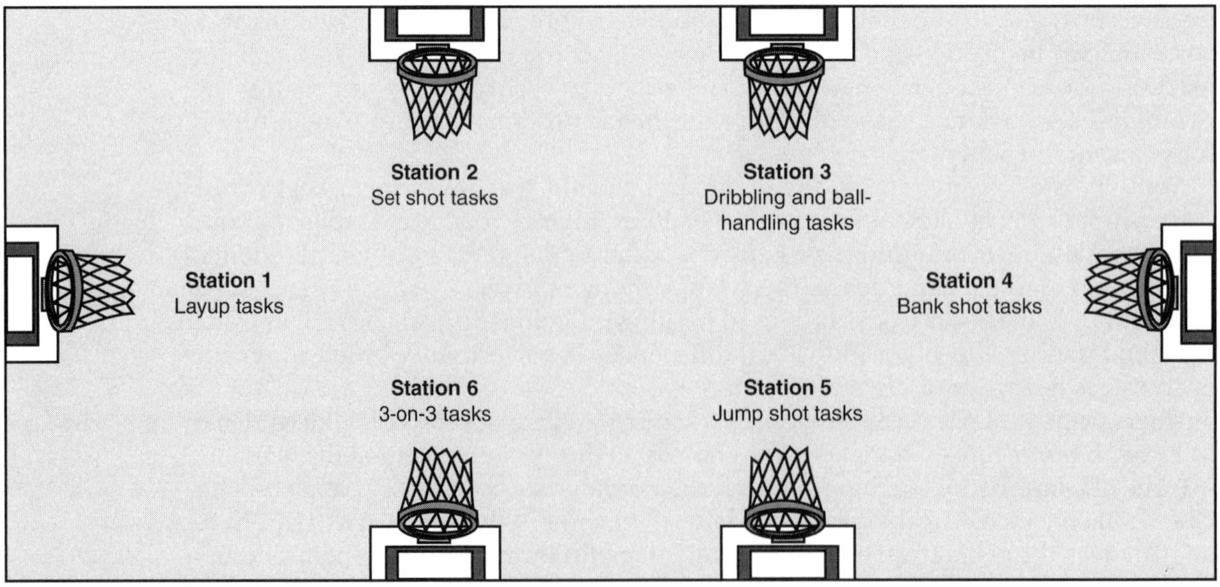

FIGURE 4.7 Six basketball stations can be set up using each basket in a gymnasium.

Commercial CDs are available for station or circuit work, or you can make your own on/off ratio of music. That way, the programmed music CD becomes the timer; you are not tied to a stopwatch and a CD player.

Sometimes, teachers want students to have a bit more freedom to choose and practice skills on their own or with a partner. Providing students with a list of skills or tasks to practice or complete gives them direction and accountability, while at the same time allowing them the freedom to select practice tasks. This style of teaching is referred to as a **self-check style** and requires students to chose tasks and check them off as they complete them (mastery learning) during part of a lesson. Task, or check, sheets can be used to help guide students through parts of a skill (see figure 4.9) or as lists of tasks they can select and practice (see figure 4.10 on page 96). It is important to offer a variety of tasks from easier to more challenging to give all students the chance to be successful.

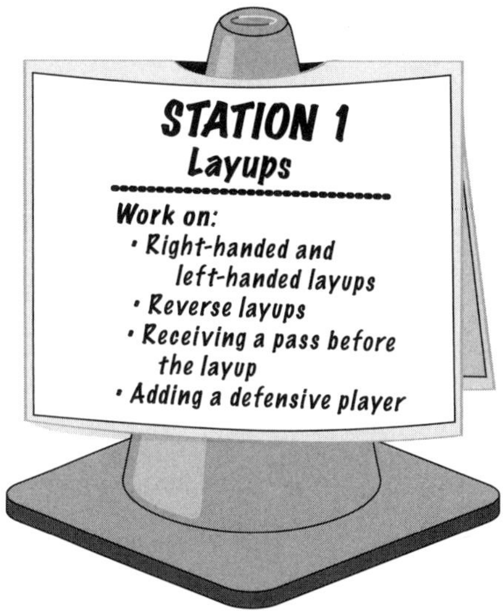
STATION 1
Layups
Work on:
• Right-handed and left-handed layups
• Reverse layups
• Receiving a pass before the layup
• Adding a defensive player

FIGURE 4.8 A cone caddy is one effective way to display station poster signs around the gym.

Both the practice and self-check teaching styles allow students to practice skills in an environment that offers them some freedom and choice; thus, these styles often enhance their motivation to participate and learn. In addition, these two teaching styles give you ample opportunity to roam the gymnasium and offer feedback to students.

Student-Centered Styles

Teachers use student-centered teaching styles when they want students to become more cognitively and creatively involved in learning. Student-centered, or indirect, styles usually require students to find answers or solutions to questions or problems instead of teachers telling or showing them (spoon-feeding) the answers.

Volleyball Float Serve Task Sheet

Directions: Starting with the first task, practice five attempts of the each of the following. Check off tasks (✓) when complete.

TASKS

- ☐ Toss the ball in front of your hitting shoulder. The ball should land on the poly spot next to your forward foot.
- ☐ Add the hitting arm position to task A (arm back and elbow high). No ball contact.
- ☐ Serve into the wall while standing on or behind a black line. Concentrate on making contact on the lower third of the ball with the heel of your hand. The ball should hit the wall above the target line.
- ☐ Same as the preceding. Concentrate on not following through (make the ball float). The hitting arm remains extended after ball contact.
- ☐ Serve the ball over the net into the other court. Stand on the red, white, or blue line.

FIGURE 4.9 Example of a self-check task sheet for practicing a volleyball float serve.

Volleyball Self-Check Sheet

Directions: Select the tasks to perform. You can select any or all tasks in any order. When you have completed a task, check it off in the space provided.

FOREARM PASSING

- ☐ Large space to self 10 times
- ☐ Narrow space to self 10 times
- ☐ Consecutive above the wall tape 10 times

With a Partner

- ☐ Toss and pass 5 times
- ☐ Toss, pass, and move 5 times
- ☐ Pass 10 times consecutively
- ☐ Toss over net or pass to target 5 times

SERVING

- ☐ From 10-foot (3 m) line 5 times
- ☐ From midcourt 5 times
- ☐ From back third 5 times
- ☐ From end line 5 times
- ☐ Short serves 5 times
- ☐ Deep serves 5 times

FIGURE 4.10 Example of a self-check task sheet for various volleyball skills.

When teachers want students to take more responsibility for learning a skill or task, they may use a **reciprocal, or peer, style** of teaching, which has students work cooperatively in small groups to teach each other or assess each other's skills. Teachers often create task sheets or peer critique sheets for students to follow to help keep groups focused and on the task. Students can use the compass learning task sheet in figure 4.11 as they teach each other about a compass as part of an orienteering unit. One student verbally describes the tasks listed on the sheet, while the other performs the tasks. When the tasks are completed, the partners switch roles.

You can create task sheets to help students gain a better understanding of skill technique by allowing them to critique each other's performances. When using the reciprocal, or peer, teaching style in this situation, one student is the performer (the doer), while the other partner(s) observes the performance, gives feedback, and marks the task sheet (see figure 4.12 on page 98). Your role when using this format is to facilitate the learning process and provide feedback to the observer, not the performer. As you might guess, it would *not* be wise to use this teaching for an entire lesson; rather, the reciprocal, or peer, teaching style is best used to complement part of an overall lesson.

If you want to lead students to determining an outcome or the solution to a problem, you may use the **guided discovery style** of teaching. For example, instead of teaching first-graders how to do a standing long jump correctly, you might elect to guide them to performing a mature long jump through a series of planned activities that eventually lead them to the final product. You might first ask them to try to jump to marked distances any way they can with their hands placed on their hips or clasped together. You may then ask them to do this same task by keeping their ankles or knees "tight" (straight) at the beginning of the jump. Finally, you ask them to find a way to jump the farthest without any body restrictions. After these trials,

Compass Learning

Directions: One partner reads each introduction step to the other. When the other partner has completed the first step, check it off and move on to the next step. When all steps have been completed, reverse roles and begin again as the other partner reads each step.

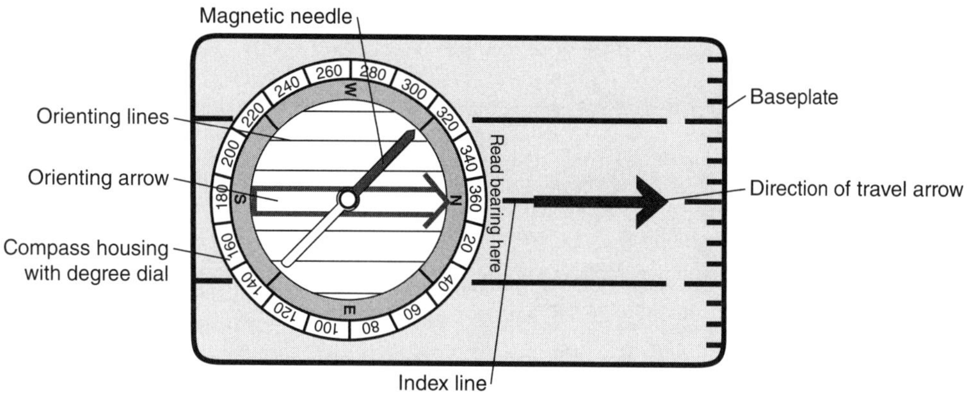

INTRODUCTION STEPS

___ ___ **1.** A compass is used to determine direction when traveling. As you hold the compass flat (level), notice how the compass needle moves freely. The red part of the compass needle *always* points toward the earth's magnetic north pole—it points north.

___ ___ **2.** Hold the compass level with the base of the compass near your belly button and the direction of travel arrow pointing straight ahead of you.

___ ___ **3.** Notice how you can turn the rotating ring (compass housing). Turn the rotating ring until the red compass needle is pointing to N (North). Now you are ready to use the compass.

___ ___ **4.** To determine the direction you are facing, find the direction of travel line (index line) on your compass scale. Match that line to the direction on the compass. Are you facing directly north, south, east, or west? Perhaps you are facing a direction in between, such as southwest (SW), southeast (SE), northwest (NW), or northeast (NE). What direction are you facing?

___ ___ **5.** You can determine the specific direction (bearing) you are facing by looking at the degrees found inside the compass housing that align with the direction of travel line. For example, north is at a bearing of 0°, south is at 180°, east is 90°, and west is 270°. You could be facing 120° SE or 330° NW. What is the bearing you are facing?

___ ___ **6.** What bearing would you be facing if you took two steps clockwise? After you take two steps and face that new direction, remember to rotate your compass housing so the red needle points to N before you read your compass bearing.

___ ___ **7.** Pick out something around you and face it. What is the bearing you need to walk in order to get to that object? Remember to make sure the compass and red needle align to N, and that you are reading the degrees in line with the direction of travel line on the compass scale.

Switch roles after step 7.

FIGURE 4.11 Task sheet used when peers teach each other how to use a compass.

Peer Teaching: Basketball Set Shot

Doer: Perform set shots from areas around the key while your partner(s) watches your form.

Observer: Use the following criteria sheet. Record the performance you observe after several shots and offer feedback to your partner. Switch roles after 12 shots.

Observer(s):______________________________ Doer:______________________

Things for the observer to look for:	All of the time	Most of the time	Not there yet
1. **Balance is maintained.** Feet are shoulder-width apart and knees are slightly bent. (Observe three shots, record, and give feedback.)			
2. **Elbow forms an L.** Elbow and hand are positioned under the ball. (Observe three shots, record, and give feedback.)			
3. **Eyes are looking at the basket.** (Observe three shots, record, and give feedback.)			
4. **Follow-through occurs after the shot.** The arm remains extended up and out and the wrist flicks down. (Observe three shots, record, and give feedback.)			

FIGURE 4.12 Reciprocal, or peer, teaching style check sheet used for skill assessment.

you ask students what they did to long jump the farthest, leading them to describing a mature long jump technique. As you can tell from this simplified example of the guided discovery teaching style, you initially had a question or problem in mind (i.e., What is the best way to jump the farthest when doing a standing long jump?), and then channeled students through a series of tasks to come up with the answer.

Helping students learn game tactics or strategies is another use for the guided discovery style. Through a series of lead-up games and questioning strategies, you can help students inquire about and determine how to develop various game tactics and strategies, such as how to spread out to maintain possession of the ball in a team sport, or set up for a point-scoring shot in tennis or badminton (Griffin, Mitchell, and Oslin1997).

When you want individuals or groups of students to cooperatively come up with solutions to a problem or question on their own, you can use a **divergent style** of teaching. When using this teaching style, you need to keep in mind that many answers or solutions are correct. For example, you might want children to come up with a variety of ways to volley an object in the air. Some children may keep an object in the air by kicking it, others may do so using their knees, and others may strike it with their hands. Each student has a solution to the problem, yet all solutions are correct. You may ask students to develop a series of offensive plays or create a unique aerobic dance, tumbling routine, or strength training program based on skills and concepts they have previously learned. By following your guidelines (i.e., a rubric), students have the freedom to come up with their own solutions to the problem (see figure 4.13). The divergent teaching style promotes creative problem-solving, recognizes individual differences, and encourages cooperative learning.

Tumbling Routine

Directions: Create your own tumbling routine that has the following four parts:

1. A **balance** pose
2. A **travel** skill
3. A **tumbling** move
4. A **weight transfer** example

You can chose from any number of skills practiced during class, and you can arrange your routine in any order. For each part of your routine, circle one part and write in the skill you will perform on the line above. A mark (+) will be recorded if each part of the routine is performed accurately. Finally, your entire routine should be smooth and flow from one skill to the next.

ROUTINE OUTLINE

Skill: ______________________________

Circle one: Balance Travel Tumble Weight transfer

Skill: ______________________________

Circle one: Balance Travel Tumble Weight transfer

Skill: ______________________________

Circle one: Balance Travel Tumble Weight transfer

Skill: ______________________________

Circle one: Balance Travel Tumble Weight transfer

SMOOTH TRANSITIONS

Balance: knee-to-floor, jump your toe, elbow, wall walk-up, thread needle, tripod, lever, V-sit, Turkish stand, up-spring, dip, jump foot

Travel (locomotor): Skip, hop, jump, leap, gallop, slide, lunge, grapevine

Tumbling (rolls): Forward (straddle, stand), side, egg, backward (straddle, stand), dive

Weight transfer: Tripod to head stand, lower the boom, forward drop scale, kip up, back bend, handstand, cartwheel, round-off, up-spring, shoot through, teeter-totter

FIGURE 4.13 This fifth-grade checklist is a way for students to demonstrate their ability to create and perform four basic tumbling movements.

Created by Corinne Morgan, Koelsch Elementary, Boise, ID.

Clearly, a variety of ways exist for teaching physical education lessons. Teaching styles allow for various levels of teacher and student control over what is taught, how it is taught, and how it is learned. It will be up to you to determine the type of teaching style that would be best in various lessons. More than likely, your lessons will eventually include several teaching styles. As you gain more confidence and experience in your teaching abilities, try to incorporate other teaching styles into your lessons.

Summary

There are many factors to consider when organizing a class, strategies to use when delivering instruction, and concepts to remember when planning for lesson content. Using efficient and effective classroom organizational strategies and routines will help lessons flow smoothly and alleviate student misbehavior (see chapter 6), and will help you use your time wisely. Using stop signals, arranging students into class formations, grouping students, and distributing equipment are all examples of classroom organization tasks physical education teachers perform every day. In addition, physical education teachers need to follow appropriate teaching practices during instruction, including using effective demonstrations, using meaningful cues, and providing useful feedback to students.

Effective skill practice is based on extensions and applications, closed-and open-skill practice settings, whole or part practice, and distributed practice considerations. Using these concepts will help you create effective skill progressions and help students develop their skills. Finally, by using a variety of teaching styles, you can provide students with various ways of practicing, learning, and applying physical education skills and content.

Discussion Questions

1. Why is using an effective stop signal important, and what stop signal options might you use?
2. In addition to asking students to find a partner or two to work with, what are some other creative ways to organize students into groups?
3. Select four skills and develop teaching cues you could use when demonstrating the parts of each skill.
4. How might you design learning tasks progressions for performing the forearm pass in volleyball or fielding a ground ball in softball or lacrosse, using open- and closed-skill practice concepts?

CHAPTER 5

Motivation

CHAPTER OBJECTIVES

After reading this chapter, you will be able to:

- ☐ Recognize an assortment of motivational theories.
- ☐ Describe various factors that can motivate students to increase effort and participation in physical education.
- ☐ Explain strategies for developing a positive motivational environment.

KEY TERMS

ego orientation
extrinsically motivated
intrinsically motivated
motivation
personal interest
perceived competence
self-efficacy
situational interest
task orientation
TARGET

What motivates you? What makes you decide to do or try something? What makes you put forth more effort in some tasks than others? **Motivation** is something (i.e., need or desire) that causes a person to act. In physical education, students choose to act (participate) based on many factors. Some decide to participate because the task looks fun and interesting. Others decide to try it because they believe they have the skills to be successful, whereas others engage in the task because they know that if they work hard and practice, they'll be able to do it eventually.

Motivation is an important part of learning. Learning is most likely to occur in physical education when students are motivated to be actively engaged in the lessons; however, it's extremely hard to motivate students who don't want to participate. You can't *make* students be motivated to learn and be active, but you can modify the learning environment to enhance the motivational climate. The purpose of this chapter is to provide basic motivational theories and strategies to help you increase the motivational climate in your gym.

Motivational Theories

To be an effective physical education teacher, you should be familiar with the assorted motivational factors that trigger students to participate actively during class. The following theories were selected from a vast array of information on motivation to help you gain a basic understanding of why students may or may not be motivated to participate in class.

Motivated by Expectations: Social Learning Theory

Some students are motivated when they weigh the expectations of an outcome based on **self-efficacy,** or their perceived confidence in performing a certain skill or specific parts of a skill (Bandura 1977). For instance, certain students may have high self-efficacy in performing a forearm pass in volleyball and may be motivated to practice various forearm passing tasks, but do not have confidence in setting or serving the ball, which could affect their motivational level to try those skills. As such, after the teacher demonstrates a task and explains the activity, some students (1) estimate the outcome of performing the task (e.g., *Will it be meaningful to me? Will it be a positive experience?*), (2) weigh the outcome (e.g., *Can I do it? Do I have the ability?*), and (3) decide whether to participate. Usually, students who are motivated by expectations participate if they think they will be successful at the task or that a positive outcome will occur; if they think they won't be able to handle it, they avoid the situation. Thus, self-efficacy is noted when students put forth effort and try, even when faced with a challenge or the possibility of failure (Bandura 1986; Chase 2001).

Motivated by Confidence: Competence Motivation Theory

Some students are motivated to participate and try because they believe they are generally skillful movers (e.g., good at sports, athletic); they have high self competence. For example, some students may not know how to perform a forearm pass in volleyball, but because they have high self-competence in their overall abilities, they are motivated to try. Students who perceive themselves as competent in performing physical skills are usually intrinsically motivated to demonstrate their competence by participating in challenging and interesting tasks. In addition, students who have higher levels of competence or confidence often demonstrate higher levels of self-esteem, enjoyment, and achievement (Harter 1982). Successful attempts and outcomes, along with positive role models and support from teachers, parents, and friends, help these students develop confidence in themselves as movers.

Motivated by Interest: Interest-Based Motivation Theory

Some students are motivated by their **personal interest** in an activity or by a certain **situational interest** that is sparked by the novelty of the task, a special challenge, some type of attention-getter (e.g., a teacher wearing unique clothing to fit the lesson), an opportunity to explore, or something that causes instant enjoyment (Chen and Darst 2001; Hidi 2000). Situational interest may help attract and motivate students who are first learning how to perform a new skill, even though their personal interest in that activity is low (Shen et al. 2003). In addition, tasks that challenge students to think and become cognitively engaged spark situational interest and enhance motivation (Chen and Darst 2001).

Motivated by Needs: Self-Determination Theory

Some students are motivated by a need to satisfy their own intrinsic desire, not because someone or something else controls their environment (Deci and Ryan 1985). Self-determination theory addresses three needs that drive people to reach positive outcomes: the need for (1) a feeling of competence (self-efficacy), (2) relatedness (belonging, feeling secure), and (3) autonomy or self-determination (Deci and Ryan 2000). For example, some students are **intrinsically motivated** based on their need to be competent at the task and in charge of their situation. The desire to accomplish challenging tasks, along with a belief in their own competence, encouragement

Modifying a game in an interesting or unique way may help spark situational interest and motivate students to participate.

from the teacher, and a desire to choose and control their own situation, motivates them to participate.

On the other hand, students who participate because they will receive something in return or who believe they have to participate because of the teacher are **extrinsically motivated**. For example, some students participate because they think it is good value for them (e.g., *I will get fit; this will help me lose weight; this is good for my health; this will help improve my basketball shot*), whereas others decide to participate because they want to be good students in the eyes of the teacher or because they believe they have to. Some students are motivated by an award or prize, such as getting their name up on a recognition board, a ribbon, or free choice of an activity.

Although fostering intrinsic motivation in students is a goal of most physical education teachers, extrinsic motivational factors should not be dismissed. It is important to help students value being physically active, which can help motivate them to become more active and participate in physical activity both in and outside of class (Rink 2010). Occasionally awarding a class with an extrinsic reward for a job well done or reaching a goal is an effective motivator; however, using too many extrinsic rewards can undermine the development of intrinsic motivation and may downgrade the perception of the reward to a bribe.

Motivated by Success: Attribution Theory

Some students are motivated based on their own perceptions (attributes) of why they succeed or fail. These attributes determine how much effort they put into the

Recognizing successful student performances can help elevate their self-esteem.

task at hand and in the future (Weiner 1979). For example, when students are successful at a task, they may attribute that success to their hard work, effort, or ability. If they fail, they might attribute their failure to external factors outside of their control, such as bad luck, bad teaching or officiating, or lack of help. They often quit or give up if they are not successful and use excuses to avoid acknowledging their shortcomings.

The attributes or explanations students make for their successes or failures when performing a certain task or skill fall into three categories: *internal or external* (factors within them or external factors found in the environment), *stable or unstable* (whether attributes are always the same when performing a task, or whether they will change during a future attempt), and *controllable or uncontrollable* (factors that are perceived to be easily controlled or not) (Weiner 1985). Overall, students who have higher perceived confidence in their skill contribute their success to internal, controllable, and unstable factors, even if they accept that failure is possible (Nicholls 1984a; Rudisill 1989). They demonstrate more effort, more persistence in the task, and better performance than those who have lower perceived confidence (Rudisill 1989).

Sometimes those who demonstrate an external locus of control (belief that someone, something, fate, or luck controls events that affect them) and have low self-efficacy develop an attitude of learned helplessness, which means that they believe that no amount of effort or practice will lead to success (i.e., *What's the use of trying*?). Learned helplessness results from repeated failure over time, along with perceptions of poor ability (Maier and Seligman 1976).

Motivated by Task Achievement or Success: Achievement Goal Theory

Achievement goal theory includes concepts from attribution theory and explains how students are motivated to achieve a skill, task, or goal within an intrinsic or extrinsic motivational focus, based on their perceived confidence in a skill. Some students have a **task orientation**. They believe their success is based on hard work and effort, and they are intrinsically motivated to improve and master their skill technique. Students who are task oriented seek challenging activities, like to try new and interesting things, and persist when the task becomes more difficult.

On the other hand, some students have an **ego orientation.** That is, their perceived confidence is based on outperforming others or comparing their ability to that of others. Students who are ego oriented demonstrate effort and feel successful when they perceive their abilities to be greater than those of their peers. However, if they perceive their abilities to be less than those of others, their effort will be low or they may seek easier or more difficult tasks to hide their ability level. They often give up quickly when a task becomes too difficult (Ames 1992; Nicholls 1984b). Ego-oriented students who perceive themselves as having low self-efficacy in a skill tend to believe that there is little or no reason to engage in the lesson (Deci and Ryan 2000; Standage, Duda, and Ntoumanis 2003).

Clearly, there are a lot of factors to consider when attempting to develop a positive motivational learning environment in physical education (see figure 5.1 on page 106). The theories presented earlier share some common motivational factors, or themes. The first and most important is that of perceived ability, or one's **perceived competence** at performing a skill, also called self-efficacy. How students perceive their ability in various skills is contingent on a number of issues. They may have siblings, parents, or friends who model being active. This social network provides inspiration and encouragement that helps shape perceived competence. Teachers

FIGURE 5.1

Factors Affecting Motivation

Motivational Factors

- Confidence
- Effort
- Ego orientation
- Enjoyment
- Expectations
- Extrinsic motivation
- Feedback
- Intrinsic motivation
- Perceived competence
- Persistence
- Personal interest
- Role models
- Self-efficacy
- Situational interest
- Success
- Support
- Task orientation
- Wants

and coaches who show concern and offer encouragement and feedback add to the development of perceived competence. Personal emotions and the value they place on a task also affect perceived competence. Finally, of course, students need to experience success to enhance their perceptions of self-efficacy.

Many of the motivations theories suggest offering challenging tasks and giving students opportunities to make choices. These factors help create an intrinsic motivational climate that gives students opportunities to succeed, put forth effort, and enjoy learning and being active.

Strategies to Enhance Motivation

Undeniably, you and the teaching methods you use during a lesson will affect student motivation. The bottom line is that you must play an active role in constructing positive perceived competence and a healthy motivational climate (Treasure and Roberts 1995). The following considerations and strategies, based on the motivational theories presented, will help you develop a positive motivational climate when you become a physical education teacher.

Be a Caring Teacher

As part of creating a positive emotional climate for your students, you need to show that you care about your students as individuals and that you care about their learning (Solmon 2006). Taking the time to communicate with students and acting in their best interest shows that you care (Owens and Ennis 2005). Establishing a caring environment in the gymnasium goes a long way in motivating students and helping them develop a sense of competence.

> Students like to have fun in physical education. What is fun? Is the concept of fun the same for everyone? How will you ensure that your students have fun when you become a physical education teacher?

Enhance Value and Interest

You need to convey the value you place on what you teach. Help students understand why doing well on a task or activity is

Professional Profile: Jaime Amezaga

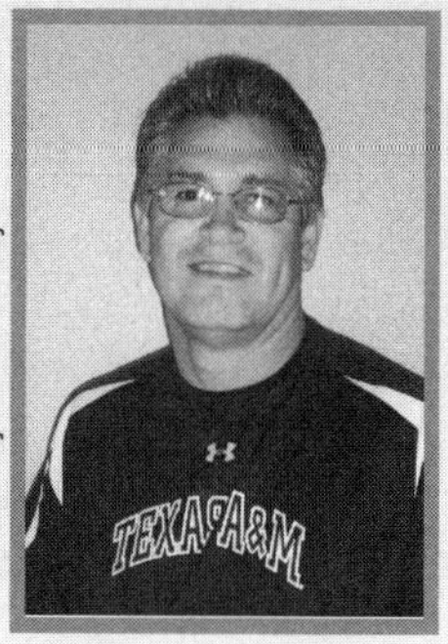

Photo courtesy of Don Disney

BACKGROUND INFORMATION

I received a bachelor's degree in education from the University of Texas at El Paso. I have taught in the El Paso Independent School District (EPISD) since 1988 and am currently a middle school physical education and health teacher at Canyon Hills Middle School. I strive to be the epitome of the teacher and coach. Teaching is my priority. In addition to teaching, I coach high school track and am the athletic coordinator at my campus. I am on the physical education and health steering committee and am involved in several exciting initiatives: heart rate monitors, pedometers, Fitnessgram, Activitygram, and an exciting project using I-Touch devices to assess students. I am a member of the Texas Association for Health, Physical Education, Recreation and Dance (TAHPERD). I am married and have four children.

Why did you decide to become a physical education teacher?

My junior high school physical education teacher was a major influence on my life. He made physical education class fun while stressing the importance of fitness. I always wanted to be involved in sports and fitness. My first 19 years of teaching were in the classroom as well as athletics, but physical education has always been my passion.

What do you like most about your job?

I love the fact that I can influence the well-being of so many students. I can make a difference in their lives, especially here on the border. They can use the things I teach them to make their lives productive and healthy into adulthood.

What is the most challenging part of your job?

The health issues that affect our border students, such as diabetes and obesity, are a big challenge. I also find that having to justify the need for physical education is a big challenge, but one well worth doing. I consider myself a health promoter. How can I prepare our students for the future and to be healthy, safe, and productive?

How have you continued to grow professionally?

I attend as many workshops and conferences as I can. There is so much to learn, and professional growth is so important. I also am very involved in various committees in my district that promote health and physical education. Giving back is the key ingredient for success in our profession.

What advice would you give a college student who wants to become a PE teacher?

Get involved in promoting health and wellness and our profession. You will be an asset to the children you teach and the community you serve. Learn all you can from top physical education teachers, and use that information to make your program the best it can be.

important. Show students what you value by promoting feelings of enjoyment and fun during class. Help them establish an intrinsic sense of the importance of being active (Solmon 2006). In addition, it is important to establish interesting tasks that grab students' attention and motivate them to try new things.

Promote Intrinsic Motivation

You can help students enjoy moving by creating an intrinsically motivated climate. The following are some ways to stimulate intrinsic motivation (Alderman, Beighle, and Pangrazi 2006; Solmon 2006):

Give Choices

One way to motivate students is to give them the freedom to make choices. You could offer, for example, the following choices during practice: practicing set shots by themselves at marked areas around the key, dribbling, making some moves on a fake defender before setting up for a shot, or working with a partner and setting up for a shot after receiving a pass. When using a station format during a lesson, you could include several choices for students to select from at each practice station.

Dressing the part for unique lessons, such as international dance, enhances the fun and authenticity.

In addition, students could use self-check or task sheets from which they can choose tasks to complete.

Offer Challenges

Offering choices also challenges students based on their developmental levels. To enhance student learning, the range of tasks must include ultimate challenges for those who have advanced skills, as well as lower-level challenges for beginners (Shen and Chen 2006). Based on their perceived competence, students can select the option that will give them opportunities for success and challenge.

Modify

Providing students with choices can also be accomplished by allowing them to modify (1) their environment (e.g., selecting shorter or longer distances, smaller or larger working areas, or different size targets to use during a task), (2) the equipment (e.g., larger or smaller balls, longer or shorter rackets), or (3) the activity itself. Students are good at modifying their working environment and equipment to meet their own needs; allow them to do so.

Enhance Perceived Skill Competence and Success

As you now know, perceived competence is a huge motivational factor, perhaps one of the most important to address. It is critical that you design lessons and curricula that foster perceived competence in a variety of skills. How can you help all students in your class experience success and improve their confidence levels when performing skills? The following suggestions may help answer that question.

- *Student demonstrations.* To facilitate perceived competence, it may be beneficial to use a student model during demonstration rather than an expert model (see chapter 4). When students see one of their peers learning how to do a skill, their outlook on performing that same skill themselves is heightened (Darden 1997). Conversely, some students become discouraged after observing an expert (i.e., the teacher) demonstrating the skill.
- *Time:* It is critical that you allow enough quality practice time during lessons for students to develop and improve their skills and gain confidence in their abilities. Too often teachers rush through a few days of skill practice and move right into game play. At that point, many students have not developed the basic skills needed for playing the game, nor do they have the confidence to try. The use of extensions and application activities (see chapter 4) will help accommodate all levels of students as they practice and develop their skills.
- *Feedback:* Reinforce skill practice with positive, corrective, and informative feedback. Feedback encourages students to work hard and provides them with information to improve skill performance and gain more confidence in their abilities (see chapter 4).

Small-sided games played on modified, shortened fields maintain a level of active participation.

Foster a Mastery-Oriented Climate

A mastery-oriented climate helps to develop intrinsically motivated students who believe that effort and hard work will help them become successful, thus increasing their confidence and their ability to learn (Alderman, Beighle, and Pangrazi 2006; Martin, Rudisill, and Hastie 2009; Solmon 2006). You can develop a mastery-oriented climate in your gymnasium by considering the acronym **TARGET** (Epstein 1988). You will find that TARGET encompasses most of the separate strategies mentioned earlier.

***T**ask.* Designs tasks and learning activities to help encourage effort, positive feelings, and satisfaction (success). Create varying levels of challenging tasks, and offer students choice (e.g., choice of tasks, choice of equipment, choice of groups).

***A**uthority.* Provide students with a sense of authority, or ownership, in the lesson by allowing them the freedom choose tasks, make decisions within their groups, and monitor and evaluate their own progress and outcomes.

***R**ewards and Incentives.* Offer individual recognition for progress and improvement; this helps students develop satisfaction and pride in their skill and effort. In a mastery-oriented environment, rewards and incentives are not commonly used to recognize achievements and accomplishments compared to others.

***G**rouping.* Allow students the freedom to select their groups, emphasizing working cooperatively within the groups. If you are working with larger groups, select groups randomly and change them often.

Evaluation. Evaluate student progress and individual improvement based on reaching goals, participation, and effort. Students can take part in the evaluation by logging the outcomes of their skill attempts over time to demonstrate their improvement.

Timing. Give students ample time during lessons to accomplish the tasks.

Play Music

You can help enhance the motivational climate of the gymnasium by playing invigorating music while students are engaged. Music energizes the playing area for children and adults alike. Although music CDs specifically for physical education are available, many physical education teachers make their own CDs or capture music on iPods from the Internet. Make sure the music you play is appropriate, meaning that the language is free of foul words and the message is clean. Use caution if you allow students to bring in their own music, because some of the music students listen to is not appropriate to use in an educational setting. Finally, make sure the volume of music isn't so loud that it distracts students from the learning tasks (Shen et al. 2003).

Provide Competition

What? The concept of competition has not been highlighted in any of the motivational theories or strategies thus far because it often fosters an ego-oriented climate. Yet, physical education teachers use games and competitive play as part of their curricula. Teachers often design end-of-the-unit tournaments for many of their activities. The sport education model and the tactical games approach (see chapter 1) use game play and competition. In addition, many students really enjoy and are motivated by a competitive atmosphere. Competition also can be used to develop a mastery-oriented climate that focuses on intrinsic motivation.

When using competitive activities and games in physical education, it is helpful to shift the focus of the game from that of winning or losing (outcome, or product) to the process. For example, during a competitive activity or game, attention can be directed toward the following:

- Partner cooperation or teamwork
- Game tactics and strategies
- Skill technique
- Effort
- Individual or group improvement

Additionally, you could offer students a choice of competition levels, such as professional league games or recreational games. Students often select a level of competition based on their perceived motivational level for the day or their skill competency. This option allows you opportunities to provide more assistance to students who select the recreational level of play.

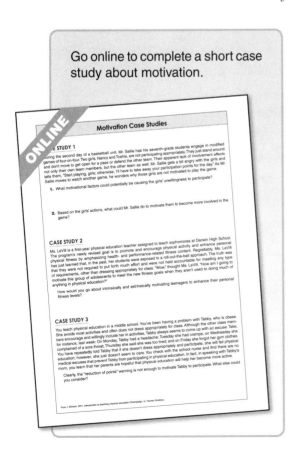

Go online to complete a short case study about motivation.

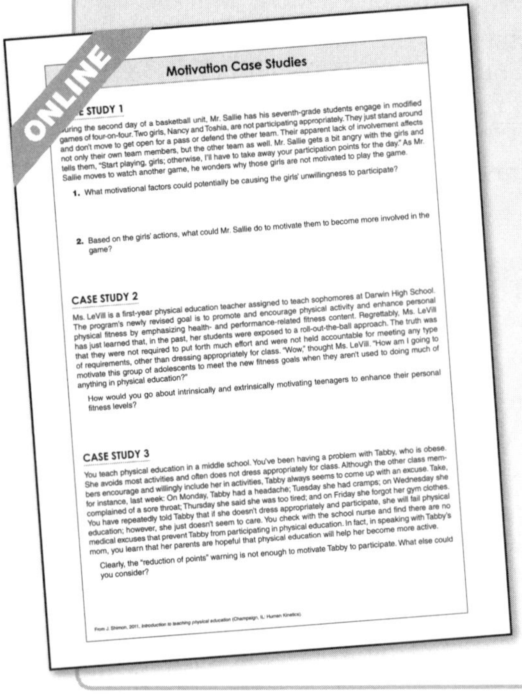

Motivation Case Studies

E STUDY 1

uring the second day of a basketball unit, Mr. Sallie has his seventh-grade students engage in modified games of four-on-four. Two girls, Nancy and Toshia, are not participating appropriately. They just stand around and don't move to get open for a pass or defend the other team. Their apparent lack of involvement affects not only their own team members, but the other team as well. Mr. Sallie gets a bit angry with the girls and tells them, "Start playing, girls; otherwise, I'll have to take away your participation points for the day." As Mr. Sallie moves to watch another game, he wonders why those girls are not motivated to play the game.

1. What motivational factors could potentially be causing the girls' unwillingness to participate?

2. Based on the girls' actions, what could Mr. Sallie do to motivate them to become more involved in the game?

CASE STUDY 2

Ms. LeVill is a first-year physical education teacher assigned to teach sophomores at Darwin High School. The program's newly revised goal is to promote and encourage physical activity and enhance personal physical fitness by emphasizing health- and performance-related fitness content. Regrettably, Ms. LeVill has just learned that, in the past, her students were exposed to a roll-out-the-ball approach. The truth was that they were not required to put forth much effort and were not held accountable for meeting any type of requirements, other than dressing appropriately for class. "Wow," thought Ms. LeVill. "How am I going to motivate this group of adolescents to meet the new fitness goals when they aren't used to doing much of anything in physical education?"

How would you go about intrinsically and extrinsically motivating teenagers to enhance their personal fitness levels?

CASE STUDY 3

You teach physical education in a middle school. You've been having a problem with Tabby, who is obese. She avoids most activities and often does not dress appropriately for class. Although the other class members encourage and willingly include her in activities, Tabby always seems to come up with an excuse. Take, for instance, last week: On Monday, Tabby had a headache; Tuesday she had cramps; on Wednesday she complained of a sore throat; Thursday she said she was too tired; and on Friday she forgot her gym clothes. You have repeatedly told Tabby that if she doesn't dress appropriately and participate, she will fail physical education; however, she just doesn't seem to care. You check with the school nurse and find there are no medical excuses that prevent Tabby from participating in physical education. In fact, in speaking with Tabby's mom, you learn that her parents are hopeful that physical education will help her become more active.

Clearly, the "reduction of points" warning is not enough to motivate Tabby to participate. What else could you consider?

From J. Shimon, 2011, Introduction to teaching physical education (Champaign, IL: Human Kinetics).

Summary

Providing a positive motivational climate is important to student learning. If students aren't motivated to participate, they will not learn to their fullest potential. Therefore, it is your responsibility to develop a learning climate that motivates your students. Because a variety of motivational factors are in play during a lesson, you need to thoughtfully plan lessons that address motivational theories and strategies. Designing activities that challenge students, yet allow them opportunities to succeed, as well as giving them opportunities to choose challenging tasks based on their level of perceived competence, can increase motivation. Students need to believe that they can be successful. Providing positive and corrective feedback during the lesson is also critical. Feedback not only motivates students to try, but also helps them correct technique, achieve success, and develop self-efficacy. Finally, the overall motivational environment can be improved by demonstrating a caring disposition and using music to create an energetic atmosphere.

▶ Discussion Questions

1. Based on your own experiences, which of the motivational theories presented reflect your motivational tendencies?
2. Why is choice an important motivational tool to consider in physical education?
3. How might you include choice within a tennis, golf, or soccer lesson?
4. How can you develop a mastery-oriented climate?
5. Which motivational strategies are best to use when teaching children at the elementary level? Which strategies would be best for adolescents at the secondary level?

CHAPTER 6

Behavior Management

CHAPTER OBJECTIVES

After reading this chapter, you will be able to:

- ☐ Describe behavior management safeguards you can use to help prevent misbehaviors from occurring.
- ☐ Explain various behavior management strategies you can apply when misbehavior does occur.
- ☐ Recognize positive behavior management techniques.

KEY TERMS

consequences
ignore with a purpose
instant activity
pinpointing
Premack principle
proximity control
time-on-task
time-out
verbal prompts
wait time
with-it-ness

The constant stress of dealing with student misbehavior is a major reason some physical education teachers leave the profession (Gordon 2003). Why do some students misbehave? Is it because they are "bad," or could other factors be contributing to the misconduct, such as personal issues, poorly designed lessons, meaningless tasks, or teacher behavior? Needless to say, many factors can contribute to misbehaviors. Accordingly, it is important for you to begin thinking about a prevention plan and a behavior management system that will help you address behavior issues that may occur when you begin your teaching career.

Behavior Management Safeguards

Although you will certainly deal with misbehavior in your physical education class, you can take some steps up front to help curb or prevent misbehavior from occurring in the first place (Lavay, French, and Henderson 1997; Rink 2010; Siedentop and Tannehill 2000). Many of the following safeguards have been discussed in previous chapters. They are mentioned here as reminders of things to consider as you develop your behavior management plan.

Develop a Routine

A daily routine in your lessons provides students with a regular schedule they know will occur every time they come to class. This consistency helps alleviate the anxieties some students harbor when they don't know what to expect. Three things you can do to establish a routine are to have students perform a warm-up or instant activity at the start of class, post the day's activities for students to see as they come in, and use a regular effective stop signal.

At the elementary level, teachers sometimes lead a quick warm-up or **instant activity** or list warm-up instructions on a whiteboard for children to follow as soon as they come into the gym. At the secondary level, the warm-up is most often the first activity students do during every class, usually after attendance is taken. After students complete the warm-up routine, they know the main lesson is about to begin. You can always change the activities within the warm-up to add challenge or prevent boredom. At the end of each lesson, some physical education teachers routinely plan a game, whereas others include a static-stretch cool-down routine or other form of class closure (see chapter 8). When routines are established, students know what to expect and are less likely to act out or misbehave.

Another way to develop a routine is to post the day's activities on a board for students to read as they come into the gym or locker room. One question physical education teachers repeatedly hear from students, especially at the secondary level, is, "What are we doing today?" By listing the day's activities on a board, you let students know right away what the content will be and whether they will be indoors or outdoors. This simple task helps establish a physical education routine and alleviates the unnecessary anxiety some students hold.

Using an effective stop signal, as described in chapter 4, is another way to establish a routine. When students hear the signal, they know to stop what they're doing and pay attention to directions. An effective stop signal decreases the time students take to respond during a lesson, otherwise known as response latency (Darst and Pangrazi 2009). A routinely used stop signal provides consistency for students and gives you a quick way to gain student attention.

Be Organized and Prepared

Careful attention to lesson planning can help ward off student misbehaviors. Although your lessons may not go exactly as planned, by being well prepared and organized, you will be able to respond to unexpected situations that may arise. Being well prepared involves planning for more content than anticipated. In other words, be overprepared. Planning for several learning tasks, activities, and games will allow you the flexibility to alter tasks quickly if you see students getting bored, having difficulty, or playing a game that is not working out as expected.

Thorough planning also includes paying attention to lesson flow and student grouping strategies (see chapter 4). In addition to developing tasks for your students to work on during a lesson, you must also take time to work through the organization of those tasks and how you will transition students from one task to another. For example, once you determine the tasks students will perform, will you have all students organized along certain lines, behind cones, in specific areas in the gym, or scattered in any free space while practicing their skills? How will you transition them from one activity to the next, especially if different equipment is needed or group sizes change? How will you organize your class into games of two-on-two or three-on-three after they have been working individually or with a partner or two? These organizational issues must be thought through prior to teaching the lesson. Poor planning that results in disorganization may be just the thing to spark misbehavior in some students.

Being organized also involves careful attention to the learning tasks. Students have few reasons to misbehave when they are interested and engaged in learning. Students tend to act out when they become bored; when tasks are too easy, too hard, or meaningless; and when they get tired. Therefore, it is vital that you provide a variety of tasks that are challenging and meaningful and that give students the opportunity to make choices (see chapter 5). Paying attention to learning tasks and your teaching style (see chapter 4) will help you safeguard against misbehavior (see figure 6.1).

Use Effective Instruction

Applying quality teaching practices is another way to prevent misbehaviors from occurring during a lesson. One important factor to consider is **time-on-task**. As you recall from chapters 3 and 4, time-on-task refers to the amount of time students are engaged in productive activities. When students must listen to lengthy demonstrations or explanations, when they have to wait in long lines for a turn to actively participate or use a piece of equipment, and when learning tasks or games involve large groups and limited equipment, not only is active learning time limited, but also the chance for misbehavior increases. Therefore, it is important that you enhance the time students are actively engaging in learning tasks and manage class organization and instruction time wisely. The following are some suggestions for maximizing time-on-task:

- Keep demonstrations and explanations short (one to two minutes long).
- Use a stop signal to gain students' attention quickly.

FIGURE 6.1

Safeguards to Discourage Misbehavior

Allow for challenge and success.
Be prepared and organized.
Develop classroom rules.
Develop daily routines.
Foster motivation.
Implement time-on-task strategies.
Monitor the periphery.
Plan for meaningful tasks.
Provide feedback.
Think through transitions (flow).
Turn on your teacher radar.

- Arrange students into groups or teams quickly.
- Use a system to quickly issue and collect equipment.
- Maximize the use of individual or partner work.
- Keep group sizes small using ample equipment.
- Lessen the number of students per team (e.g., three-on-three instead of six-on-six).
- Modify court or playing areas to maximize participation.
- Avoid elimination-type activities.

Effective instruction also requires that you be actively engaged in the lesson (Owens 2006). One way to actively engage is to walk around providing feedback to individual students and groups while they are practicing or playing games. This not only increases student motivation and enhances skill development, but also reminds students to stay on task. Moreover, by constantly monitoring the learning area while keeping your back to a wall or periphery, you can keep your eyes on the entire class. If students know you are watching them, they are less likely to become off task or misbehave.

Create a Motivating Environment

Chapter 5 offered suggestions for creating a motivating learning environment to encourage students to participate in physical education. Those suggestions are also important safeguards against misbehavior. Creating meaningful and challenging tasks and giving students opportunities to succeed and make choices are important motivators. Demonstrating a caring disposition, along with providing feedback and energizing the learning environment with music, is also important.

Maximize passing skill practice with partner drills that offer lots of ball-touch opportunities.

Develop and Enforce Class Rules

All teachers, of course, are required to enforce the school's policies for major behavior offenses such as fighting, insubordination, drug use, or weapon possession. School administrators are responsible for handling the consequences for those behaviors, often resulting in some sort of school suspension or further action from law enforcement. As such, it is important that you familiarize yourself with the school's rules, even when you are working at a school during a field experience or student teaching.

What correlation exists among classroom organization, instruction, motivation, and student behavior?

In addition to upholding school rules, you must also develop your own set of class rules that describe clear expectations and appropriate conduct while students are in physical education (see appendix A for an example of class rules and policies). Often, general classroom rules mirror the expectations of the school. They also often consist of value-laden words such as *responsibility, respect, integrity,* and *safety.* Whatever rules you develop for your class, state them positively (see table 6.1). Also, try to limit rules to no more than five (Darst and Pangrazi 2009). Remember, the more rules you have, the more you will have to enforce. On occasion, you may want to develop additional rules pertaining to certain activities such as archery, swimming, or gymnastics for safety reasons. Some teachers have only one class rule: *Be appropriate* (Mahle 1989). Giving students examples of appropriate and inappropriate behaviors will help teach them what you expect of them. Essentially, students need to know your expectations for acceptable behavior.

Elementary physical education teachers (as well as secondary-level teachers) develop class rules to help deal with distractions that occur during class such as water and bathroom breaks. When one child gets a drink of water or uses the restroom, all of them may want to do the same. Therefore, many elementary physical education specialists have a rule that only one person can be at the water fountain or use the bathroom pass at a time. Other class rules teachers might have at the elementary level includes raising one's hand to answer questions or lining up quietly before leaving the gym when class is over.

Secondary-level physical education teachers usually create rules for class management as well as behavior management. For example, they may require students to wear physical education uniforms or appropriate clothing and tennis shoes to receive daily credit. They may have rules for absences, tardiness, not having appropriate clothing, making up work, or excuses. These rules are needed for developing consistency within the structure of the class.

What class rules might you develop when you become a physical education teacher? What are some of the class rules established by elementary- and secondary-level physical education teachers in your town or city?

Regardless of age level, students learn rules through repeated training. Simply stated, going over the rules once on the first day

Table 6.1 Stating Classroom Rules Positively

Negatively stated rules	Positively stated rules
Do not damage equipment.	Treat equipment with care.
No fighting.	Control your emotions.
No pushing or shoving.	Maintain your own personal space.
Do not make fun of others.	Demonstrate respect for others.

of class is not enough. Teaching students about appropriate behavior is a yearlong training process. You will have to provide constant and consistent reminders to help your students learn and develop appropriate behavior while in your class. Posting written class rules on a wall also provides a daily reminder.

Demonstrate With-It-Ness

Developing behavior management safeguards also involves the use of teacher radar (Owens 2006). Your teacher radar is on when you are alert and take notice of what is happening around you during class, or when you demonstrate **with-it-ness** (Kounin 1970). You can gather a lot of information by watching the way students interact with each other and their moods. For example, are groups of students beginning to get restless? Are some students instigating poor behavior, teasing others, or becoming too aggressive in their play? Being alert to these types of things will help you be proactive in behavior management, rather than reacting to misbehavior after the fact. Demonstrating with-it-ness during a lesson not only fosters better decision making when dealing with behavior issues, but it also demonstrates to students that you have a handle on what is occurring in the class.

Learn Names

Finally, it is critical that you learn students' names as quickly as possible. By learning their names, you not only show them that you care enough to learn their names, but also gain an advantage when you have to implement a behavior management strategy. You have a lot more authority when you say a student's name than when you say, "Hey you over there."

Learning names is a difficult task, especially at the elementary level where physical education specialists may see every child in the school at least once each week. That's a lot of names to remember, especially in large schools; many specialists at the elementary level teach well over 400 students a week. At the secondary level, physical education teachers usually see the same students in each class period all week long, which makes learning names a bit less troublesome. Nonetheless, learning names is easier said than done. Figure 6.2 offers some suggestions for learning names quickly.

Behavior Management Strategies

Sometimes the safeguards you create to prevent student misbehaviors do not work. All your careful planning, routines, rules, and best teaching practices may not be enough. Certain students may act out no matter what. Perhaps they are having a bad day; maybe their home life is in turmoil; they could be under the influence of alcohol or drugs. For whatever reason, they are causing disruptions in your class and depriving others of their right to learn. What can you do when inappropriate student behavior becomes a problem? The following sections offer suggestions for dealing with misbehavior.

Implement Waiting Techniques

Using basic waiting techniques can take care of a lot of the little problems that can occur during a lesson, including students talking or fidgeting with their equipment while you are leading activities or giving directions. These behaviors can lead to larger problems if they are not addressed. Waiting techniques are subtle movements or prompts you can use to quickly address inappropriate behaviors while you are talking to the class. When students are talking, not paying attention, or causing minor annoyances while you are teaching, try the following:

■ **Proximity control.** Slowly position yourself near those students who are talking or off task while giving instruction or directions. Your mere presence (proximity) is often enough to remind those students to listen and pay attention.

■ **Verbal prompts.** While giving instruction or directions to the class, make eye contact with those students who are talking and quickly say their names or use a general term to address the talkative group (e.g., "girls/boys") while continuing with your instruction. Your subtle alert reminds those students to listen and pay attention. When those students do stop talking and pay attention, positively recognize the appropriate behavior by saying something like, "Thanks for paying attention" or giving them a thumbs-up sign. Your action positively reinforces the appropriate behavior, which sends a message to the entire class.

■ **Wait time.** Quietly wait to begin your instruction if too many students are talking or not paying attention. Although this takes some time, those students who are listening will eventually make it clear to others to be quiet. Again, when you have the attention of all your students, positively thank them for their attention. This strategy can also be used when you are explaining something during the middle of a lesson and too many students are off task and not paying attention. Just stop what you're saying and wait for everyone to get refocused before continuing.

■ **Ignore with a purpose.** If some students exhibit inconsequential or annoying behaviors (e.g., tapping something on the floor or making vocal noises), ignore the behavior and continue to teach. Most minor nuisances disappear within 30 seconds or so (Latham 1998). While teaching, you can always make eye contact with those students to let them know you are aware of their actions. If the behavior continues or other students join in, you can apply any of the previous techniques to address the problem, or you can focus your attention on the positive behaviors occurring in class as described in the next section.

FIGURE 6.2

Strategies for Learning Students' Names

Ask individual students their names when addressing them.

Associate a name with something familiar.

Issue name badges for a short time.

Meet and greet students in each class.

Study the class roster and connect with names with a class photo.

Take daily attendance.

Use name games.

Write names on student uniforms.

Use Positive Behavior Management

For some reason, many teachers tend to address all the negative and inappropriate behaviors that occur during class. Certainly, misbehaviors need to be dealt with; however, many of the appropriate behaviors students demonstrate never get noticed. When you refocus your attention and acknowledge positive behaviors, students often begin to feel valuable and capable, which can lead to more responsible behavior (Stiehl, Morris, and Sinclair 2008). This is called positive behavior management.

When you see students doing something appropriate, tell them. Positively acknowledge those behaviors by saying something like, "I am happy with the way

Why do you think teachers tend to focus more on negative behaviors? Do you think this is a societal behavior?

you came up with a solution to the problem," "I appreciate the way you all are ready to listen," or "Thank you for putting the equipment in its proper place." In addition to using praising words, you can also use expressions, such as smiling, clapping, or giving a thumbs-up signal. Giving students a high-five is another way to positively acknowledge appropriate behavior.

Situational reinforcements is another positive behavior management tool (Downing, Keating, and Bennett 2005). Point out and praise students who are on task or behaving appropriately rather than focusing on those who are misbehaving. This is called **pinpointing.** When teachers ignore the inappropriate behavior and recognize appropriate behavior occurring nearby, students who are off task often change to more appropriate behaviors. For example, if your elementary students are talking while you are asking them to be quiet, you might say something like, "I like the way this group is sitting quietly and ready to listen" or "I like the way some of you are sitting quietly." Using this same technique at the secondary level, you might say, "I appreciate all of you who are listening and ready to get started." Those who are talking or not sitting quietly may change their behavior as a result.

Positive behavior management needs to be used with care, however. When praise is overused, the words become meaningless and behaviors often remain unchanged. When using praise, do the following:

- Be selective; acknowledge behaviors that are deserving of positive recognition.
- Be sincere with your comments.
- Be causal and brief.
- Emphasize the value of positive behavior ("Thank you for…") (Latham 1998).

Enforce Rules and Consequences

A majority of physical education teachers teach students how to behave appropriately through the use of rules and **consequences.** As previously stated, you are responsible for developing your class rules. In addition, you are also responsible for developing the consequences for breaking them. Students have more responsibility for their behaviors when they know the rules and penalties for breaking them. Unfortunately, some students still elect to misbehave. It is important that you uphold the consequences when students violate the rules.

Upholding the rules and issuing consequences may be a tricky task for you at first: on one hand you want to establish class control, and on the other, you want students to like you and be your friend. If you follow the friendly path when you first start teaching, you will more than likely become relaxed in upholding class rules, which could lead to a classroom that is out of control. Keep in mind that you can establish a caring relationship with your students while still being the leader in charge of your class. For the most part, students value and appreciate teacher leadership. The following are suggestions to consider as you develop your rules for behavior management.

Be Firm and Consistent

It is vital that you be firm and consistent when holding students accountable for their behavior. If you let some rules slide or are inconsistent with upholding the rules (e.g., give too many warnings), you may lose credibility with your class, students may regard consequences as nothing more than verbal threats, and some students will continue to misbehave. Stated more simply, students may have a tendency to walk all over you if they know your consequences are meaningless. This doesn't mean that you have to be an ogre. You can still laugh and have fun with students; however, they need to know that you are the leader and in charge of the class.

Issue Warnings

Teachers often issue warnings for first-time behavior offenses ("Karla, you can hit the ball over the fence again and sit out for the remaining lesson, or keep the ball inside the court and continue playing," or, " Fred, it's your decision whether to work cooperatively with your group or earn zero points for the day."). Warnings give students a chance to redeem themselves and correct their behavior. If the inappropriate behavior occurs a second time, however, a consequence must be issued. Otherwise, students quickly learn that warnings are meaningless, and the misbehaviors will continue. To maintain control over your class, you must take an early stand and act on your warnings, especially at the start of a school year or semester.

Some students need a brief cooling-off period in time-out to reset their temper and behavior.

Demonstrate Fairness

It is important that you be fair when issuing consequences. Showing favoritism or being lenient with certain students may demonstrate a bias toward a particular group (e.g., gifted athletes, girls, or boys) and undermine your credibility with the others. Fairness also involves being flexible. Students are individuals and come to class with individual issues and problems. Your decision to issue a warning or consequence should also be based on your knowledge of your students and their individual needs (Buck et al. 2007).

Uphold Consequences

Time-out is one example of a consequence you can use when elementary students misbehave. Time-outs have been shown to reduce or decrease the occurrence of misbehavior (Johnson 1999) when they involve removing a child from a rewarding environment such as physical education (Heron 1987). Because most children enjoy physical education and do not want to sit out and miss the fun, behavior often improves following a time-out warning.

Time-out is a teaching tool to help children understand and learn appropriate behavior. Designate a time-out space in the gym that is away from others, yet clearly in view. Children should be seated facing the class (not a wall) and remain in time-out for no more than five minutes (Henderson et al. 2000). While the class is actively engaged in a task, converse briefly with the child about his or her poor behavior and the appropriate behavior expected when the child chooses to return to activity. Time-outs can be effective at the secondary level as well, although they're not labeled as such. Set aside a space in the gym where students can go to sort out or "cool off" disruptive emotions or poor behaviors before they do or say something that will get them into further trouble.

Consequences of misbehavior also include losing daily points or privileges, detentions, and having parents or guardians called. Sending a student to the main office is usually a last resort; many administrators request that all teachers handle behavior issues in class. Nonetheless, sending a student to the office is an option when the student cannot be controlled and is disrupting the learning environment of others.

Give Students Responsibilities

Giving the class some control over developing class rules and consequences can empower students and increase buy-in, which often results in better behavior and adherence to the rules. Although this process takes some time during the first few days of class, the results are well worth the time spent.

Briefly mentioned in chapter 1, Don Hellison's model of responsibility (2003) is another way to develop student responsibility by using group talks, individual meetings, or reflection time (time-outs) to help students acknowledge their behavior and make improvements. Some teachers hang a large poster illustrating the behavior levels near the door (see figure 6.3). On the way out of the gym, students tap the level they believe best represents their behavior during the lesson. This action serves as a daily recognition of individual behavior.

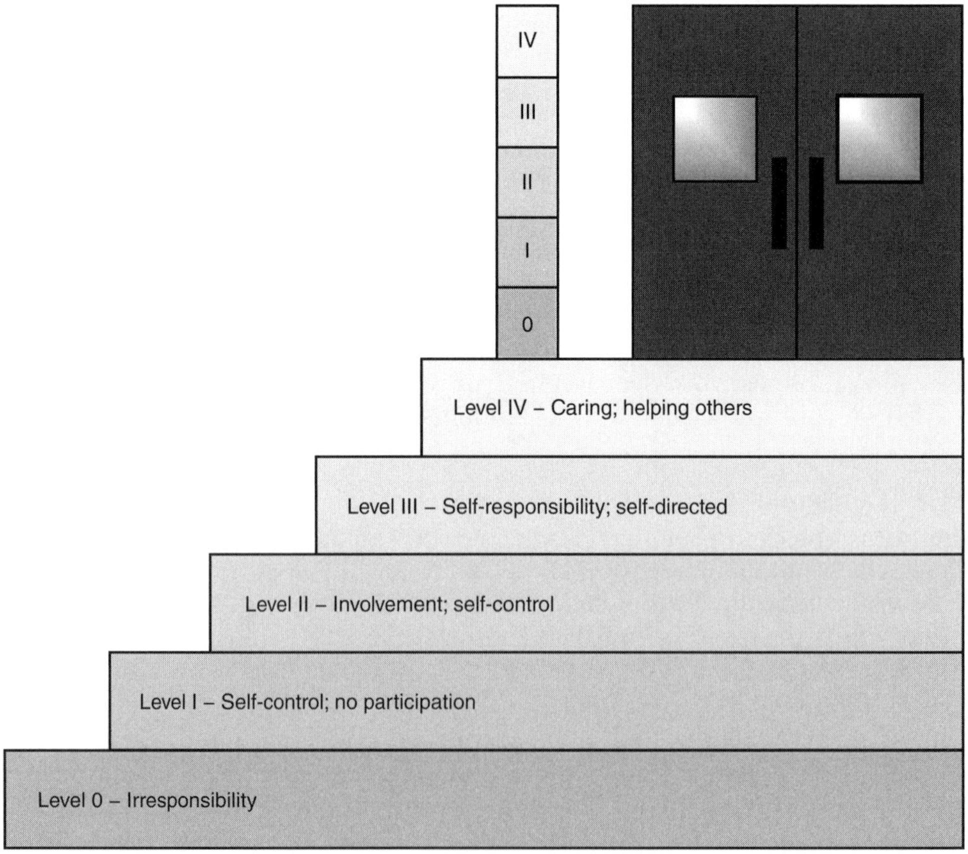

FIGURE 6.3 Students are asked to indicate their level of responsibility during class or as they exit the gym.

Based on Hellison 2003.

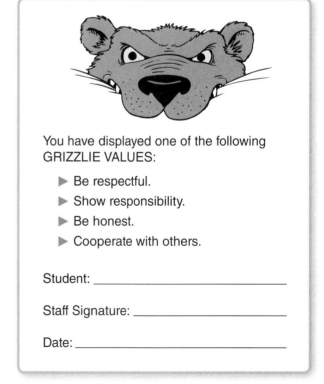

Offer External Rewards and Contingencies

You may choose to control student behavior through the use of positive external consequences, or rewards. You might say, "If you are all good and try the drill, we will play a game," or "If you do all the practice drills, you will have a free day tomorrow." These rewards are contingent on good behavior. This is an example of the **Premack principle** (Premack 1965), which bases a preferred behavior (reward) on completing a less desirable behavior. You also can reward good behavior by issuing extra points, special shoe tokens, certificates, or other types of material rewards. Sometimes entire schools have awards systems set up in which students who demonstrate certain values receive special cards (see figure 6.4). Keep in mind, however, that using too many extrinsic rewards may have a negative effect on intrinsic motivation (see chapter 5).

> Do you think extrinsic rewards are a way of bribing students to be good, or are there benefits to rewarding students for appropriate behavior?

Hold Individual Conferences

When students act up in class, it is not in your best interest to publically reprimand, scold, or punish them in front of their peers. This tactic often backfires and may lead to a confrontation between you and the students, often resulting in a shouting match and loss of control. If you do find a student who is being defiant or callously disruptive, deal with that person individually during class while the rest of the class is actively engaged in a task, or at a determined time during the school day.

When conducting an individual conference during class, use the corner of the gym or an area away from the rest of the class but from which you can still keep an eye on the class. A cool and calm demeanor is critical to maintain at this point, even though you may be fuming inside. If a dialogue is possible between you and the student, try to determine what is going on. You may be surprised to find that the student is dealing with a life issue you had no idea about. Nonetheless, it is important to express your disapproval of the behavior, not the student. For instance, you can say something like, "I'm disappointed in the way you handled that situation. It upsets your classmates when you're rude and disrespectful," or "I'm truly dismayed with your behavior" (Stiehl, Morris, and Sinclair 2008).

Negotiating with the student may be helpful. You may ask the student to identify and judge the behavior. In addition, you might ask what changes need to occur in his or her behavior and what should be done if the behavior occurs again. Approaching the problem from this angle puts the responsibility of appropriate behavior back on the student instead of on you.

You have displayed one of the following GRIZZLIE VALUES:

- Be respectful.
- Show responsibility.
- Be honest.
- Cooperate with others.

Student: ______________________

Staff Signature: ______________________

Date: ______________________

FIGURE 6.4 This card is awarded to students who demonstrate a positive behavior.

Prevent Fighting

Many school policies address fighting as a major offense with some type of school suspension as a consequence. It is your responsibility to follow school procedures for handling a fight if it occurs in your class, in the locker room, or in the hallway. Turning on your teacher radar and demonstrating with-it-ness can help you head off a

Go online to complete a brief case study about behavior management.

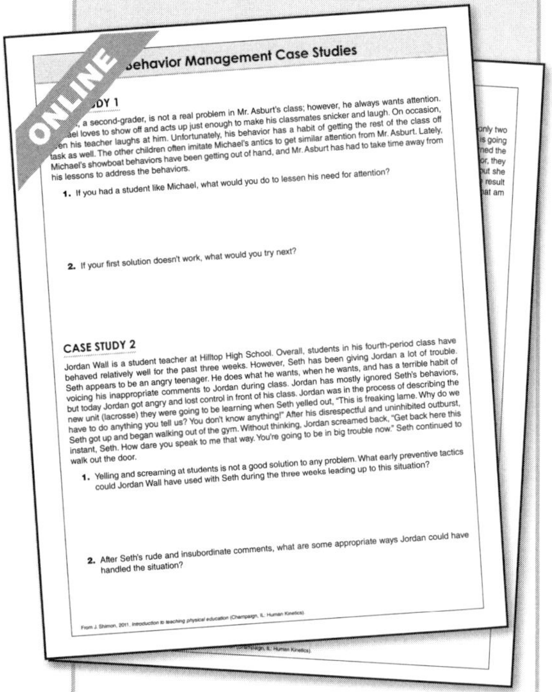

potential fight. If you see tension brewing between students, it is important to intervene before punches begin to fly.

Unfortunately, sometimes you may not be able to prevent a fight. School policies often require teachers to send for immediate help in violent situations or when weapons are present. It is important that you act quickly and remain composed. The safety of the class should be your main concern, along with your own personal safety. Most experts recommend not touching students in order to break up a fight; instead, use a loud voice or a whistle to distract them from fighting.

Summary

Managing student behavior is a daily task for most physical education teachers. However, the undertaking doesn't have to be a dreaded part of teaching. By embracing behavior management as a way to help students learn how to behave appropriately, it becomes part of the overall teaching process instead of a disciplinary campaign. The following are essential dos and don'ts of successful behavior management:

Do:

- Get to know your students.
- Be organized and prepared.
- Create challenging, meaningful lessons.
- Use student names.
- Acknowledge positive behaviors.
- Use positive and sincere praise.
- Use basic waiting techniques.
- Be firm and consistent.
- Use occasional extrinsic rewards.
- Expect students to behave.

Don't:

- Use coercion.
- Downgrade students.
- Engage in confrontations.
- Give threats.
- Ridicule.
- Use group punishment for only a few.
- Use corporal punishment.

▶ Discussion Questions

1. How does being mindful of time-on-task help curb behavior problems?
2. How do you plan to quickly learn students' names when you begin teaching?
3. What are some waiting techniques that can help minimize misbehavior?
4. What are the benefits and consequences of using contingencies for good behavior?
5. When dealing with a student one-on-one for behavior issues, why is it important not to do it behind closed doors (i.e., in your office)?

PART III

LESSON PLANNING AND OUTCOMES

When you decide to go on a long trip or take a vacation, you usually make plans and consult a map to make sure you know what you're doing and where you're going. You carefully pack your bags, anticipating what you will need on your journey. The camera is among those items packed so you can take plenty of pictures to reflect all those memorable events.

If the preceding example makes sense to you, then the purpose and benefits of careful planning and preparation when teaching physical education will make sense as well. The chapters in part III will help you plan and develop safe and successful lessons and provide strategies to determine whether outcomes are achieved and learning has occurred. It's important to know what you're going to teach, how you're going to do it, and whether you've succeeded. Needless to say, planning is important. Thoughtful preparation may not guarantee a successful lesson; however, the time spent organizing your lessons will help you adapt and respond to those unexpected events that often occur during a school day. Plan away!

CHAPTER 7

Scope and Sequence

CHAPTER OBJECTIVES

After reading this chapter, you will be able to:

- Define *scope* and *sequence*.
- Describe the scope of elementary, middle, and high school physical education programs.
- Explain how movement concepts can be used in combination with fundamental movements.
- Describe components of health- and performance-related fitness.
- Identify ways scope and sequence can be used in overall curriculum, unit, and lesson planning.

KEY TERMS

axial skills
dynamic movements
fundamental movements
health-related fitness
invasion games
inverted supports
locomotor skills
manipulative skills
movement concepts
net or wall games
performance-related fitness
scope
sequence
specialized movements
springing movements
stability skills
striking or fielding games
target games
upright supports

We know that the goal of physical education is to develop physically educated people who have the knowledge, skills, and confidence to enjoy a lifetime of healthy physical activity (NASPE 2004). We also know that participating in physical activities is critical to the development and maintenance of good health. However, what content and skills are needed for enjoying a lifetime of physical activity? What content will you be responsible to teach students at the elementary, middle, or high school level? In other words, what is the **scope** (content) of a physical education program? When discussing the content of a physical education program, you will often hear the phrase *scope and sequence*. This chapter will help you understand scope and sequence and the essential content you will be expected to teach at the K-12 level.

Scope: Elementary School

At the elementary level (usually grades K-5 or K-6), the scope is well established. Within the psychomotor domain, elementary physical education specialists are responsible for making sure children develop mature or correct movement patterns for basic fundamental movements (Gallahue and Cleland-Donnelly 2003; Graham, Holt/Hale, and Parker 2010; Pangrazi and Beighle 2010). **Fundamental movements** combine the movement patterns of two or more body segments, such as running, throwing, and balancing, which combine movements of the arms and legs. Fundamental movements are broken down into three categories: (1) locomotor skills, (2) manipulative skills, and (3) stability skills.

Locomotor Movements

Locomotor skills are those that help children move, or travel, from one place to the next in either a horizontal or vertical direction (Gallahue and Cleland-Donnelly 2003). The nine locomotor skills are shown in figure 7.1. Even though some children can perform basic locomotor skills prior to entering school, it is the job of the elementary physical education specialist to make sure children develop these skills using proper form. Consider, for example, walking and running skills. You may think these skills are too simple to teach; however, many children have immature or incorrect walking or running forms, such as poor foot placement or arm swing. If children continue to use improper walking or running forms, they will more than likely be inefficient movers as adults.

At the elementary level you may cluster running and leaping skills together, because the leap can be easily extended from a running form. If you can remember from your elementary years, a leap is when there is a longer flight phase (no ground contact) between stepping off one foot and landing on the other, such as when bounding over a puddle of water.

The hop and jump are two other locomotor skills developed at the elementary level. What is the difference between jumping and hopping? How would you explain the difference to students? A jump is when you take off from one or both feet and land on

FIGURE 7.1

Locomotor Skills

Walk	Gallop
Run	Slide
Hop	Skip
Jump	Climb
Leap	

Encourage students to add unique moves while practicing their jumping skills.

two feet at the same time, such as in a long jump or triple jump. The hop, on the other hand, is when you take off from one foot and land on that same foot. It is important that you use these terms correctly when asking children to either hop or jump.

Children usually learn the gallop and slide prior to the skip, but they are performed in a similar fashion. The gallop is completed by always facing and stepping forward with the same lead foot, while the trail foot steps in behind it. Teachers often use the phrase or teaching cue *step, together*, meaning that the lead foot *steps* (forward) while the back foot meets up with the front foot and comes *together* prior to taking another step.

The slide is similar to the gallop except that it is performed in a sideways direction, such as when doing a defensive shuffle in basketball. Skipping is usually more difficult to learn because of the opposition of body movements or cross-lateralization of the arms and legs (Gallahue and Cleland-Donnelly 2003).

The skip is accomplished by alternating a sequence of steps and hops, starting with a small hop on the lead foot. You may use the phrase or teaching cue *step, hop* when teaching children to skip. Children will first step and hop on one foot; then step and hop on the other. Eventually, an even skipping rhythm will develop.

FIGURE 7.2

Manipulative Skills

Throw	Trap
Catch	Volley
Strike	Bounce/dribble
Kick	Underhand roll
Punt	

Manipulative Skills

The second area of fundamental movements is **manipulative skills**, or those skills that require an object to be directed or controlled (see figure 7.2). Objects are directed or controlled by either propulsive actions, such as striking, kicking, or throwing a ball, or absorbing actions of catching or trapping a ball (Gallahue and Cleland-Donnelly 2003). All types of balls, as well as bats and rackets, are equipment that can be manipulated. Teaching manipulative skills at the elementary level usually involves the use of various types of equipment. You can easily guess a variety of games and sports that use manipulative skills as part of their **specialized movements.**

Two of the manipulative skills listed in figure 7.2 require further mention. Striking skills can be taught using an array of equipment or even the hand. Equipment can include rackets or paddles (e.g., foam paddles, short-stemmed rackets), clubs (e.g., putter in golf), a foam bat, or the hand when serving a volleyball or hitting a balloon in the air. Volleying skills are similar to striking skills; however, in volleying, the repeated force to an object is directed upward. Hitting a balloon up in the air over and over is an example of a volleying skill, as is setting a volleyball, juggling or heading a soccer ball, and kicking up a footbag (Hacky Sack).

All types, sizes, and colors of striking implements and balls can be used when teaching manipulative skills to children. Allowing students to select their equipment, such as balloons, lighter or smaller balls to heavier or larger ones, or foam paddles to short-stemmed rackets, enables them to achieve successful attempts while practicing and developing manipulative skills.

Stability Skills

The final fundamental movement category addresses the broad concept of stability. **Stability skills** are any movements whose main emphasis is maintaining or

FIGURE 7.3

Stability Skills

Axial skills

Bend, turn, stretch, twist, lift, push, pull, dodge

Springing movements

Diving board, trampoline, springboard, vertical jumps

Upright supports

Symmetrical and asymmetrical balances, balance beam, partner stunts

Inverted supports

Tripod, headstand, handstand, cartwheel

gaining equilibrium, or balance, whether stationary (static) or moving (dynamic) (Gallahue and Cleland-Donnelly 2003). The four categories of stability skills are axial skills, **springing movements**, upright supports, and inverted supports (see figure 7.3).

Axial Skills

Axial skills involve static and dynamic actions in which a body segment rotates around an axis (a fixed point such as the spine, hip, or shoulder joint) while balance is maintained. Movements such as twisting and bending are axial movements. A diver or gymnast must have control of her body as it twists or turns in space, just as a person needs to find balance while bending to execute a yoga pose. Axial skills are also used to pull, push, and lift objects. Just think of the axial skills you use when performing a variety of strength training exercises in the weight room. Changing directions quickly or being able to stop and go rapidly are other examples of dynamic axial skills. Teaching children how to dodge, pivot, or fake are ways to help them learn how control and balance their bodies in dynamic situations.

When teaching throwing skills, emphasize the importance of stepping forward with the opposite foot of the throwing arm.

Photo courtesy of Jane Shimon

Springing Movements

Springing movements—or movements that cast the body in an airborne state for a period of time—also require balance and are included in the list of stability skills (Gallahue and Cleland-Donnelly 2003). Have you ever jumped on a trampoline, tried a round-off handspring, or launched off a diving board into a pool? During your brief space flight, your body had to make adjustments as it momentarily lost contact with the ground so it could return to a balanced base of support. Children need to learn not only how to spring off the floor or a platform, but also how to land properly, especially after jumping really high or jumping off a box or other platform. Additionally, they need to learn accurate landing techniques to decrease the risk of knee injuries, which sometimes occur from participating in sports (Hewett, Ford, and Myer 2006; Hewett, Myer, and Ford 2006). Overall, the children you teach will have to learn how to gain control of their bodies as they experience springing-type **dynamic movements**.

Balancing Supports

Balancing supports are the final two components of stability skills. **Inverted supports** are those skills that help children learn how to maintain their equilibrium or gain energy against outside forces (i.e., gravity) when the body is upside down (Gallahue and Cleland-Donnelly 2003). Inverted supports (e.g., a headstand) use static balancing skills, whereas other feats (e.g., a forward roll) use dynamic stability skills. Various types of **upright supports**, including symmetrical (i.e., both sides of the body holding the same pose) and asymmetrical, or unequal, balances, place students in upright postures. Can you think of other upright supports or balance stunts individuals or groups of students can practice? Just think of all the ways to balance on one, two, or three points of body contact with the floor.

Tumbling stunts such as the forward roll help develop stability skills.

Photo courtesy of Jane Shimon

Because fundamental movements are the foundation for most physical activities, children should develop mature fundamental movements early on, usually beginning in preschool or kindergarten (for those schools that offer physical education to three- to five-year-olds) and during the primary grades (grades 1 and 2). If they do not, there is a good chance they will have difficulty with specialized sport skills in later childhood, in adolescence, and as adults (Gallahue 1996). Needless to say, the elementary physical education specialist has a huge responsibility in helping children develop mature fundamental movement skills.

Movement Concepts

When teaching fundamental movement skills to children, allow them to experience the movements and learn about how their bodies move in as many ways as possible in a variety of situations. Using **movement concepts** is one way you can help children refine their movement skills. As highlighted in figure 7.4, children can learn how to move while exerting varying amounts of force and performing a fundamental skill (effort). They can learn how to move while their

FIGURE 7.4

Movement Concepts to Use When Teaching Fundamental Movement Skills

Moving With Effort

Force: Light/heavy, soft/hard, delicate/strong

Time: Slow, medium, or fast

Flow: Free flowing/restricted movements

Moving Within Space

Level: Low, medium, or high body levels

Direction: Forward/backward; diagonal/sideways; up/down; curved, straight, or zigzag; clockwise/counterclockwise

Range: Curved- straight-, or wide-body; personal space/general space; large/small

Moving With Relationships

Objects: In/out; over/under; between/among; in front of/behind; above/below; through/around

People: Mirror (face to face); shadow (follow); alternate; in unison; with a partner/in a group

How might you use movement concepts when teaching children to hand or foot dribble a ball, strike a balloon, or run around the gym?

bodies are positioned at various levels or going in various directions (space). And, they can learn to move in relation to the objects or people around them (relationships). As an example, you can have students hop on one foot really fast or slow as they lightly travel backward, or they can skip while traveling under a bar or around a cone. These are examples of movement concepts being used to help students experience fundamental movement skills in a wide variety of conditions.

Climbing through a hoop is an example of moving with relationships.

Fundamental movement skills, along with movement concepts, comprise a large portion of the scope for the primary grades. In addition, rhythmic skills are also included in the scope for this level. It is important to help children develop a steady beat, or a movement rhythm to the constant beat of a drum, clap, or music. If children do not learn how to hear a rhythm and move to that beat early on, they will have difficulty dancing to the beat of a rhythm found in music as they get older. It is often the case that adolescents and adults who have difficulty discerning the beat of the music or stepping to the beat of the music were not exposed to rhythmic skills when they were youngsters.

What about the scope for intermediate grade levels, grades 3 through 5 or 6? Physical education specialists commonly help children refine or polish their fundamental movement skills while transitioning those skills into a variety of games, sports, dances, and fitness activities (Gallahue and Cleland-Donnelly 2003). Using lead-up games and modifying various individual, dual, and team activities give children ample opportunities to practice their skills, as well as expose them to concepts of game tactics, teamwork, and fair play that they will need as they enter middle or junior high school.

In addition to enhancing sport-specific skills, elementary physical education specialists also begin teaching children about basic health-related fitness concepts and the value of being physically active. Children are taught about heart-healthy intensity levels by learning about working easy, moderately, and hard. They learn the fundamental concepts of stretching safely and are taught about muscle function and exercises that help strengthen the prime muscle movers of the body (see figure 7.5).

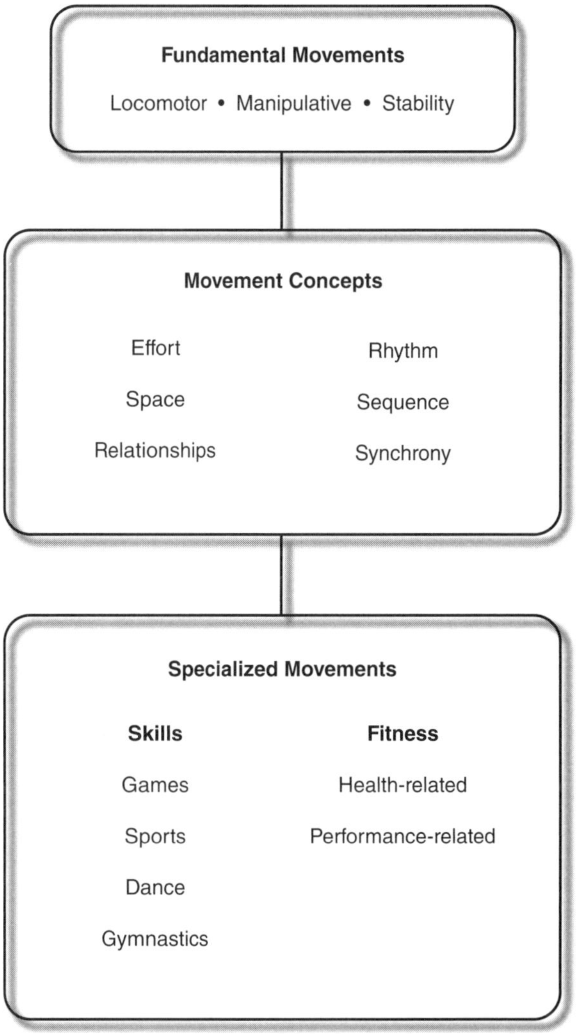

FIGURE 7.5 Overview of the elementary scope.

Scope: Middle School and Junior High School

What is the scope for students in middle school (grades 6 to 8) or junior high school (grades 7 to 9)? More than likely, you are thinking that students at this age should be exposed to a variety of sports. Many middle school programs do concentrate largely on team sports, with added emphases on individual and dual sports, fitness, and dance (Buck et al. 2007). Usually, middle or junior high school physical education programs are activity based with a scope that includes a wide selection of sport, dance, aquatic, outdoor adventure, and fitness activities in the hope that students find a few activities they really enjoy (Rink 2009). If you teach physical education at the middle or junior high school level, your job will be to help your students continue to develop the sport-specific skills they developed during elementary school, to enhance their fitness levels, to help them work on team-building skills, and to teach them a variety of new activities.

Figure 7.6 lists activities taught by physical education teachers at two middle schools. As you can tell, teachers at this level are expected to teach a wide range of activities. Can you add to the list of possible physical activities to teach found in table 7.1 on page 136?

FIGURE 7.6

Comparison of Activities Taught at Two Middle Schools

Jefferson Middle School, Denver, Colorado

Archery	Floor hockey	Table tennis
Badminton	Football/arena	Team building
Baseball/softball	Kickball/mat ball	Team handball
Basketball	Pickleball	Tennis
Bowling	Rock wall	Ultimate
Conditioning	Roller skating	Volleyball
Dance	Soccer	

Morey Middle School, Champaign, Illinois

Badminton	Lacrosse	Teamwork
Basketball	Soccer	Tsegball
Dance	Softball	Tumbling
Fitness	Swimming	Volleyball
Flag football	Table tennis	Weightlifting
Gymnastics apparatus	Team handball	Wrestling
In-line skating		

To teach at the middle school level, you will have to not only have a basic understanding of all the games and activities you will be teaching, but also be competent to teach the specific skills and content comprising each one. Consider all the activities taught in the two physical education programs in figure 7.5. That's quite a bit of information for those teachers to know!

Middle school physical education programs do not all include the same activities. Some activities are specific to certain locations or geographical regions. For example, physical education teachers in the central mountain region of the United States (e.g., Salmon, Idaho) include snowshoeing, cross-country skiing, and downhill skiing in their programs; curling is a popular activity taught in Bemidji and Wilmar schools in Minnesota; and Trikkes are used in a unit taught in the flatland coastal community of Myrtle Beach, South Carolina. (Trikkes are three-wheeled scooters that move and turn based on body lean.)

Sometimes, facilities dictate what activities can be taught. For instance, swimming is taught at Morey Middle School, but a pool is not available for the Jefferson Middle School physical education program; however, they have use of a climbing wall, so students work on traversing and climbing skills. Students who attend Spearfish Middle School in South Dakota have opportunities to develop fly fishing skills because the Spearfish River is nearby.

High school gyms that offer a variety of aerobic equipment help minimize boredom and monotony, which aid students in reaching their cardiovascular goals.

Additionally, the scope at the middle and junior high school level often includes improving students' understanding of game tactics. Physical education teachers often refer to the teaching games for understanding framework when teaching students about game tactics and strategies (Griffin, Mitchell, and Oslin 1997; Werner, Thorpe, and Bunker 1996). Within this model, similar strategies can be used when teaching various **invasion games** such as flag football, basketball, and soccer. Because invasion games involve moving into an opponent's side of the field or court to score, many similar tactics can be used across those game forms. For example, ways to get open to receive a pass or to defend a space are similar for all invasion games. **Net or wall games**, such as volleyball, tennis, and racquetball, follow their own sets of comparable game strategies including ways to gain an offensive advantage. Other activities that share similar game tactics are **striking or fielding games** (e.g., softball and kickball) and **target games** (e.g., golf, bowling, and archery).

Are specific or unique units taught in physical education programs in your area based on geographic location, regional interest, or facilities?

Table 7.1 Potential Physical Activities for Secondary-Level Physical Education Programs

Team activities	Fitness activities	Solo/dual activities	Outdoor adventure	Rhythmic activities	Recreational games
Basketball Field hockey Flag football Floor/ice hockey Kickball Lacrosse Soccer Softball Speedball Team handball Ultimate Volleyball	Aerobic dance Cardio/conditioning Kickboxing Martial arts Medicine balls Pilates Strength training Walking/running Yoga	Archery Badminton Disc golf Gymnastics/tumbling Golf Pickleball Tennis Track and field	Backpacking Canoeing/kayaking Cycling Fishing Ice skating In-line skating Orienteering Rock/wall climbing Roller skating Skateboarding Skiing/snowboarding Snowshoeing	Ballet Country line dance Folk and square dance Jazz dance Modern dance Social dance	Bocce ball Bowling Croquet Horseshoes Shuffleboard

Scope: High School

Finally, we come to the high school level. What should the scope include for high school physical education? This is an important question, because many high school physical education programs continue to follow what was taught at the middle or junior high school level, resulting in teaching the "same old things." High school physical education programs that mimic middle or junior high school programs do not stimulate the diverse physical activity interests and needs of high school students.

Unfortunately, there is often a lack of scope at the high school level because there is not a clear purpose for physical education at this level. Some schools emphasize individual and dual sport activities, whereas others allow students to choose from a list of individual, dual, team, and fitness activities. A number of programs emphasize lifetime activities that help students develop or improve skills they can use on their own or with a partner after graduating from high school, such as tennis, golf, swimming, fitness walking, bowling, rock climbing, canoeing, fishing, cycling, fitness and strength conditioning activities, yoga, and Pilates. Some schools access community resources as an extension of the gym, allowing classes to travel to local YMCAs, bowling centers, golf courses, or rock climbing facilities. Ultimately, high school physical education programs should offer a wide range of activities and allow students to choose to help spark their interest and motivation to participate in physical education activities as adolescents and future adults (Rink 2009).

> What did you learn or play in physical education when you were in high school? Were the activities the same as in junior high school or middle school? Did you learn anything new or participate in activities that helped prepare you to be an active adult?

As stated in chapter 1, some high school programs have an exclusively health-related fitness program, which means that the scope revolves around helping students enhance their fitness levels by following a more adult fitness center approach. **Health-related fitness** addresses improving in the following areas: (1) cardiorespiratory fitness, (2) flexibility, (3) muscular endurance, (4) muscular strength, and (5) body composition. High school programs with this emphasis have students doing conditioning exercises to improve aerobic endurance, stretching to improve

Professional Profile: Meg Greiner

Photo courtesy of Meg Greiner

BACKGROUND INFORMATION

I am a national board-certified elementary physical education teacher at Independence Elementary School in Independence, Oregon. I have been teaching elementary physical education since 1989 and regularly receive student teachers and practicum students into my setting. I have received numerous national awards and accolades for my innovative physical education program and the development of TEAM Time, including the 2005 NASPE National Elementary Physical Education Teacher of the Year, 2005 *USA Today* All-USA Teacher Team, and the 2006 Disney Outstanding Specialist Teacher of the Year. I am currently working with NASPE as a Head Start Body Start trainer of trainers, serving on the AAHPERD Physical Best Committee, and presenting NASPE Pipeline workshops all over the United States.

Why did you decide to become a physical education teacher?

I didn't really choose it; it chose me. When I graduated from college there were not many physical education jobs open. I applied for many—every area elementary school, middle school, and high school—and was rejected by many. Finally I landed a position teaching elementary physical education, fell in love with the age group, and continued working at that level. I love the elementary children's desire to learn and move. At the elementary level I feel that I can have a huge impact on whether or not they will learn to love being physically active for a lifetime.

What do you like most about your job?

I love the children and the fact that I can plan and deliver amazing lessons using a variety of equipment that does not have anything to do with the typical traditional physical education curriculum. I teach lessons on dynamic and static balance, circus arts, skateboarding, how the heart works, and various rhythmic activities using equipment like jump bands, rubber tubs, and PVC pipe (like stomp and tinikling).

What is the most challenging part of your job?

Not getting to see my students enough. I see my students once a week for 30 minutes—hardly enough time to make a difference or teach them the things I know that they need to know to be physically educated.

How have you continued to grow professionally?

I belong to the Oregon Alliance for Health, Physical Education, Recreation and Dance and the American Alliance for Health, Physical Education, Recreation and Dance. I continue to attend local, regional, and national physical education conferences and have gotten involved at the state, district, and national levels serving on various boards and committees. I also work with practicum and student teachers from neighboring colleges to help the next generation to become great teachers and good professionals. By being involved, I keep abreast of the new curriculums, research, and trends and keep myself fresh and challenged, which helps me to continue delivering outstanding content to my students.

What advice would you give a college student who wants to become a PE teacher?

Get as much experience as possible with children in the schools. Work at summer camps and sport camps. Play and master as many sports and activities as possible. Learn to juggle both scarves and balls. Learn to dance—take as many rhythm and dance classes as possible. Become professionally involved early by going to professional conferences. When at the conferences, go to the rhythm and dance sessions. Learn a second language. If I could do things over, I would have learned to speak Spanish and taken sign language classes. That would have helped me immensely. Never quit learning! Keep evolving as a teacher; don't let yourself get stuck in a rut! Don't ever be afraid to be silly! Enjoy yourself!

flexibility, lifting weights to enhance muscular strength and endurance, and monitoring their body weight and body composition.

Many high school physical education programs adopting a fitness-based approach have added cardio machines to their weight rooms including stationary bikes, treadmills, elliptical and rowing machines, and stair steppers. Physical education departments often purchase used fitness and strength training equipment at reduced rates from local fitness clubs or area colleges or universities because of the high cost of this type of equipment.

Because some high school weight rooms are too small to accommodate large physical education classes, many programs supplement their resistance training equipment with stretch bands or other multiuse training devices, such as the Targitfit portable gym. These mini-gyms offer over 100 different exercises and can be set up in a gymnasium to service all students in a class. Many schools also use exercise balls and Bosu balls (half moons) to add variety and challenge to strength and conditioning activities.

Some high school programs also include a **performance-related fitness** component in their scope, which focuses on developing (1) speed, (2) power, (3) coordination, (4) balance, and (5) agility. Physical education teachers often teach drills and activities used in athletics, skill performance centers, and fitness clubs to help develop performance-related fitness skills. For example, teachers may have students go through a series of agility ladder exercise. Ladders are stretched out across the floor or grassy area. Students practice a variety of agility and coordination tasks while stepping over or in each segment of the ladder. Ladders can be purchased through fitness supply companies; however, teachers also can paint ladders on the floor using water-based paint or make ladders using duct tape to save money. Some teachers also use step boxes as platforms for plyometric-type exercises. Many progressive stepping and jumping activities can be performed with step boxes to help develop power and balance.

High school physical education programs that follow a fitness-based model usually include some type of classroom work to help students learn how to apply health-related fitness concepts to their personal lives, often following content found

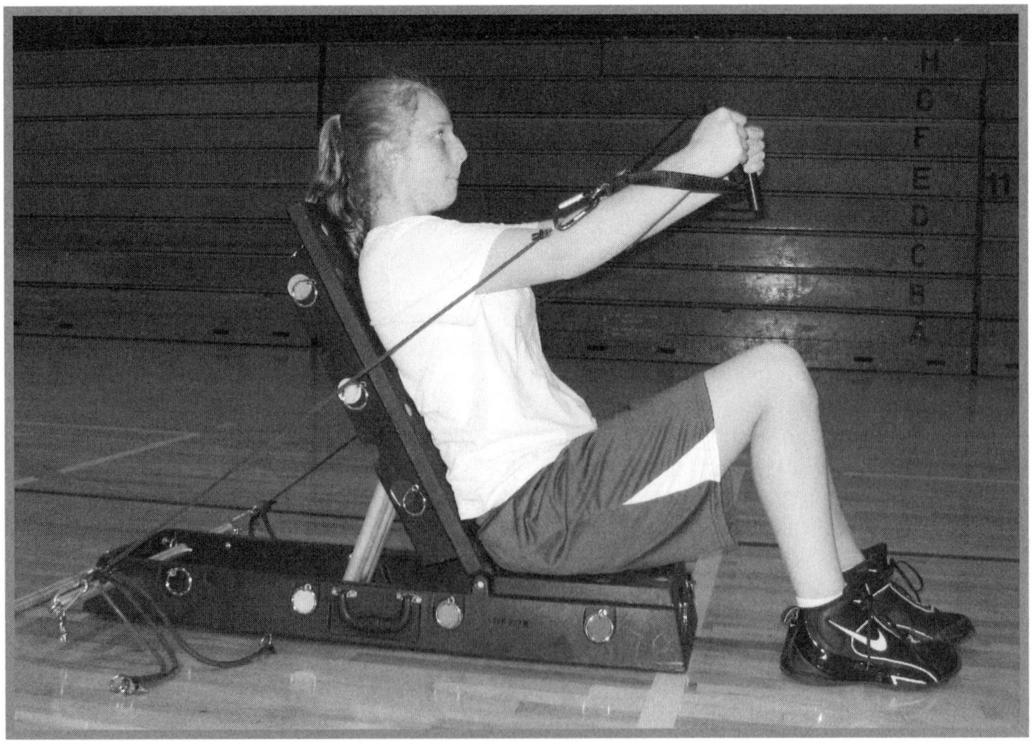

A student uses the Targitfit gym to develop upper body strength.

Photo courtesy of Jane Shimon

in Fitness for Life (Corbin and Lindsey, 2007). For example, students receive in-depth instruction on fitness concepts such as the FITT (frequency, intensity, time, and type) and overload principles, along with strength training information. They learn how to calculate their heart rate for various intensity levels and determine what activities are best for maintaining specific heart rate intensities. They learn about specific muscles and the types of muscular contractions (i.e., isometric, isotonic [concentric and eccentric], and isokinetic), safe breathing and lifting techniques, and muscular strength and endurance factors such as sets and repetitions.

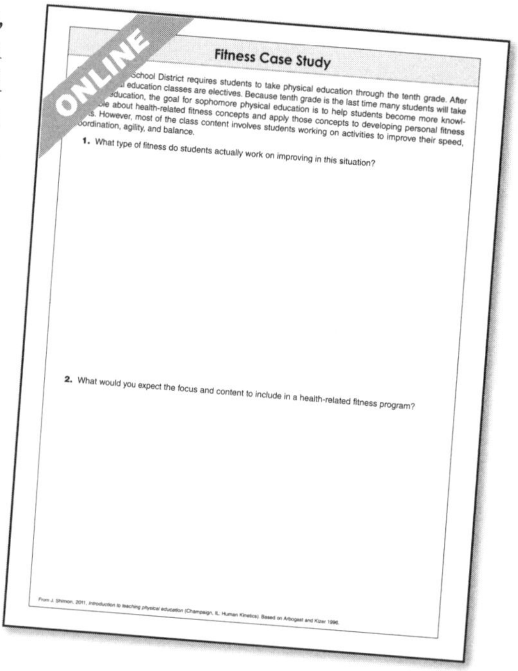
ONLINE

Fitness Case Study

School District requires students to take physical education through the tenth grade. After ... education classes are electives. Because tenth grade is the last time many students will take ... education, the goal for sophomore physical education is to help students become more knowl... about health-related fitness concepts and apply those concepts to developing personal fitness ... However, most of the class content involves students working on activities to improve their speed, coordination, agility, and balance.

1. What type of fitness do students actually work on improving in this situation?

2. What would you expect the focus and content to include in a health-related fitness program?

From J. Shimon, 2011, *Introduction to teaching physical education* (Champaign, IL: Human Kinetics). Based on Arbogast and Kizer 1996.

High school students use what they learn in class to develop their own fitness goals and personalized training programs. A variety of fitness tests are used to determine baseline (starting) levels, and training logs and further fitness tests demonstrate whether they are making progress toward their goals. Teachers also have students use pedometers and heart rate monitors to check their activity levels. Some teachers include information on diet and nutrition as well.

If you have a dual major in physical education and health or are planning to earn a health minor or endorsement along with your physical education degree, you are fortunate, indeed. You will more than likely use all that content when teaching at the high school level. Physical education teachers at this level who follow a fitness-related model help prepare their students by giving them the knowledge and skills to maintain a health-enhancing level of fitness as adults.

The scope of a high school physical education program often includes introducing new activities, like archery.

AP Photo/Ed Betz

Sequence

Thus far, this chapter has concentrated on the scope of K-12 physical education programs. Although you need to determine what you will teach, you must also consider when you will teach it. **Sequence** refers to the order, or progression, of the scope. The sequence may address the time of the year you teach an activity, the order in which you teach the skills within an activity, or the progression of teaching a specific skill within a lesson.

If you are teaching volleyball at the middle school level, when will you teach the unit—in the fall, winter, or spring? Will you teach it for two weeks or three? If you are teaching volleyball, what is the sequence of skills you will teach during the unit? Will you teach the forearm pass first, or will you start with serving? If you teach the forearm pass, what progression sequence will you use to teach the skill? Will you start with students forearm passing the ball individually, or will you start teaching the pass from a partner's toss? If you are teaching volleyball at the elementary, middle, and high school levels, what will the scope and sequence include from year to year so that students will continue to grow and develop, instead of learning the same skills over and over at each grade level? Clearly, the terms *scope* and *sequence* have a variety of meanings (see table 7.2).

If you were a high school physical education teacher, what would be the purpose and scope of your program? Go online to complete the scope and sequence case studies.

Summary

Scope addresses content; sequence addresses order and progression. Together, the terms reflect the physical education content being taught and the order in which it is taught. Content can range from specific games and activities to the specific skills of those games. The scope for elementary physical education is clear and purposeful. Helping children develop fundamental movement skills and transitioning those

Table 7.2 Examples of Scope and Sequence

	Scope	Sequence
Curriculum	Tennis	Three weeks: August-September
	Soccer	Two weeks: September
	Weight training and fitness activities	Six weeks: October-November
	Dance	Two weeks: November-December
Specific activity	Badminton	Overhead clear Overhead and underhand drop Serve Drive and smash
Specific skill	Kicking	Ball stationary, child stationary Ball stationary, child moves Ball moves, child stationary Ball and child move

skills into specialized sports, activities, and fitness skills is the main focus at this level. Middle school and junior high school programs normally focus on enhancing those fundamental movements by teaching a wide variety of sports, games, dances, and aquatics and fitness activities. Often, high school physical education programs do not have a clear purpose; hence, many programs do not provide meaningful physical education classes for older adolescents. The scope for high school physical education programs can consist of traditional team and dual sports, lifetime activities, fitness and conditioning activities, or a choice from a number of options. Whatever the scope, the high school program should prepare adolescents to become active for a lifetime.

The various activity and methods classes you will be required to take as part of your physical education teaching program will prepare you to determine effective scope and sequence schemes for the lessons, units, and curricula you develop. Based on those classes, you will be able to determine what skills are best to teach first, and what skills can be added in later lessons. You will learn the recommended sequences for teaching various skills, whether by breaking skills into workable parts or adding complexity or challenge to the learning tasks. Scope and sequence concepts will follow you throughout your undergraduate course work and into your professional teaching career.

Discussion Questions

1. How can the development of fundamental movements contribute to successful performance in sport-specific activities?
2. If you had limited time available to teach at the elementary level, what specific fundamental movements would you emphasize and why?
3. Describe the activities that are taught in the middle schools in your area and compare that list to the activity courses you are required to take as part of your teacher preparation program. How do you plan to learn those activities you may have to teach, but are not required to take?
4. What is the scope of the high school programs in your area? Do you agree with their content offerings, or do you believe a different focus should be considered?

CHAPTER 8

Lesson Planning

CHAPTER OBJECTIVES

After reading this chapter, you will be able to:

- ☐ Explain the purpose of a performance objective in a lesson plan.
- ☐ Write performance objectives containing two or three components.
- ☐ Describe the parts that comprise a lesson plan.
- ☐ Explain the difference between dynamic warm-ups and instant activities.

KEY TERMS

anticipatory set
condition
criteria
performance objectives
task

What do I want my students to be able to do today? This question is the driving force for every lesson you will develop. Answering this question will not only provide a specific purpose, or objective, for the lesson, but also be a guide for planning the scope and sequence of activities students will learn and perform. In addition, the answer to this question will offer a means for evaluating lesson effectiveness and student outcomes. Developing lesson objectives and thorough lesson plans is an integral part of being an effective teacher, especially for the novice physical educator.

Writing Performance Objectives

Performance objectives are clear and specific statements of what students will be able to do (outcome) as a result of a lesson (Mager 1997). A performance objective for a basketball lesson plan, for instance, might be something like this: *Students will be able to dribble up and down the court without losing control of the ball,* or: *When working cooperatively in groups, students will be able to develop two ways to get open to receive a pass.* Having established your objective for the lesson, you can then plan a variety of learning activities and lead-up games to help students maintain control of the ball, or develop various group tasks to help students learn and practice offensive ways to dodge a defender to get open for a pass.

Performance objectives need to be *observable, measurable,* and *attainable.* The preceding performance objective examples are observable: Students can be observed dribbling a ball (demonstrating, or executing, a skill) or working together in groups to solve a problem during a lesson. These performance objectives are also written so that you can determine (measure, or assess) whether students have achieved them—that is, whether students maintain control during their dribble or whether they work cooperatively. Finally, these objectives are attainable.

Sometimes performance objectives are written in ways that make them not observable or measurable. Objectives that use words such as *learn* or *understand* cannot be observed or measured; as such, they are ineffective (see table 8.1). An incorrect performance objective might be something like this: *Students will learn how to dribble up and down the court without losing control of the ball* or: *Students will understand how to get open to receive a pass.*

When writing a performance objective for a lesson plan, include (1) the task, (2) the condition, and (3) the criteria.

Table 8.1 Examples of Verbs Used in Observable and Nonobservable Performance Objectives

Observable		Nonobservable/not appropriate
Students will be able to ____________.		
apply	execute	develop
demonstrate	follow	grasp
design	identify	learn
define	solve	like
discuss	synchronize	understand

■ **Task** (what): The main part of a performance objective involves a task or behavior. In other words, *what* do you want students to be able to do? Do you want students to be able to dribble a ball, perform a forward roll, work cooperatively in groups, take a test, or develop a conditioning program? These examples describe various tasks students will do during the lesson.

■ **Condition** (how): The condition of a performance objective describes a circumstance or situation of performing the task. In other words, *how* will students do the task? How do you want students to dribble a ball? Do you want them to dribble a ball in their own space, against a defender, by following a line along the floor, up and down the court, or between cones? Do you want them to dribble the ball while walking or running? Describing the condition of a performance objective makes the task specific.

■ **Criteria** (how well): Finally, a performance object includes some type of standard, or level, of performance. In other words, *how well* do you want students to perform the task? Do you want students to perform the task in a certain amount of time, perform a skill correctly, or complete a certain number of successful attempts (e.g., 8 out of 10)? Do you want students to work together in groups without complaining, or pass a written test at 80 percent accuracy? Including criteria in a performance objective provides a way to measure or assess it (Rink 2010).

Can you identify the three parts of the following performance objectives?

1. Students will be able to serve a tennis ball into the correct service court three out of five times.
2. Students will be able to perform an overhead volley 10 consecutive times over a line on the wall.

Some physical education teachers write performance objectives with a broader focus by including only the task and condition components; others add criteria to make the objectives more precise. Your teacher will specify the type of performance objectives you will be required to write for your lesson plans.

Performance objectives can also be written for each learning domain, depending on the learning outcomes of the lesson. Because learning outcomes for a lesson may involve more than one domain, teachers often include several performance objectives within a lesson. For example, you may want your students to be able to dribble a basketball around cones without losing control (psychomotor domain) and to describe various ways to get open to receive a pass (cognitive domain).

Overall, performance objectives provide direction as you develop your lesson plans. They help you clarify the purpose of each lesson and offer a foundation on which to design it. Performance objectives also help you become more accountable for what your students are learning and achieving in class, and help you demonstrate to parents what their children are learning. Finally, performance objectives can inform students about what they will be learning or expected to do during the lesson (Buck et al. 2007; Rink 2010).

Go online to complete the exercise in writing performance objectives.

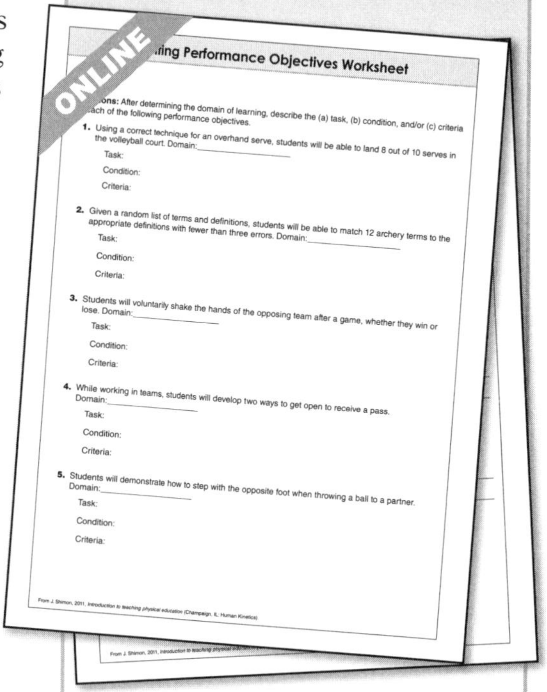

...ing Performance Objectives Worksheet

...ons: After determining the domain of learning, describe the (a) task, (b) condition, and/or (c) criteria ...ach of the following performance objectives.

1. Using a correct technique for an overhand serve, students will be able to land 8 out of 10 serves in the volleyball court. Domain:________
   Task:
   Condition:
   Criteria:
2. Given a random list of terms and definitions, students will be able to match 12 archery terms to the appropriate definitions with fewer than three errors. Domain:________
   Task:
   Condition:
   Criteria:
3. Students will voluntarily shake the hands of the opposing team after a game, whether they win or lose. Domain:________
   Task:
   Condition:
   Criteria:
4. While working in teams, students will develop two ways to get open to receive a pass. Domain:________
   Task:
   Condition:
   Criteria:
5. Students will demonstrate how to step with the opposite foot when throwing a ball to a partner. Domain:________
   Task:
   Condition:
   Criteria:

From J. Shimon, 2011, *Introduction to teaching physical education* (Champaign, IL: Human Kinetics).

Creating Lesson Plans

How do lesson plans fit within the design of a physical education curriculum? In the global scheme of a school year, physical education teachers usually follow a curriculum guide for meeting state, district, or national standards and the general goals of the program. Physical education curricula include general goals, activities, and what students will learn and achieve during the semester or year. Based on the scope and sequence of activities to be taught during the semester or school year, teachers often create unit plans for each activity within the curriculum, describing unit objectives, content they will cover, and assessments they will use. Finally, they develop specific lesson plans and performance objectives for each day of a unit. In Figure 8.1, the scope and sequence of this curriculum example indicates activities that will be taught during the fall, winter, and spring. The tennis unit plan illustrates a refined scope and sequence of skills and concepts that will be taught during a 10-day unit within the curriculum. Finally, teachers develop daily lesson plans for each day of the unit, describing specific progressions and learning tasks.

Lesson plans are specific guidelines teachers follow that are developed from the units or teaching strands found within the curriculum. They outline an organized scope and sequence of learning experiences based on the general objectives of the unit and the specific performance objective(s) of the lesson. In addition, lesson plans are often continuations or expansions of previous lessons that help students progressively develop the skills and knowledge necessary for participating successfully in the unit and achieving overall curriculum goals.

Lesson plans are not only an important tool for teachers to use during the lesson, but also a form of legal written evidence of instruction. As such, they are used by substitute teachers when covering class. In addition, some school administrators require teachers to submit weekly lesson plans or keep copies of their lesson plans for periodic review.

Lesson plans can be difficult to develop, especially the first time. Initially, you will have to make assumptions about your students' skill levels or related knowledge, and plan learning tasks and activities based on those assumptions. Sometimes your assumptions will pay off and your lesson plan will work; other times, you will have to make adjustments to the plan during the lesson if it is not working as anticipated. It is important that you also reflect on the effectiveness of each lesson you teach and make necessary changes for future use.

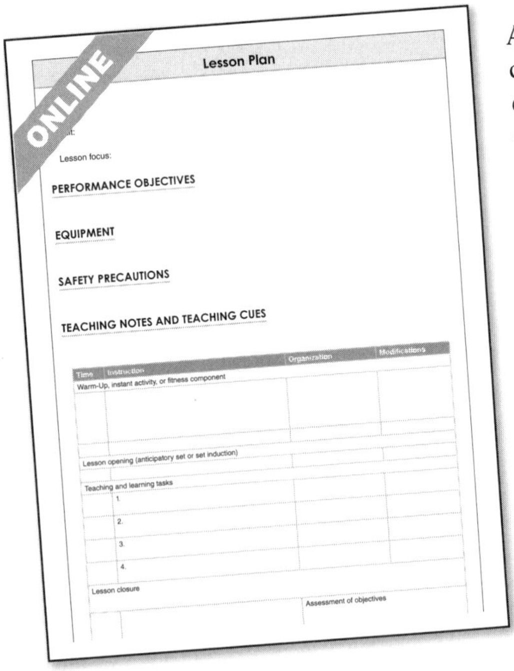

Components of a Lesson Plan

Although there are many ways to format a lesson plan, they all contain the same basic information. Lesson plans include basic descriptive information such as equipment needs, safety concerns, and special gym setup instructions, as well as a space in which to write performance objectives. The instructional component of a lesson plan includes a detailed description of the scope and sequence of teaching and learning tasks. A variety of lesson plan formats are available in the online student resource.

Some physical education teachers divide the instructional component of a lesson plan into parts: a warm-up or fitness part, a lesson opening, and a lesson closure.

Warm-Up

A majority of physical education lesson plans begin with a warm-up. Traditional warm-ups usually include a few minutes of easy running, followed by static (stationary) stretching. However, more programs are beginning to implement dynamic warm-up activities, which include low-, moderate-, and then high-intensity hops, skips, jumps, lunges, and other upper- and

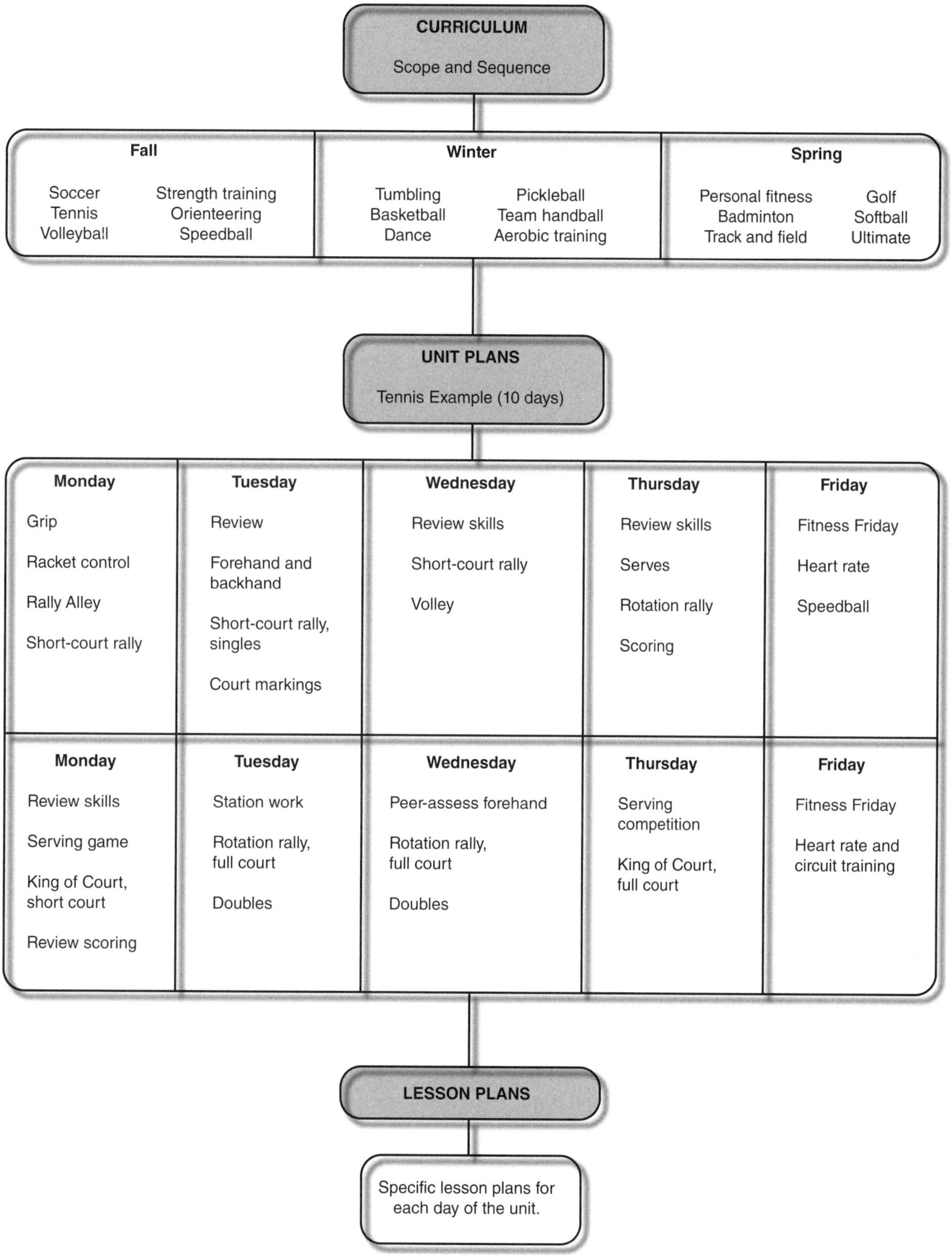

FIGURE 8.1 An example of how lesson plans fit within a simplified scheme of a middle school physical education curriculum.

Professional Profile: *Phil Abbadessa*

Photo courtesy of Phil Abbadessa

BACKGROUND INFORMATION

I have a master's degree in secondary education and exercise science plus 60 hours. I taught elementary physical education for 5 years; this is my 25th year teaching at the high school level and my 30th year in education. I have also taught adapted physical education, health education, and driver education. I am the physical education chair at Mountain Pointe High School in Phoenix, Arizona. Since 1991, I have helped Dr. Chuck Corbin on research and implementation of the Fitness for Life curriculum. In 2008, I received the Council of Exceptional Teacher Excellence Award for adapted physical education.

What do you like most about your job?

I like working with high school students and helping them be successful.

What is the most challenging part of your job?

The most challenging part of my job is dealing with large class sizes.

How have you continued to grow professionally?

I continue to grow professionally by reading, attending conventions, and working with Dr. Hans Van Der Mars from Arizona State University.

What advice would you give a college student who wants to become a physical education teacher?

You should get certified to teach K-12 subjects other than physical education. It can be very challenging to land a high school physical education teaching job. You will probably be required to coach more than one year of high school sports. You also should consider teaching science, social studies, or any other subject. We have teachers who have physical education degrees, but they end up getting classroom positions.

lower-body movements to help elevate core body temperature, maximize active ranges of motion, and excite motor units and kinesthetic awareness (Faigenbaum and McFarlane, 2007). Dynamic exercises prepare the body for physical education lessons, athletic practices, and competition. Examples of dynamic exercises can be found in appendix B.

Some physical education teachers include instant, or introductory, activities in lieu of warm-up exercises or as a supplement to warm-ups. Instant activities are fun, low-organized games or activities that quickly get students moving and elevate heart rates. Instant activities can include challenging partner and small-group activities or activities that involve the entire class, such as various tag games (Darst and Pangrazi 2009; Pangrazi and Beighle 2010). No matter the age level, instant activities are a quick and fun way to motivate children and adolescents to get moving at the start of class.

In addition to a warm-up or instant activity, some lesson plans also include a separate section dedicated solely to health- and performance-related fitness activities (Darst and Pangrazi 2009; Pangrazi and Beighle 2010). Teachers use this part of the lesson to plan for fitness-specific activity. Examples include various agility drills, partner resistance exercises, station or circuit work, or other creative activities to enhance health- and performance-related fitness.

Main Instruction: Teaching and Learning

The teaching and learning tasks comprise the main instruction portion of the lesson plan. A lesson opening, often referred to as the **anticipatory set** or set induction, often begins this portion of the lesson plan. The anticipatory set is a quick opening statement (one to two minutes) prior to instruction that informs students about what they will be doing during the lesson. You can approach the anticipatory set in a variety of ways. You can use the lesson opening as a way to get your students

Instant activities get students moving and ready to actively participate in PE class. Make the activities fun and engaging!

excited about the lesson by telling an interesting tale or by relating the upcoming lesson to previous experiences they have had. You can show a short video clip that relates to the lesson to spark their interest, or you can just quickly tell them the objectives of the lesson. No matter what you chose as the anticipatory set, your opening will ultimately inform students of the lesson's focus.

After determining the anticipatory set, you will develop the main instructional component of the lesson plan. As you know, this part of the plan outlines the progressions of skills and tasks you will have students learn and do based on your performance objectives. Chapter 4 provides some helpful guidelines to keep in mind when designing your instruction. The following are some factors to consider as you develop the instructional portion of your lesson plan:

- Skill and developmental level of students
- Demonstrations
- Checks for understanding
- Progressions of closed to open practice opportunities
- Whole versus part practice
- Extensions to adapt or modify the activity and challenge students
- Application tasks
- Student choice

Figure 8.2 (page 150) shows one physical education teacher's instructional plan for the first day of a seventh-grade tennis unit. Based on the performance objective, the focus of this tennis lesson is control. The teacher has outlined when demonstrations and checks for understanding will occur, along with skill progressions that work on racket control using extensions, applications, and student choice. A tentative timeline for the teaching and learning tasks is also included. This timeline provides a general sense of how much time to allocate for each task.

Lesson Plan

Lesson No. *1*, Grade:*7*

- Unit: *Tennis*

Lesson Focus: *Racket control*

PERFORMANCE OBJECTIVES

Students will be able to demonstrate racket control by consistently rallying back and forth with a partner over an alley and in the service court (short court).

EQUIPMENT

- One racket per student or bucket of tennis balls
- ropes for rat-tails
- 15 poly spots

SAFETY PRECAUTIONS

Have space when hitting the ball. Students who hit two balls hit over fence are removed from the activity and lose participation points.

TEACHING NOTES AND CUES

Grip: Handshake

Play rattail tag within the service court areas as a way to outline service court boundaries for the short-court game.

Treat equipment with care—no spinning, twirling, or hitting the racket on the ground when angry

Time	Instruction	Organization	Modifications
	WARM-UP/INSTANT ACTIVITY/FITNESS		
5 min	Dynamic warm-up routine + 1 min of crunches and 30 s bridge		
2 min	Instant activity: rattail tag		
	LESSON OPENING (ANTICIPATORY SET/SET INDUCTION)		
2 min	How many of you have played or watched tennis on TV? Tennis is a great lifetime physical activity for you to learn. Today we're going to get comfortable hitting the ball under control; control is the focus of today's lesson. [Remind students about equipment care.]		
	TEACHING AND LEARNING TASKS		
2 min	**1.** Demonstrate grip (handshake). Check for understanding by having students show it.		

(continued)

FIGURE 8.2 This lesson plan outlines the instructional planning of teaching and learning tasks for a tennis lesson.

Time	Instruction	Organization	Modifications
5 min	**2.** Racket control—individual tap work a. Palm up/tap up b. Palm down/tap up c. Palm down/rebound against ground d. Moving in personal space/choice e. 30 s time challenge/choice. Repeat to improve.		
10 min	**3.** Demonstrate alley rally with two students. Stress control. a. Partner practice b. 30 s time challenge c. Challenge: poly spot(s) in middle of alley for target d. Rotate partners		
10 min	**4.** Demonstrate short-court rally with two students. Stress control. a. 30 s time challenge b. Rotate partners		
	LESSON CLOSURE		
2 min	It is important to develop racket control. You all demonstrated great control during some of your rallies today. Tomorrow we will concentrate more specifically on technique.	**Assessment of Objectives** ☐ Observation ☐ Skill critique ☐ Group work ☐ Task sheet ☐ Peer assessment ☐ Oral check ☐ Quiz or test ☐ Other	

From Jane M. Shimon, 2011, *Introduction to teaching physical education* (Champaign, IL: Human Kinetics).

FIGURE 8.2 *(continued)*

As mentioned in chapter 4, you must also take time to think through the organizational strategies for teaching and learning tasks within the instructional part of the lesson plan. Thoughtful planning of class formations, equipment distribution and collection, and grouping combinations will help your class transition smoothly from one activity to the next, without taking too much time away from the lesson. Figure 8.3 on page 152 shows a further development of the lesson plan in figure 8.2, illustrating the organizational strategies for each task in the tennis lesson. The teacher has predetermined how students will be organized and how equipment will be issued and collected. The plan also outlines informal assessment strategies the teacher will use to determine whether lesson objectives are being met. Chapter 9 addresses student assessment in detail.

Lesson Closure

The last part of the lesson plan is a quick lesson closure or wrap-up. Some teachers use a lesson closure to check for student understanding of certain concepts or techniques taught during the lesson; others use a closure to inform students about

Lesson Plan

Lesson No. *1*, Grade:*7*

- Unit: *Tennis*

Lesson Focus: *Racket control*

PERFORMANCE OBJECTIVES

Students will be able to demonstrate racket control by consistently rallying back and forth with a partner over an alley and in the service court (short court).

EQUIPMENT

- One racket per student or bucket of tennis balls
- Ropes for rattails
- 15 poly spots

SAFETY PRECAUTIONS

Have space when hitting the ball. Students who hit two balls over the fence are removed from the activity and lose participation points.

TEACHING NOTES AND CUES

Grip: Handshake

Play rattail tag within the service court areas as a way to outline service court boundaries for the short-court game.

Treat equipment with care—no spinning, twirling, or hitting the racket on the ground when angry

Time	Instruction	Organization	Modifications
	WARM-UP/INSTANT ACTIVITY/FITNESS		
7 min	Dynamic warm-up routine + 1 min of crunches and 30 s bridge	Squads: Play within the boundaries of the service court. Squad leaders gather ropes or tails for the squad.	
2 min	Instant activity: rattail tag		
	LESSON OPENING (ANTICIPATORY SET/SET INDUCTION)		
2 min	How many of you have played or watched tennis on TV? Tennis is a great lifetime physical activity for you to learn. Today we're going to get comfortable hitting the ball under control; control is the focus of today's lesson. [Remind students about equipment care.]	Semicircle around the teacher	
	TEACHING AND LEARNING TASKS		
2 min	**1.** Demonstrate grip (handshake). Check for understanding by having students show it.	Each girl gets a racket and one ball; then each boy; back to semicircle around the teacher.	

(continued)

FIGURE 8.3 Organization and assessment planning is added to the tennis lesson plan.

Time	Instruction	Organization	Modifications
5 min	**2.** Racket control—individual tap work a. Palm up/tap up b. Palm down/tap up c. Palm down/rebound against ground d. Moving in personal space/choice e. 30 s time challenge/choice. Repeat to improve.	Use two courts; have students spread out within the service court boundaries.	Allow the use of short-stemmed rackets and different types of balls.
10 min	**3.** Demonstrate alley rally with two students. Stress control. a. Partner practice b. 30 s time challenge c. Challenge—poly spot(s) in the middle of the alley for targets d. Rotate partners	Groups of two or three (choice) on opposite sides of the alleys (use two courts). The tallest partner gets one or two poly spots.	Allow students to modify the alley space.
10 min	**4.** Demonstrate short-court rally with two students. Stress control. a. 30 s time challenge b. Rotate partners		
LESSON CLOSURE			
2 min	It is important to develop racket control. You all demonstrated great control during some of your rallies today. Tomorrow we will concentrate more specifically on technique.	**Assessment of Objectives** ☑ Observation ☐ Skill critique ☐ Group work ☐ Task sheet ☐ Peer assessment ☑ Oral check ☐ Quiz or test ☐ Other	

From Jane M. Shimon, 2011, *Introduction to teaching physical education* (Champaign, IL: Human Kinetics).

FIGURE 8.3 *(continued)*

what they will do the next time they have physical education. At the elementary level, a lesson closure also helps settle children down prior to sending them back to their classroom teacher. Finally, some teachers incorporate static stretching exercises into lesson closures.

Lesson Plan Tips

It can be awkward to carry your lesson plan with you to your class. One tip you may consider is to transfer the main information from your lesson plan to a three-by-five index card. This card can be attached to a lanyard worn around your neck or alongside a whistle (see the photograph on page 154). The card is readily available to view at any time during the lesson, and you don't have to worry about managing a large piece of paper. Another helpful tip is to transfer an abbreviated lesson plan to a whiteboard in the gym. The lesson outline is an excellent visual prompt to refer to during an indoor lesson. Some teachers also refer to their lesson plans on handheld computers or smartphones.

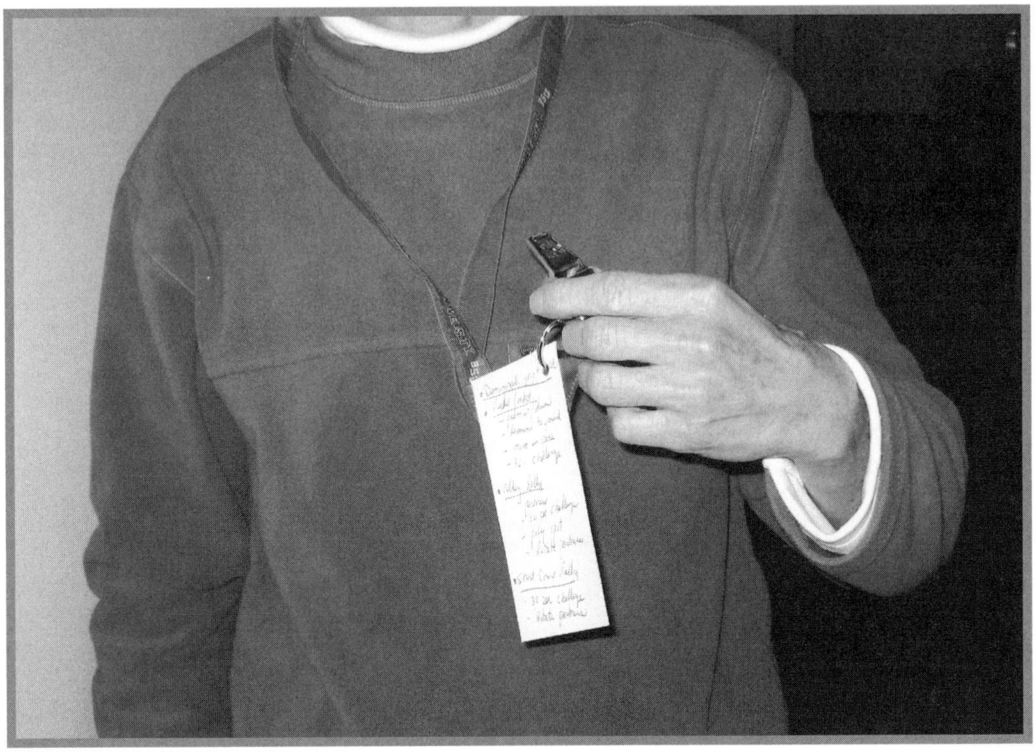

An abbreviated lesson plan (three-by-five card) secured to a whistle.

Photo courtesy of Jane Shimon

Teachers often refer to their lesson plans year after year. After teaching a lesson, many teachers pencil-in changes, make adjustments, and improve the lesson plan for the next time they teach the lesson. Therefore, it is important to keep your lesson plans; don't throw them away! After you teach from your lesson plans, add comments, make necessary changes, and file the plans until you need them again. When you refer to those old lesson plans, you'll be thankful that you took the time to write in notes and suggestions to make the lessons better.

The last lesson plan tip involves creating a rainy-day fund of lesson plans and activities. Rainy-day lessons are preplanned lessons that you can use if some unforeseen circumstance affects your originally planned lessons. Let's say you have developed a wonderful outdoor flag football lesson, full of group work and team play. However, during fourth period, a thunderstorm rolls in and you have to keep your class indoors. You can't teach your lesson indoors because of space limitations. What do you do? What happens if you are just informed by the school principal that your gym will not be available for classes because a last-minute assembly has to be set up in the gymnasium? Your intended lesson plans and learning activities are useless, and the weather may prohibit you from going outside. What do you do? Or, let's say that an imminent holiday or vacation break is wreaking havoc on students' attention span and focus, and you know your planned lesson will not be effective. What do you do?

Indeed, having a backup plan is wise. You can thumb through your collection of rainy-day activities and select a lesson plan that fits your current situation—group initiative and problem-solving activities, various knot-tying or juggling activities that can be done in a limited space, orienteering lessons with treasure hunts, cup-stacking tasks, silly relay challenges or games tied to holiday themes, or classroom content activities. No matter the situation, if you have rainy-day activities, you will be prepared to make immediate and stress-free changes when unexpected events occur.

Summary

Performance objectives are the cornerstone of each lesson. They describe what students will be able to do as a result of the lesson and provide a specific foundation for developing teaching and learning tasks. Needless to say, you will need an objective for every lesson; otherwise, there's no reason to plan or teach it.

Lesson planning is a fundamental part of teaching and provides a road map to delivering smooth and successful lessons. Although some seasoned teachers may not develop lesson plans as extensively as novice teachers do, effective teachers definitely have performance objectives and lesson plan content determined prior to each lesson.

Discussion Questions

1. What is the purpose of writing a performance objective for each lesson?
2. Why is it important that performance objectives be observable, measurable, and attainable?
3. What are the benefits of performing dynamic warm-ups compared to standard static stretching routines?
4. How might a lesson plan look for the first day of teaching the forward roll to second-graders or badminton to seventh-graders?

CHAPTER 9

Student Assessment

CHAPTER OBJECTIVES

After reading this chapter, you will be able to:

- ☐ Recognize common assessment terminology.
- ☐ Explain the meaning and purpose of rubrics.
- ☐ Compare and contrast the various types of rubrics.
- ☐ Recognize grading options in physical education.
- ☐ Describe the benefits of Fitnessgram and the tests offered within the program.
- ☐ Describe tips for writing an assortment of test items.

KEY TERMS

assessment
criterion-referenced standards
evaluation
formative assessments
measurement
objective assessments
objectivity (of a test)
process
product
reliability (of a test)
rubrics
subjective assessments
summative assessment
validity (of a test)

How will you know whether your students have achieved the objectives of a lesson or the goals of your physical education program? How will you know whether your program has met district, state, or national standards, and how will you determine final grades for student report cards or progress reports? The answers to these questions lie in the use of assessments.

Unfortunately, many physical education teachers do not assess student outcomes. Whatever the reasons cited (e.g., too many students in class, grading skill is not fair, testing students takes too much time), perhaps the underlying culprits are administrators who do not hold physical education teachers accountable for demonstrating student learning and meeting local or state standards. Regardless, physical education teachers cannot dismiss their professional responsibility to measure student outcomes. Those who do assess in physical education not only hold themselves accountable for student learning, but also demonstrate the educational value of physical education and improve the image and integrity of the discipline among colleagues, administrators, parents, and the community.

In this age of budget cutbacks, program scrutiny, and standards-based education, physical education teachers must be able to demonstrate student achievement and show that objectives and standards are being met. Although assessing student learning is no easy task, this chapter provides the essentials for getting started on a routine of student assessment.

Terminology

As part of your teacher preparation program, you may be required to take a class called something like Tests and Measurements or Measurement and Evaluation. The words found in those course titles—*tests, measurement,* and *evaluation*—are closely related and are often referred to as assessment. **Assessment** is an umbrella term in education used to describe the process of measurement and evaluation. **Measurement** basically means the process of administering a test and collecting test scores (data). **Evaluation** involves your analysis and interpretation of data, which gives meaning to the information (Baumgartner et al. 2007). Evaluating results allows you to determine the extent of student learning or progress, your own effectiveness, or the quality of your program.

Physical education assessments are either objective or subjective. **Objective assessments** involve a standardized or well-defined scoring system that eliminates teacher bias in determining a score. Written test items (i.e., multiple choice, true or false, matching), pedometer or heart rate readings, and timed or counted events (i.e., fitness testing) are all examples of objective assessments. On the other hand, **subjective assessments** do not include a standardized scoring system and often require you to make personal judgments regarding the score or outcome. Examples of subjective assessments are determining a score for an essay on a written test, the quality of skill performance, or a grade for a project or assignment.

Assessments can be administered at any time during the learning process. **Formative assessments** are conducted during a lesson or throughout a unit of instruction as a form of feedback to students regarding their progress or to determine whether they have mastered a certain task. You may observe skill development; give mini short-answer quizzes; have students chart heart rates; check for understanding; or use task sheets to assess physical skills, knowledge, or fitness levels during a lesson. In contrast, you will use **summative assessments** at the end of a unit of instruction or semester to determine the extent of learning that has occurred. Summative assessments are often used to establish student grades for report cards and to determine whether unit or course objectives have been met, and include end-of-course exams and skill or fitness testing.

Finally, three important assessment characteristics you need to keep in mind are **validity, reliability,** and **objectivity.** When an assessment measures what it's supposed to measure, it is considered valid. For example, the 1-mile run is a valid, or relevant, measure of aerobic capacity, whereas the 50-yard dash is a valid measure of speed. To be valid, an assessment must also demonstrate **reliability**. A reliable assessment measures scores consistently. That is, assessment scores should be identical if administered twice to the same student whose ability has not changed (Baumgartner et al. 2007). Last, assessments should reflect a level of **objectivity,** or impartiality. For instance, if two physical education teachers use the same assessment to measure the set shot technique of a student, both final scores should be the same; the assessment tool should allow both teachers to come to the same conclusion on the performance. A lack of objectivity reduces both the validity and reliability of the assessment (Baumgartner et al. 2007).

Student Assessment Options

There are a variety of ways to assess student learning and demonstrate that standards have been met (see figure 9.1 on page 160). You can use traditional assessment methods, such as formal skill and fitness testing, along with written tests, or more alternative or authentic methods. Authentic assessments help you determine relevant knowledge or skill performance in realistic, or authentic, situations, in addition to positively influencing students' self-concept, motivation, and skill achievement (Mintah 2003). For example, the execution of a certain skill, understanding of rules, or good sporting behavior can be assessed during game play instead of as separate and isolated events (Doolittle and Fay 2002). Students can also demonstrate their current knowledge, skill performance, or both, by creating an instructional video or informational pamphlet.

Make use of all assessment opportunities. For example, you can assess running form while students are completing warm-up laps.

Although demonstrating skill competency is found in many physical education program objectives, many teachers do not like to assess skills. It is often a misconception of physical education teachers that assessing physical skills isn't fair because some students are gifted athletes while others struggle to perform even the most basic movements. This notion has merit if tests measure an end product of a skill, such as the number of baskets made in 30 seconds or the number of serves made to a certain part of a court. Students need considerable practice

FIGURE 9.1

Assessment Options

Traditional Forms	*Alternative or Authentic Forms*
Specific skill tests (end product)	Skill technique (process)
Counted (frequency) events	Videos or photos of performance
Timed events	Personal fitness logs
Fitness tests	Peer assessments
Quizzes	Portfolios
Written tests	Checklists or task sheets
	Self- or group assessments
	Presentations or projects
	Rating sheets
	Drawings
	Pamphlets or brochures
	Reflective journals
	Interviews
	Inventories or surveys
	Game play

time to improve their accuracy or develop the strength to produce an acceptable end product of a skill. How can teachers expect students to develop a high level of skill after a few days of instruction or within a short unit (one or two weeks) when athletes often take years developing their skills?

This rationale does not mean that skills should not be assessed. Students can be held accountable for learning skills, and you can assess them quickly and equitably by assessing specific movements associated with executing the skill. You can assess the **process** of skill achievement or the quality of skill technique, instead of whether a ball makes it over the net, makes into a basket, or hits a target (**product**). In addition, when students know that they will be graded on a skill or behavior, most will be motivated to put forth more effort to practice and improve.

Types of Rubrics

Physical education teachers develop rubrics as a tool to assess a variety of student outcomes, including skill technique and various types of alternative or authentic tasks. **Rubrics** are a type of rating scale or scoring guide that indicates the specific elements of a skill or task that will be assessed (Lund 2000). Rubrics clarify to both teachers and students what is expected and how the tasks will be scored. They can be used to determine scores for a final grade or as evidence that objectives and standards have been met.

Rubrics range from general to more complex systems of assessment (Lund 2000). Some rubrics assess whether students have demonstrated specified skill elements or tasks, whereas others assess the quality of the performance.

Checklists

Checklists are a general type of rubric that assesses whether students have mastered specified elements or tasks. A simple check box or (yes or no) option can be marked by either teachers or students when required elements have been observed. Checklist rubrics can be helpful for quickly determining students' current levels of achievement. As you can tell by viewing figure 9.2, checklists indicate only whether skills or tasks have been completed; they do not indicate the level or quality of those skills or tasks.

A point system can also be added to a checklist rubric. In addition to listing elements or tasks, points are assigned to the tasks, allowing you to use the scores in a grading scheme. As with the checklist rubric, the point system does not address the quality of the performance (see figure 9.3).

TENNIS FOREHAND GROUNDSTROKE

Skill Elements	*Yes*	*No*
Racket back early	☑	☐
Firm wrist and arm	☐	☑
Swing in arc low to high	☑	☐
Finish across and up	☑	☐

THROWING FORM

☑ Body in T position
☑ Forward arm points to target
☐ Throwing elbow leads
☑ Steps with opposite foot first
☐ Follows through across and down

FIGURE 9.2 Checklist rubrics that assess a forehand tennis stroke and throwing technique.

PERSONAL RESPONSIBILITY DURING TEAM PLAY

Elements	*Yes*	*No*
I played fairly within the rules.	☑	☐
I didn't argue with others.	☐	☑
I offered encouragement.	☑	☐
I respected the effort of the other team.	☑	☐
Total: 7/8		

AEROBIC DANCE PRESENTATION—50 POINTS

☑ Warm-up activities (5 points)
☑ Aerobic component (20 points)
☑ Lower-extremity strength component (10 points)
☑ Core component (10 points)
☐ Cool-down (5 points)
☐ Total: 45/50

FIGURE 9.3 Point system rubric used to assess responsibility and a dance presentation.

Rating Scales

Rating scales allow you to assess not only specified elements of a performance or behavior, but also the quality of those elements. They can be numerical, worded, or holistic.

Numerical Rating Scales

Numerical (quantitative) rating scales allow you to develop levels to help differentiate the quality of each element or task. Similar to the point system rubric, numerical rating scales also allow you to award a grade value to the outcome if you so choose. Figures 9.4 and 9.5 illustrate examples of numerical rating scales.

Tennis Forehand Groundstroke

	3	2.5	2	0
Skill elements	Always	Usually	Rarely	Never
Racket back early	X			
Firm wrist and arm			X	
Swing in arch low to high		X		
Finish across and up	X			
Total: **10.5/12**				

FIGURE 9.4 Numerical rating scale for assessing the skill elements of a forehand tennis stroke.

Physical Activity and Fitness Brochure

Required elements	10: All are present	8: Most are present	6: Incomplete	5: Few are present
1. Description of FITT principle: Includes frequency, intensity, time, and type	X			
2. Examples of FITT: Includes examples for each component of FITT		X		
3. Physical activity recommendations: Includes recommendations for vigorous and moderate activities and strength for youth and adults		X		
	Excellent	**Good**	**Needs work**	**No attention**
4. Attention to presentation: a. Visual organization (layout, typed)	X			
b. Spelling, grammar, and punctuation			X	
Total: **42/50 (84%)**				

FIGURE 9.5 Numerical rating scale for assessing a physical activity and fitness brochure.

Worded Rating Scales

Worded (qualitative) rating scales allow you to describe the specific quality expected within each level. The description gives both you and your students a clear and precise illustration of what will be assessed. Points can also be allotted to each level as part of a grading plan (see figures 9.6 and, on page 164, 9.7).

Assessing student performance with worded rating scales can be difficult because some students may exhibit some elements found in more than one level. For example, in figure 9.6, some students may demonstrate a forearm tennis stroke that has a consistent sweeping C motion from high to low (mature level), yet occasionally break or bend their wrist when hitting the ball (elementary level). You may have to use a half-point option (e.g., +2.5) or average scores when parts of a skill performance are found within two or more levels.

Holistic Rubrics

Holistic rubrics describe all the elements that should be present within each level, thereby requiring that you rate the entire performance as a whole (see figure 9.8 on page 165). To receive the total points allotted for each level, students must exhibit all of the elements described. As with the worded rating scale, issues may arise when a student's performance falls within two or more levels. In that case, an average score or a half-point option will have to be used to determine a final score.

Rubric Construction

There are basic steps to follow when creating a rubric, depending on whether you want to use a checklist rubric to assess completed skill elements or tasks or a more advanced rubric to determine the quality of the performance. Regardless of the type, you will have to determine the elements or tasks to be assessed. If you want

Elements	Mature (+3)	Elementary (+2)	Initial (+1)
Preparation	Racket is consistently drawn back early; racket head is high; anticipates and moves into position.	Racket is occasionally drawn back early; racket head is positioned midlevel; reaction and position to ball is sometimes delayed.	Racket is not drawn back early; racket head is kept low; reaction and position to ball is late.
Execution	Weight shifts forward; swing initiated with sweeping C motion; wrist/arm and racket are one —no bend.	Inconsistent weight shift and use of C motion; wrist/arm bends occasionally.	No weight transfer on contact; parallel swing; wrist/arm breaks or bends during swing and contact.
Follow-through	Continues swing up, across, and back after hit; gets into ready position.	Continues swing up, yet inconsistent with racket motion across and back; usually gets into ready position after contact.	Contacts ball and stops swing; does not resume a ready position after hit.

FIGURE 9.6 Worded rating scale for assessing a tennis forehand groundstroke.

Twenty-Minute Aerobic Dance Presentation

WARM-UP

A: Neck, shoulder, trunk, hip, leg, and calf range of motion; uses low-impact aerobic movements.

B: Includes most of the listed body areas with low-impact movements.

C: Three or four static stretches; no accompanied low-impact movements.

D: Limits warm-up to static stretches of one or two body areas; no accompanied low-impact movements.

AEROBIC COMPONENT

A: 10 min; three different step sequences; two different arm actions; movements in beat with the music.

B: 7-9 min; three different step sequences; two different arm actions; movements in beat with the music.

C: 6-7 min; two different step sequences; one different arm action; movement rhythms inconsistent.

D: 5 min; same step sequence; same arm action; may or may not be in rhythm with the music.

STRENGTH COMPONENT

A: Three different exercises for two lower-extremity areas (hip, quad, hamstring, calf).

B: Two different exercise for two lower-extremity areas.

C: Two different exercise for one lower-extremity area.

D: One strength exercise for one lower-extremity area.

CORE COMPONENT

A: Four different core exercises.

B: Three different core exercises.

C: Two different core exercises.

D: One core exercise.

COOL-DOWN

A: Range of motion movements; checks heart rate at end of 20 min routine.

B: Range of motion movements; checks heart rate at end of 16 to 19 min routine.

C: Range of motion movements; checks heart rate at end of 15 min routine.

D: Range of motion movements; does not check heart rate; less than 15 min routine.

A = 10 points; B = 8 points; C = 7 points; D = 6 points

FIGURE 9.7 Worded rating scale for assessing a group aerobic dance routine presentation.

12: QUALITY FORM

The racket is consistently drawn back early. The racket head is high while the student anticipates and moves into position to hit the ball. Body weight shifts forward, the swing is initiated with a sweeping C motion, and wrist/arm and racket are one—no bend on ball contact. The swing motion continues up, across, and back on follow-through. The student gets into a ready position after hitting the ball.

10: PRETTY GOOD FORM

The racket is usually drawn back early and held in a semi-high position. The student anticipates and moves into position before hitting the ball most of the time. Body weight shifts forward, the swing demonstrates a C motion, and the wrist/arm and racket remain somewhat firm. The swing motion continues up, and follow-through across and back usually occurs. The student assumes a ready position.

8.5: GETTING THERE

The racket is occasionally drawn back early with the racket head positioned midlevel. The reaction and position to the ball are sometimes delayed. The student inconsistently shifts weight forward and sometimes uses a C motion. The wrist/arm bends frequently. Follow-through motion is inconsistent, and the student usually gets into a ready position after contact.

7: NOT THERE YET

The racket is not drawn back early, and the racket head is kept low. The reaction and position to the ball are most often late. Limited or no weight is transferred forward on contact. The swing is parallel while the wrist/arm breaks or bends during swing and contact. The swing stops after ball contact. The student does not resume a ready position after hitting.

FIGURE 9.8 Holistic rubric for assessing a forehand tennis groundstroke.

to measure the quality of those tasks, you will also have to develop a rating scale and corresponding performance expectations or criteria.

Determine Assessment Elements

The first step in creating a scoring rubric is to determine what you want to assess. If you are assessing a skill technique, for example, it often helps to use the teaching cues or main skill elements that you used during instruction. It also helps to limit the number of skill elements requiring assessment to six. Assessing too many elements at one time may not be realistic given the allotted time or number of students in your class. In addition, if students will be using the rubric to assess their peers, fewer skill elements to observe will make the assessment process easier for them as well. As an example, the following skill elements could be included in a rubric based on the teaching cues used for the basketball set shot described in chapter 4: (1) Knees are slightly bent, (2) wrist is cocked under ball, (3) arm pushes up and out to the basket, and (4) wrist flicks on follow-through. These four basic skill elements can be clearly assessed using a checklist rubric.

Rubrics also can be used to score other performance-type tasks. If students are required to do a project, presentation, or group of tasks in a portfolio, the required parts of those tasks will become the elements to assess within the rubric. For instance, if you want students to develop their own fitness plans, the elements to assess might include (1) a purpose statement, (2) short-term goals, (3) prefitness assessments, (4) application of the FITT principle (various activities that demonstrate frequency, intensity, time, and type), (5) periodic improvement assessments, and (6) a reflection. The required elements make it easy for you to assess the fitness plan, and students will know exactly what to include in the project.

If you want to use a checklist or point system rubric, you need only include a yes or no check box or assign a point value to each of the elements. However, if you want your rubric to assess the quality of skill elements or tasks, you will need to add two more steps to develop a rubric that has a rating scale and specific levels of expectations, as outlined in the next two sections.

Determine a Rating Scale

If you want your rubric to assess the quality of a task or element, you will first have to determine the type of rubric you will develop: numerical, worded, or holistic. Once you have made that decision, you will have to determine a rating scale or the number of scoring levels you will use to distinguish levels of performance. A minimum of three levels is recommended (Lund 2000), although the number is ultimately up to you. Some levels may be represented by a point value, whereas others may be designated by a grade or word descriptor (see table 9.1).

Table 9.1 Level Examples for a Three-, Four-, and Five-Point Rubric

<table>
<tr><th colspan="5">THREE LEVELS</th></tr>
<tr><td>2
Mature
Good
Rapid progress</td><td colspan="2">1
Elementary
Acceptable
Steady progress</td><td colspan="2">0
Initial
Poor
Needs more time</td></tr>
<tr><th colspan="5">FOUR LEVELS</th></tr>
<tr><td>A
Exceeds
Exemplary</td><td colspan="2">B
Meets
Acceptable</td><td>C
Partially meets
Needs improvement</td><td>D
Does not meet
Unacceptable</td></tr>
<tr><th colspan="5">5 LEVELS</th></tr>
<tr><td>A
Excellent</td><td>B
Good</td><td>C
Satisfactory</td><td>D
Fair</td><td>F
Poor</td></tr>
</table>

Level elements	3 (Expected or desired)	2 (Least accepted)	1 (Unacceptable)
Knees bend	Knees have slight bend	Knees are bent near 90 degrees (too much)	Knees are locked/legs are straight
Wrist cocks	Wrist is cocked under ball	Wrist is slightly cocked behind ball	Wrist is held firm
Arm extends	Arm extends up and out to basket smoothly	Arm extends up and out in a jerky motion	Arm extends either up or out, but not both
Wrist flicks	Obvious wrist flexion on follow-through	Slight wrist flexion	No follow-through

FIGURE 9.9 Level 3 indicates desirable or expected performance criteria for the basketball set shot.

Create the Scoring Criteria

The last step in constructing a quality-based rubric is determining the criteria, or performance expectations, for each level. When you are designing a three-level rubric, it is best to designate the most desired or expected criteria for the highest level. Level 2 represents the least acceptable passing expectations (cutoff point), and the lowest level is for performances that are considered not passing or unacceptable (see figure 9.9). For a four-level rubric, you will have to determine the level that represents expected criteria. For instance, the highest level may represent the best quality of performance (i.e., A work), and the next level would include the expected or desired criteria (i.e., B work). On the other hand, you could use the highest level to represent expected or desired performances (see figure 9.10). When you describe specific performance criteria for each level, students know exactly what is expected, and you can have more confidence in the validity, reliability, and objectivity of the assessment.

It is important to remember that if you are using your rubric as part of a grading plan, the point values you place for each level must add up to the associated grade value. Sometimes teachers designate random point values to their rubrics without thought to how those total points reflect a grade. For example, if a student scores above average for each element in a rubric, that person should receive a B for above-average work; yet, if you look at figure 9.11*a* (page 168), the total score of 60 out of 80 points reflects only mid-C work (75 percent). For the rubric in figure 9.11*a* to correctly reflect the corresponding letter grades, the point allocations would have to be changed to the following: Above average (B) = 16 or 17 points (80 or 85 percent); Least acceptable (C) = 14 or 15 points (70 or 75 percent); Not acceptable (D) = 12 points (60 percent) or lower (see figure 9.11*b*). As such, it is important to pay attention to the point allocations you make in your rubrics, especially if you use the results as part of student grades.

You can develop rubrics to assess a wide variety of student performances in physical education for each of the domains of learning. Rubrics not only make you more accountable in assessing student outcomes, but also clarify for students (and you) what is expected and what constitutes expected performance (Lund 2000). Well-designed rubrics can help determine whether objectives and standards have been met, as well as contribute to student grades. If you do not want to create your own assessments, NASPE offers PE Metrics for elementary physical education teach-

4: A Highest quality of performance	3: B Expected performance	2: C Least acceptable (passing)	1: D Unacceptable
OR			
4: A Expected performance	3: B Acceptable	2: C Least acceptable (passing)	1: D Unacceptable

FIGURE 9.10 Options for determining where to place expected performance criteria in a four-level rubric.

Level elements	+20 points (A) Excellent	+15 points (B) Above average	+10 points (C) Least acceptable	+5 points (D) Not acceptable
1.		✓		
2		✓		
3		✓		
4.		✓		

a

Level elements	+20 points (A) Excellent	+17 points (B) Above average	+14 points (C) Least acceptable	+12 points (D) Not acceptable
1.		✓		
2		✓		
3		✓		
4.		✓		

b

FIGURE 9.11 *(a)* The hypothetical score equals 60 out of 80 possible points, which reflects C work (75 percent). Point values need to change to represent accurate letter grade designations. *(b)* Point allocations have been revised to accurately depict solid B work, with an overall hypothetical score of 68 out of 80 possible points (85 percent).

ers (NASPE 2008); this is a tool for assessing skills within the first standard of the National Physical Education Standards. Secondary PE Metrics is now available as well. The next section addresses some considerations for determining student grades in physical education.

Grading Considerations

Assigning students a traditional letter grade for their report cards is usually required at the secondary level; however, even some elementary school administrators are beginning to require that teachers submit a letter grade for upper grade levels. In the primary grades (K-2), teachers usually do not use letter grades; instead, they often indicate a level of achievement, such as whether students exceed, meet, or need more time to meet various objectives. Regardless of grade level, you should be able to submit a justifiable grade or rating based on the performance levels of your students. You must be able to show how grades are earned for performance and achievement (Johnson 2008). Ultimately, it is up to you to determine how best to design your grading scheme.

As stated in the opening to this chapter, many physical education teachers do not assess student learning, especially at the secondary level. Instead, they grade based on dress, participation, effort, improvement, or attitude. These factors (see table 9.2) address only compliance and do not demonstrate what students have learned or achieved (Melograno 2007). In addition, when grading on effort, improvement, or attitude, there are a few issues to consider. First, if students know they will be graded on how much they improve, some may slack off on initial assessments and perform their best at the end, thus demonstrating misleading gains. Second, some students may have lower skill or fitness levels at the onset, which allows for plenty of room for growth and improvement, whereas other students may be highly skilled or fit with limited room for improvement. Thus, grading on student improvement should be used with caution. It is best to allow students to track skill and fitness improvements over time as a way to enhance intrinsic motivation and demonstrate that they have met various objectives or standards.

Similar arguments can be made for grading on attitude. Is it fair to mark students down for a bad attitude when the lesson is boring, meaningless, too difficult, or when your own attitude is bad as well? Because grading on attitude is very subjective and often includes teacher bias, it should also be used with caution.

What factors should you consider when developing a grading plan? A final grade in physical education should reflect a certain level of performance based on achieving educational objectives. Standards and specific objectives reflect the learning targets of a physical education program and, therefore, should comprise the bulk of the final letter grade (Melograno 2007). As such, when developing a grading plan, you need to take into account the objectives and standards of the program, along with your professional judgment and philosophy of what is most important for students to know and be able to do. Thus, the overall letter grade reflects the criteria you believe are most important for students to achieve. Some teachers determine a final grade based on the overall points earned during a term and apply those points to the school's grading scale (e.g., 90–100% = A; 80–89% = B; 70–79% = C; 60–69% = D; and less than 60% = F). Other teachers emphasize or weight scores (percentages) based on what they believe is most important, such as knowledge, skill, responsibility, or fitness.

Determining a weighted score for grading criteria should not be taken lightly. Too much emphasis in one area might affect the final letter grade of students who did not do well in that area, yet performed well in other areas. Table 9.3 illustrates how weighted scores can affect final letter grades. The three students in table 9.3—designated as 1, 2, and 3—are typical students you may have in a physical education class. As you can tell by their overall score or grade for each weighted area, student 1 is someone who always dresses appropriately, participates in class,

Table 9.2 Common Grading Factors

Managerial/compliance	Learning
Participation	Knowledge
Dress	Performance (skills and fitness)
Effort	Personal and social responsibility
Attitude	

Keeping in mind the importance of accountability in physical education, how will you determine final grades for your students? What areas will your grading system address, and what weight will you assign to each area?

and completes assignments and tests with high scores; however, skill and fitness abilities are rather low. Student 2 is gifted with physical and fitness skills; however, this student doesn't like to dress appropriately and doesn't put much effort into completing assignments or studying for tests. Finally, student 3 dresses appropriately and participates most of the time, and skill, fitness, and knowledge assessments are average. As you can tell, their final grades change noticeably, based on the percentages allotted to each scoring area.

Table 9.3 Final Grades Based on Various Weighted Scores

	Participation	Performance	Knowledge	Final grade
SKILL AND FITNESS EMPHASIS				
Student	20%	60%	20%	
1	100% (A)	70% (C–)	95% (A)	81% (B–)
2	60% (D–)	100% (A)	60% (D-)	84% (B)
3	85% (B)	75% (C)	80% (B-)	78% (C)
KNOWLEDGE EMPHASIS				
Student	30%	10%	60%	
1	100% (A)	70% (C–)	100% (A)	97% (A)
2	60% (D–)	100% (A)	60% (D–)	64% (D)
3	85% (B)	75% (C)	80% (B–)	81% (B–)
PARTICIPATION EMPHASIS				
Student	70%	15%	15%	
1	100% (A)	70% (C–)	100% (A)	96% (A)
2	60% (D–)	100% (A)	60% (D–)	66% (D)
3	84% (B)	75% (C)	80% (B–)	82% (B–)
SKILL, FITNESS, AND KNOWLEDGE EMPHASIS				
Student	20%	40%	40%	
1	100% (A)	70% (C–)	100% (A)	88% (B+)
2	60% (D–)	100% (A)	60% (D–)	76% (C)
3	85% (B)	75% (C)	80% (B–)	79% (C+)
SHARED EMPHASIS				
Student	33%	33%	34%	
1	100% (A)	70% (C–)	30% (A)	90% (A–)
2	60% (D–)	100% (A)	60% (D–}	73% (C)
3	85% (B)	75% (C)	80% (B–)	80% (B–)

Participation = Final score represents overall dress and participation in class
Performance = Scores from skill assessments and fitness portfolio
Knowledge = Scores from assignments, quizzes, and end-of-unit exam

Health-Related Fitness Testing

A majority of elementary and secondary physical education teachers assess the fitness levels of their students. Often, fitness tests are conducted at the beginning and end of the school year or semester. Fitness test results may be collected by school districts as a measure of the overall physical fitness status of students in the area, and physical education teachers may use fitness scores to determine the success of their programs. Recently, fitness test scores have also been used in research to determine the positive connection between physical fitness and academic scores (see chapter 1).

There are a few things to consider as you determine the relevance and importance of physical fitness testing. If you teach at the elementary level, you may see your students only once or twice a week for 30 minutes. There is limited time to help develop sound fundamental movement skills, let alone to train children to enhance their cardiorespiratory fitness levels, especially given that preadolescent children show little training gains from high-intensity activities (Ernst, Pangrazi, and Corbin 1998).

It is also important to consider that genetic makeup can affect training performance outcomes (Lakka and Bouchard 2004). Genetic factors in some students may reduce their ability to respond to physical exercise and improve physical fitness test scores throughout the year (Bouchard and Rankinen 2001). This is especially important if you are considering using improvement in fitness test scores as part of a grade.

Finally, at the secondary level, if you do not specifically train your students to enhance health-related fitness skills during each lesson, or if your lessons do not provide moderate- and high-intensity activities, it is unrealistic to think that physical fitness scores will significantly improve by the end of a term or year. With those factors in mind, perhaps it is best to use fitness tests to assess and educate students about their personal fitness and health status, instead of determining whether they have met the goal of having a high fitness level (Darst and Pangrazi 2009).

Fitnessgram (Cooper Institute 2010) is a popular fitness testing program that evaluates and links health-related fitness performance to positive health standards. Fitnessgram uses **criterion-referenced standards** that compare student scores to a preexisting set of criteria. For example, Fitnessgram uses criterion-referenced fitness evaluations based on minimum standards for good health. If students' fitness scores fall within healthy fitness zones for the 1-mile run or PACER tests, they are considered in good health. If scores fall within healthy fitness zones for the curl-up (sit-up), push-up, and flexibility tests, students have met standards for being active. These zones help students connect their level of fitness to standards of good health. Of course, it is beneficial to remind students to try to score in the higher limits of each healthy fitness zone.

Teachers or students, or both, can enter fitness scores into the Fitnessgram computer program to generate a printable Fitnessgram report (see figure 9.12 on page 172). The printout indicates health-related fitness scores that fall within healthy fitness zones and those that do not reach the zone. In addition, recommendations are provided to help students maintain or improve those areas not in the zone. Fitnessgram reports can also be used to educate parents about the fitness and health status of their children.

Fitnessgram is supported by AAHPERD and is widely used by physical education teachers in the United States. The Fitnessgram program, including the testing CD and manual, along with a physical activity section, can be purchased through

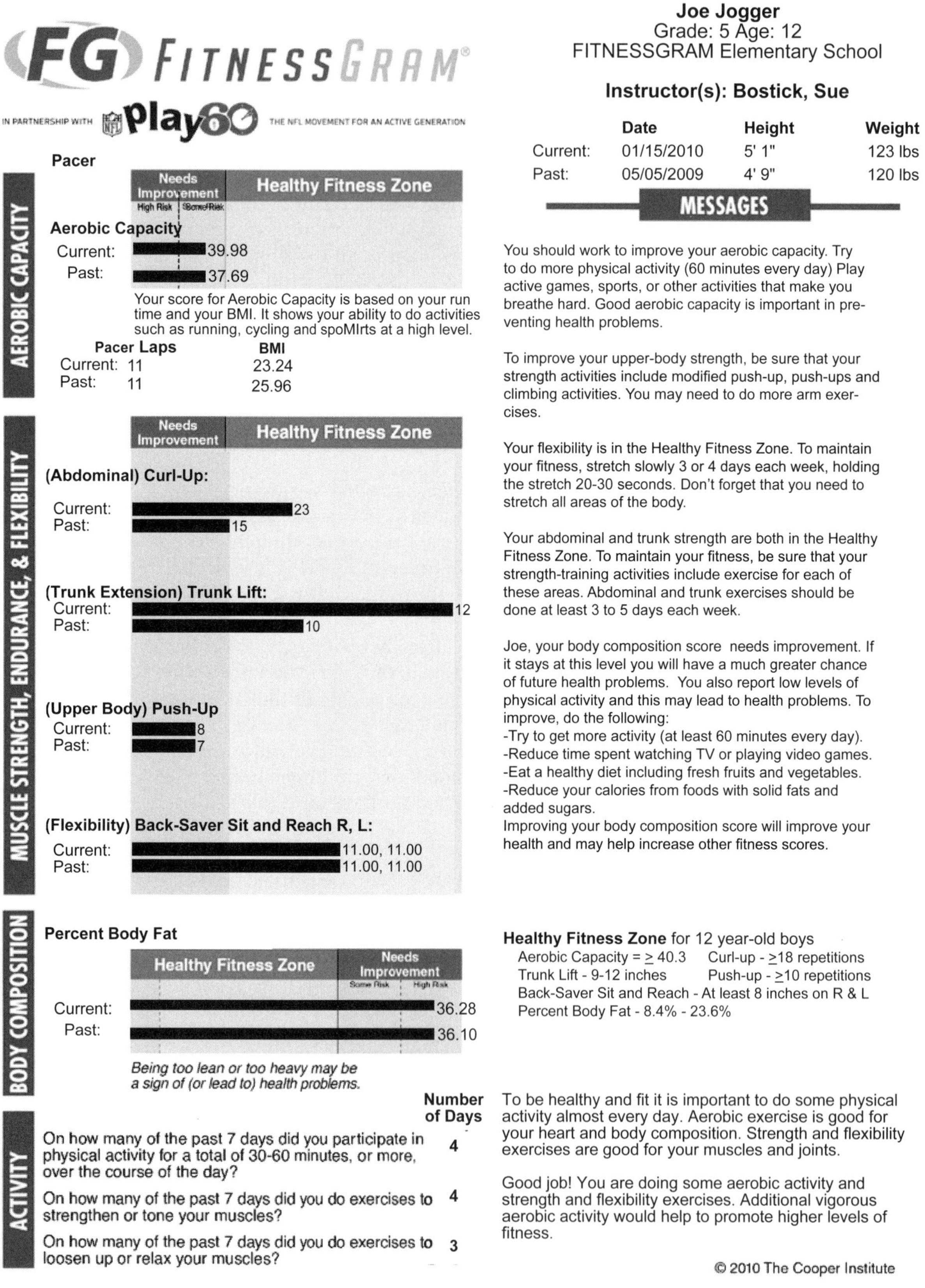

FITNESSGRAM

IN PARTNERSHIP WITH Play60 THE NFL MOVEMENT FOR AN ACTIVE GENERATION

Joe Jogger
Grade: 5 Age: 12
FITNESSGRAM Elementary School

Instructor(s): Bostick, Sue

	Date	Height	Weight
Current:	01/15/2010	5' 1"	123 lbs
Past:	05/05/2009	4' 9"	120 lbs

AEROBIC CAPACITY

Pacer

Needs Improvement (High Risk, Some Risk) | Healthy Fitness Zone

Aerobic Capacity
Current: 39.98
Past: 37.69

Your score for Aerobic Capacity is based on your run time and your BMI. It shows your ability to do activities such as running, cycling and spoMlrts at a high level.

	Pacer Laps	BMI
Current:	11	23.24
Past:	11	25.96

MUSCLE STRENGTH, ENDURANCE, & FLEXIBILITY

Needs Improvement | Healthy Fitness Zone

(Abdominal) Curl-Up:
Current: 23
Past: 15

(Trunk Extension) Trunk Lift:
Current: 12
Past: 10

(Upper Body) Push-Up
Current: 8
Past: 7

(Flexibility) Back-Saver Sit and Reach R, L:
Current: 11.00, 11.00
Past: 11.00, 11.00

BODY COMPOSITION

Percent Body Fat

Healthy Fitness Zone | Needs Improvement (Some Risk, High Risk)

Current: 36.28
Past: 36.10

Being too lean or too heavy may be a sign of (or lead to) health problems.

ACTIVITY

	Number of Days
On how many of the past 7 days did you participate in physical activity for a total of 30-60 minutes, or more, over the course of the day?	4
On how many of the past 7 days did you do exercises to strengthen or tone your muscles?	4
On how many of the past 7 days did you do exercises to loosen up or relax your muscles?	3

MESSAGES

You should work to improve your aerobic capacity. Try to do more physical activity (60 minutes every day) Play active games, sports, or other activities that make you breathe hard. Good aerobic capacity is important in preventing health problems.

To improve your upper-body strength, be sure that your strength activities include modified push-up, push-ups and climbing activities. You may need to do more arm exercises.

Your flexibility is in the Healthy Fitness Zone. To maintain your fitness, stretch slowly 3 or 4 days each week, holding the stretch 20-30 seconds. Don't forget that you need to stretch all areas of the body.

Your abdominal and trunk strength are both in the Healthy Fitness Zone. To maintain your fitness, be sure that your strength-training activities include exercise for each of these areas. Abdominal and trunk exercises should be done at least 3 to 5 days each week.

Joe, your body composition score needs improvement. If it stays at this level you will have a much greater chance of future health problems. You also report low levels of physical activity and this may lead to health problems. To improve, do the following:
-Try to get more activity (at least 60 minutes every day).
-Reduce time spent watching TV or playing video games.
-Eat a healthy diet including fresh fruits and vegetables.
-Reduce your calories from foods with solid fats and added sugars.
Improving your body composition score will improve your health and may help increase other fitness scores.

Healthy Fitness Zone for 12 year-old boys
Aerobic Capacity = ≥ 40.3 Curl-up - ≥18 repetitions
Trunk Lift - 9-12 inches Push-up - ≥10 repetitions
Back-Saver Sit and Reach - At least 8 inches on R & L
Percent Body Fat - 8.4% - 23.6%

To be healthy and fit it is important to do some physical activity almost every day. Aerobic exercise is good for your heart and body composition. Strength and flexibility exercises are good for your muscles and joints.

Good job! You are doing some aerobic activity and strength and flexibility exercises. Additional vigorous aerobic activity would help to promote higher levels of fitness.

© 2010 The Cooper Institute

FIGURE 9.12 Modified example of a Fitnessgram computerized report.

Adapted, by permission, from Cooper Institute, 2010, *FITNESSGRAM®/ACTIVITYGRAM®. Test administration manual,* updated 4th ed., edited by M.D. Meredith and G.J. Welks (Champaign, IL: Human Kinetics), 68.

Human Kinetics or at www.fitnessgram.net/home. Common Fitnessgram health-related fitness tests are described briefly in the following sections.

Aerobic Endurance

Cardiorespiratory endurance is measured by the 1-mile walk/run, a walk test (for ages 13 and older), or a distinctive progressive running test called the PACER. The PACER test is a series of repeated 20-meter runs conducted in the gym that gradually become faster as laps are completed, based on the audio prompts from the testing CD. Students start out running at a slow pace for each 20-meter segment. As the pace increases, students are asked to keep up until they are unable to maintain the pace, at which time the total number of completed laps is recorded by a peer.

Strength

A curl-up (sit-up) test is used to test for abdominal strength; however, this test is not your basic sit-up test. The test has several unique features: (1) The testing audio CD uses a three-second cadence prompt for each curl-up, and (2) students have to reach the curl-up strip on the mat for the curl-up to count. This testing protocol allows for consistent repetitions among students and minimizes the potential for cheating or questionable scores. The trunk lift is used to assess low-back strength. While lying facedown, students try to extend or lift their trunk and chest off the floor by using the muscles of the back. This position is held and a measurement is taken. The push-up test is used to test upper-body strength. As with the curl-up test, a three-second audio cadence prompt is used for each push-up. Elbows must be bent to 90 degrees for a push-up to be considered successful. Other test options for strength include modified pull-ups and the flexed arm hang.

Assess the curl-up by checking that the student reaches the curl-up strip placed on the mat.

Flexibility

The modified sit-and-reach is a common test used to determine low-back and hamstring flexibility. The shoulder stretch can also be used to measure upper-body flexibility.

Body Composition

Body composition, or percent body fat, is often determined by using calipers at two skinfold sites (calf and triceps). It takes a lot of practice to accurately gather skinfold readings; thus, many physical education teachers use body mass index (BMI) to determine whether students are at risk for health-related weight problems (Adams and Adams 2009). The body mass

FIGURE 9.13

Calculating BMI

BMI = Weight in kg / (Height in m)^2

Converting English measurements to metric:

Weight in kg = Weight in lb / 2.2

Height in m = Height in in. × 0.0254

(Height in m)^2 = Height in m × Height in m

index uses weight and height (see figure 9.13) to determine health–weight classifications: underweight, healthy weight, at risk for overweight, and overweight. It is important to remember, however, that BMI calculations do not really measure body fat. BMI identifies students who are at risk healthwise based on their body fat content compared to others of the same age (Reilly 2006). As an alternative to calipers and BMI, some schools purchase electronic bioimpedance analysis (BIA) devices to measure percent body fat. These devices analyze the electrical conductivity of tissue and fluid compartments of the body. Ultimately, you will need to determine whether measuring body composition is an important facet of health-related fitness to assess in your physical education program.

Constructing Written Tests

Physical education teachers often administer various forms of written tests to determine what students know or have learned. They use commercially written tests, tests provided by their school districts, or they develop their own. This section offers test construction suggestions to consider when writing your own test items, including true/false, multiple-choice, matching, short-answer, and essays (Green 1979).

Basic Test Construction Strategies

The questions on a written test should focus on the objectives of the unit and the content covered during class. Normally, important topics or content areas should receive more attention in the test (i.e., more questions) than less important topics. It is also helpful to use a variety of test items (e.g., multiple-choice, true/false, matching), so as not to discriminate against students who may struggle with a certain type of test item. For example, some students do poorly on true/false questions and respond better to multiple-choice and short-answer questions. The following are some other general test construction considerations:

- Use clear directions for each test item. For example, the directions for true/false questions might read: Circle T for True or F for False for each statement. Those for multiple-choice questions might be: Select one best answer and write it in the space provided for each question.
- Create a place for student to write in their answers. Using the left-hand column for true/false and multiple-choice answers allows you to check answers quickly, which can be especially helpful when you have a lot of tests to grade.
- Use appropriate spacing. Tests that are unorganized are hard to read and may be difficult to take. Make use of appropriate tabs and line spacing to present questions and answer choices clearly.

■ Make sure there is no pattern to your answers. Students who don't know an answer to a question may look for a pattern to the answers (e.g., T, T, F, F, T, __, F, F).

■ Start the test with easier questions. Begin the test with easier questions to enhance confidence and lessen test anxiety. More difficult questions can be added later. Basic knowledge–type questions include those that can be answered using rote memory or the recall of definitions, rules, or concepts. More difficult questions are those that require students to summarize concepts in their own words; apply the use of facts, rules, or principles; analyze parts of something; combine ideas into something new; or develop opinions or make decisions based on current knowledge (Bloom 1956).

Alternate-Choice Test Items

Alternate-choice test items give students a fifty-fifty chance of getting the question right or wrong; there are only two answer options. The most common example are true/false items; however, you can use other two-choice options as well (e.g., yes/no choices, diagrams, word choices) (see figure 9.14 on page 176).

Because there are only two choices, you may not know whether students have guessed the correct answer or whether they truly understand the material. Therefore, it may be wise to limit the number of true/false questions you use in a test. Teachers often use a corrective true/false option to help reduce the chance of guessing; students write in a correct word or phrase to make the statement true (see figure 9.14). The following are suggestions for creating true/false test items:

- *Make sure each statement is totally true or false.* This eliminates tricky questions.
- *Use only relevant statements.* Trivial or irrelevant statements, such as the dimensions of a court or the circumference of a ball, should not be included.
- *Include more false than true statements.* Students often mark *True* when they don't know the answer.
- *Keep statements fairly similar in length.* Students often mark *True* for longer statements if they don't know the answer.
- *Avoid using absolute wording* (e.g., *always, never, none, all*). Students often mark *False* when reading statements with absolute words (Baumgartner et al 2007).

Multiple-Choice Test Items

Multiple-choice test items decrease the probability of guessing by giving students several choices to select from. Multiple-choice test items consist of two parts: the stem and the foils. The *stem* is the main question or statement; *foils* are the choices or alternative answers. Developing four foils is recommended; however, using five foils keeps the guess factor acceptably low (Baumgartner et al. 2007). In addition, although only one foil is considered the correct or best answer, the other foils must be possible choices as well. Do not make some of the foils obviously incorrect. The following are a few other tips for writing multiple-choice test items:

- *List the order of foils (a, b, c, d) vertically in each column, not horizontally across rows.*
- *Arrange numerical foils in order* (e.g., dates, time, frequency, measurements). Listing numbers from high to low or from low to high helps students easily locate the correct answer (see figure 9.15 on page 177).

True or False. Circle **T** for True or **F** for False for each statement.

T **F** **1.** Badminton shots and serves that hit the line (liners) are declared in.

T **F** **2.** The ready position includes the racket head positioned at a low level.

T **F** **3.** Only the serving side can score points.

Large or Small. In the space provided, write **L** if the activity develops large/primary muscles or **S** if the activity develops small-mover muscles.

___ **1.** Skipping

___ **2.** Jumping over boxes

___ **3.** Tying knots in a rope

___ **4.** Climbing a tree

___ **5.** Baiting a fishing hook

___ **6.** Skateboarding

Yes or No. Based on the diagram of pass patterns, circle **Y** for Yes or **N** for No for each statement.

Y **N** **1.** A is an example of a slant running route.

Y **N** **2.** B represents a down-and-out pattern.

Y **N** **3.** Pattern C is called a post.

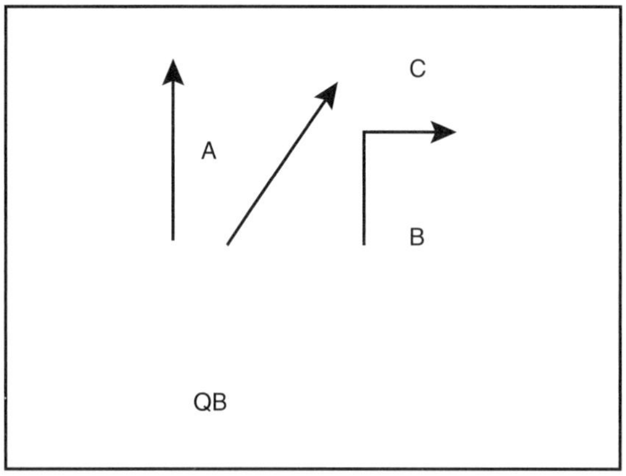

Corrective True or False. Circle **T** for True or **F** for False for each statement. If the statement is false, change the portion of the statement that is underlined and write the correct word in the space provided. (2 points each)

T **F** **1.** A basketball is generally dribbled at <u>shoulder</u> height.

FIGURE 9.14 Examples of alternate-choice test items.

Matching Test Items

Matching test items reveal whether students can make connections between stated criteria. Teachers often use matching items to determine whether students know the definitions of vocabulary words. Constructing matching test items is similar to

INCORRECT FOIL ORDER

____ **1.** After moving to hit a badminton shot, it is important to return to ____________.
a. the end line
b. the front of the court
c. the right side of the court
d. the home base area

CORRECT FOIL ORDER

____ **1.** After moving to hit a badminton shot, it is important to return to ____________.
a. the end line
b. the front of the court
c. the right side of the court
d. the home base area

INCORRECT NUMERICAL FOIL ORDER

____ **2.** What should the heart rate (bpm) be for a 16-year-old who wants to work at 60 percent of her maximum effort?
a. 160 bpm
b. 116 bpm
c. 204 bpm
d. 122 bpm

CORRECT NUMERICAL FOIL ORDER

____ **2.** What should the heart rate (bpm) be for a 16-year-old who wants to work at 60 percent of her maximum effort?
a. 116 bpm
b. 122 bpm
c. 160 bpm
d. 204 bpm

FIGURE 9.15 Incorrect and correct order of foils in multiple-choice test items.

constructing multiple-choice items in that there is a list of stems (i.e., short definitions, phrases, or concepts), followed by a longer list of foils (i.e., terms, words). The objective is for students to match the foils with stems. Use abbreviated phrases instead of exact sentences copied from a book or student handout when developing the stems. In addition, to reduce guessing, list more foils (answers) than stems. The following matching test item has short phrases, more foils than stems, and a heading for the stems and foils.

Player Action	***Referee's Call***
___ 1. Initially putting the ball into play	a. Charge
___ 2. Personal contact against a stationary defender	b. Double dribble
___ 3. Unopposed shot allowed after a shooting foul	c. Field goal
___ 4. Steps taken while holding the ball	d. Free throw
	e. Jump ball
	f. Traveling

Recall Test Items

Recall test items require students to write in their answers. They include (1) fill-in-the-blank items (blank spaces within a sentence or at the end, (2) short-answer questions, and (3) essays.

Fill-in-the-Blanks Test Items

Fill-in-the blank sentences must be plainly stated so that the answer is clear to students. If sentences are ambiguous, many different answers may be considered correct. The following are examples of fill-in-the-blank recall test items:

Fill-in-the-blank: When performing a set shot, it is important to be balanced, bend your elbow, keep your ___________ focused on the basket, and follow through.

Completion: When performing a set shot, it is important to be balanced, bend your elbow, keep your eyes focused on the basket, and ______________.

Short-Answer Test Items

Short-answer test items provide students with more freedom in answering the question than fill-in-the-blank items do. Answers can include single words, short phrases, or a few sentences. A short-answer test item may look something like the following:

Short answer: List the information you need to know when performing a set shot using BEEF? ____

____

Essay Test Items

Essay items often provide the most information regarding student knowledge or understanding of concepts. Keep in mind that although essay questions may be quick and easy to write, they take a long time to grade. If you develop essay questions on a written test, it is important that you write them as specifically as possible. In other words, clearly outline what you want students to include in their answer. In addition, develop a scoring rubric for the essay so all answers can be assessed consistently and fairly. The following are examples of a generally worded essay question and a specific essay question:

Generally Worded Essay Question

Explain what should be included in a personal fitness program. This essay is worth 40 points.

Specific Essay Question

Explain what should be included in a personal fitness program. Make sure to include the following in your answer: (1) the FITT principle, (2) examples of FITT including the progressive resistance and overload principles, (3) the connection of a personal fitness program to current physical activity guidelines, and (4) your personal advice. Thorough and accurate answers will receive the highest points. This essay is worth 40 points.

Summary

Assessment and grading are important areas of education. Assessments not only provide information about student learning, but also help to determine whether program objectives and district or state standards have been met. Final composite grades or progress reports should reflect program objectives and overall student performance. Given the current emphasis on teacher and program accountability, you will need to focus on student assessment and sound grading practices. You must be able to demonstrate to administrators and parents how students are meeting learning outcomes and the extent of their learning and achievements. In addition, students need to understand that learning outcomes comprise a letter grade in physical education. The overall rundown on assessments is this: If physical education is to be thought of as an important educational component of a school's overall program, physical education teachers must emphasize the role of assessments in their classes, as teachers do in other academic areas.

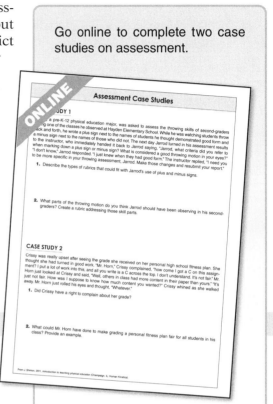

Go online to complete two case studies on assessment.

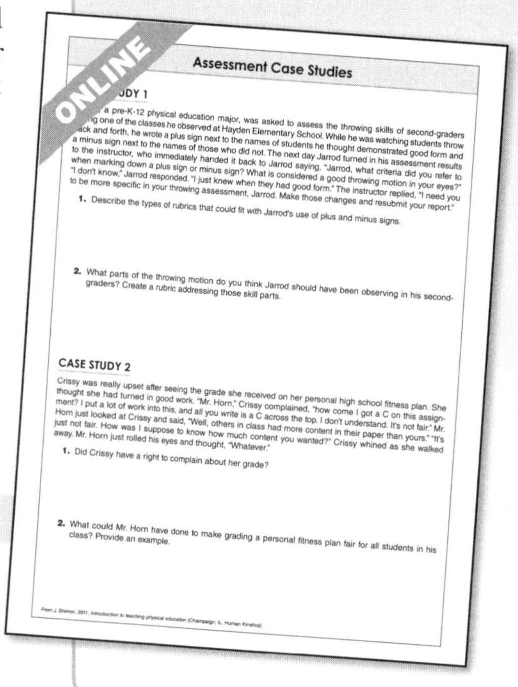
ONLINE

Assessment Case Studies

UDY 1

a pre-K-12 physical education major, was asked to assess the throwing skills of second-graders ng one of the classes he observed at Hayden Elementary School. While he was watching students throw ack and forth, he wrote a plus sign next to the names of students he thought demonstrated good form and a minus sign next to the names of those who did not. The next day Jarrod turned in his assessment results to the instructor, who immediately handed it back to Jarrod saying, "Jarrod, what criteria did you refer to when marking down a plus sign or minus sign? What is considered a good throwing motion in your eyes?" "I don't know," Jarrod responded. "I just knew when they had good form." The instructor replied, "I need you to be more specific in your throwing assessment, Jarrod. Make those changes and resubmit your report."

1. Describe the types of rubrics that could fit with Jarrod's use of plus and minus signs.

2. What parts of the throwing motion do you think Jarrod should have been observing in his second-graders? Create a rubric addressing those skill parts.

CASE STUDY 2

Crissy was really upset after seeing the grade she received on her personal high school fitness plan. She thought she had turned in good work. "Mr. Horn," Crissy complained, "how come I got a C on this assignment? I put a lot of work into this, and all you write is a C across the top. I don't understand. It's not fair." Mr. Horn just looked at Crissy and said, "Well, others in class had more content in their paper than yours." "It's just not fair. How was I suppose to know how much content you wanted?" Crissy whined as she walked away. Mr. Horn just rolled his eyes and thought, "Whatever."

1. Did Crissy have a right to complain about her grade?

2. What could Mr. Horn have done to make grading a personal fitness plan fair for all students in his class? Provide an example.

From J. Shimon, 2011, *Introduction to teaching physical education* (Champaign, IL: Human Kinetics).

▶ Discussion Questions

1. How can you use rubrics to fairly assess a skill performance or group project?
2. How might a rubric be designed to assess a high school assignment involving the development of a brochure that outlines the FITT principle?
3. If you were a physical education teacher at a middle or high school, what factors would you consider when assigning final letter grades?
4. How do checklist rubrics and rating scale rubrics compare and contrast?
5. What are different ways to write alternate-choice test items?

PART IV

BEYOND THE CLASSROOM

The technology age is here and thriving, especially in the field of education. Gadgets and tools designed for physical education teachers enhance instruction, learning, and student motivation. In addition, a wealth of information and material is available to use when you teach. Even veteran teachers use this information to stay current in the profession and enhance their effectiveness in the gymnasium. Chapter 10 outlines a variety of technological devices and resources available for you now and when you secure your first teaching position.

Is teaching in a traditional K-12 physical education program your only career option after graduation? Your first job after you graduate might not be in a school setting. What other avenues can you pursue if you can't initially find a teaching position? The final chapter in this section outlines various careers you may consider if that perfect teaching job does not materialize.

CHAPTER 10

Technology and Resources

✓ CHAPTER OBJECTIVES

After reading this chapter, you will be able to:

- ☐ Recognize the technology available to enhance instruction and motivate student learning in the gymnasium.
- ☐ Describe various physical education online resources.
- ☐ Identify the teacher resources available through NASPE.

KEY TERMS

accelerometer
exergaming
geocaching
heart rate monitor
pedometer

An assortment of resources is available to enhance professional development, physical education instruction, and student learning motivation. Many of these resources use computers or some type of computer-like device. A variety of software programs help teachers develop printed materials for class, presentation information, and spreadsheets for grading purposes (e.g., Microsoft Word, PowerPoint, Excel, school-designed software). Teachers use computers to communicate with parents and administrators about student progress (e-mail) and to search the Internet for educational information and equipment. Computers are also found in many of the fitness-related devices currently on the market, and handheld computers are often used as substitutes for pencil and paper. This chapter outlines the technology and online resources many physical educators use.

Technology

The use of technology in education has advanced with lightning speed over the past few years. Classroom teachers use various technologies to enhance learning, such as interactive whiteboards (SmartBoard), 3D projectors (Elmo), independent keyboard systems, electronic tablets, and clickers (interactive classroom response systems). Physical education teachers also use technology to stimulate student interest, augment instruction, and manage their classes. The following are just a few of the technological resources teachers use in physical education today.

Pedometers are great for tracking the amount of time you spend on the move each day. Encourage students to track and chart their daily number of steps to enhance physical fitness.

Pedometers

Worn to measure daily amounts of general physical activity, a **pedometer** is attached to the waistband (in alignment with the right or left thigh) and records the number of steps taken throughout the day by measuring the upward motion of the hip with each step. More expensive models can also calculate distance, caloric expenditure, and exercise time. Although pedometers are not suitable for all activities (e.g., swimming, cycling, skating, skiing) and are not as accurate when people walk slowly, have an uneven gait, or are highly overweight, (Crouter et al. 2003), they still provide most people with a general account of their daily physical activity.

Numerous pedometer-related resources are available for physical education teachers. A simple Internet search for pedometer activities or pedometers provides links to lessons and activities that involve the use of pedometers, along with information on the types of pedometers available. Although Yamax Digi-Walkers are considered to be the most reliable and consistent pedometers on the market to date, there are many other models to chose from, depending on your budget and need for accuracy.

You can use pedometer activities during class to motivate students to increase their physical activity and to promote the importance of daily physical activity (Pangrazi, Beighle, and Sidman 2007). Some teachers design step-count competitions among classes or with faculty, staff, and administrators (e.g., walk the entire Mississippi River, step the Appalachian or Oregon Trail, walk across Colorado), whereas others use pedometers to determine the number of steps taken in class while engaging in a variety of activities.

You can also make students more aware of their own general physical activity levels by having them calculate the number of steps taken during a specified time. As an example, during class students can check their pedometers to determine the number of steps taken after walking one mile or for one minute (steps/min). Based on the results, students can then approximate how many steps they take or miles they walk during various activities outside of school when not wearing a pedometer, such as walking with a friend, walking a dog, or walking around the mall for a certain period of time.

Daily step recommendations help people use pedometers to enhance health. For example, minimal daily step guidelines for children and young adolescents indicate that girls should attain around 11,000 to 12,000 steps per day and boys should attain around 13,000 to 15,000 (Rowlands and Eston 2005; Tudor-Locke et al. 2004; Vincent and Pangrazi 2002).

Although not everyone will be able initially to reach step-count recommendations, simple goal-setting strategies can help students increase their daily step-count levels. For instance, let's assume that after five to eight days of collecting baseline step counts, a student averages 5,000 steps per day. If this student were to add 10 percent to that baseline, the goal would be to increase the number of steps each day by 500, or to reach 5,500 steps per day. After a few weeks of maintaining this goal, the student could again increase his overall steps count by another 10 percent (550 steps), eventually reaching the step-count recommendations for youth (Darst and Pangrazi 2009; Morgan, Pangrazi, and Beighle 2003).

How many steps do you take per day? If you have access to a pedometer, record and chart your daily steps over the course of a week. You can access a chart to use on the student online resource.

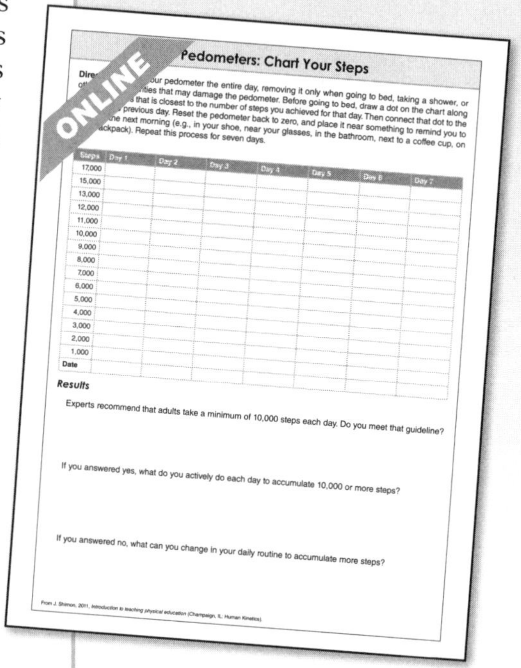

Heart Rate Monitors

We know that moderate- and high-intensity activities provide health-enhancing benefits. **Heart rate monitors** help students measure their intensity levels while participating in a variety of activities. Even though students can realistically determine their intensity levels by manually taking their pulse (i.e., at the carotid or radial pulse locations), they often can't feel or find it. Heart rate monitors provide easy and immediate feedback and prompt students to maintain a heart-healthy level of intensity during activity. The following are other advantages of using heart rate monitors during physical education classes (Nichols et al. 2009):

- Heart rate monitors hold all students accountable for maintaining a certain level of intensity, regardless of cardiorespiratory fitness levels.
- Data from certain heart rate monitors can be interfaced with a computer (e.g., Polar E600: http://education.polarusa.com/education) or manually charted on graphs to document individual outcomes and program quality.
- Heart rate monitors measure intensity levels accurately.
- Heart rate monitors help students differentiate what it feels like to work at low, medium, and high physical activity intensity levels.

Although the advantages of using heart rate monitors are numerous, there are some disadvantages to point out. First, heart rate monitors can be costly, especially those that allow data to be downloaded to a computer or are full of other features, such as programming, timing, and evaluative components. To help offset the cost, teachers often write grants to secure monies for purchasing a set of classroom heart rate monitors. In addition, heart rate monitor straps can become sweaty when used class after class. Most students don't like to put wet straps directly on their chests, even if they have been cleaned after each use. Some teachers have students place the monitor straps over their gym clothing (which is dampened) to avoid skin-to-skin contact; however, the strap often shifts, the clothing under the monitor may become dry, and data transmitted to the monitor may be unpredictable.

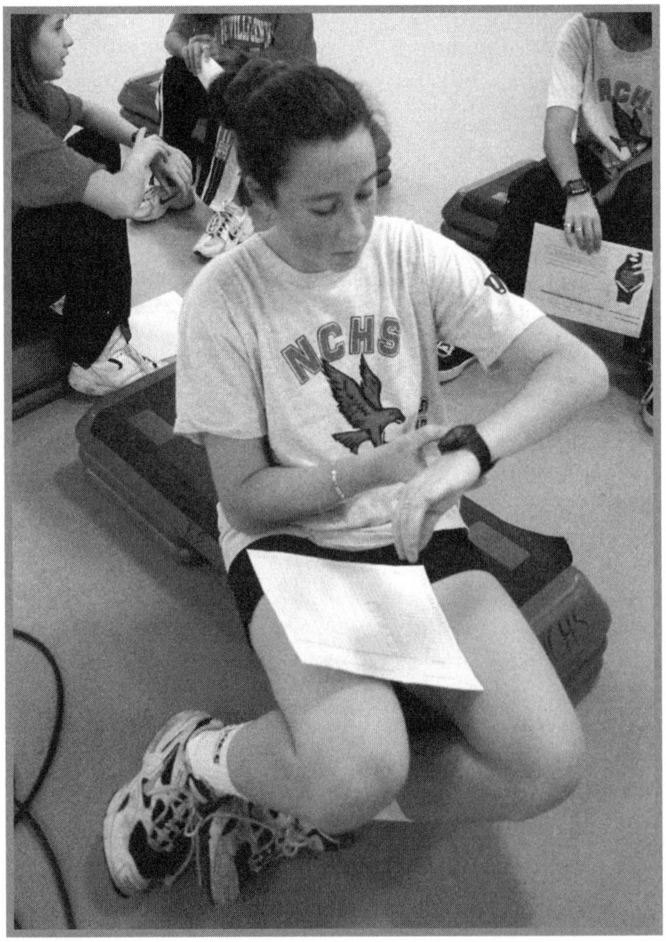

With a strapless heart rate monitor, heart rate is calculated by placing one or two fingers on the sensors located on the face of the watch.

Beltless, or strapless, heart rate monitors are being used as an alternative to those that have straps. To generate a heart rate display, students have to place one or two fingers over the sensors located on the face of the watch monitor. This usually means that they have to stop the activity or slow down to determine their heart rate. Additionally, the readings may not be as predictable or reliable as those from conventional heart rate monitors. Nonetheless, strapless heart rate monitors are an option for use in the classroom.

Accelerometers

An **accelerometer** also captures individual physical levels by recording the time and intensity of physical movements. The device looks similar to a pedometer; however, because of the cost and complex analyses involved with accelerometers, they are most often used by researchers to monitor physical activity levels in various populations. A new device called the Fitbit (www.fitbit.com) tracks motion in 3D and allows people to easily download personal physical activity data onto the Internet. As advances are made to make accelerometers more user friendly, they could become the next popular device for tracking daily physical activity levels.

Body Composition Devices

What are some ways you can use heart rate monitors during class to help motivate high school students to engage in activity?

Tools to measure body composition in physical education classes range from inexpensive skin calipers to more expensive bioimpedance devices. Because the quality of skin calipers and how they are used can greatly affect the results, some physical education programs have turned to electronic instruments to measure body composition, otherwise known as bioimpedance analysis (BIA) devices. These devices analyze the electrical conductivity of tissue (fat and muscle) and fluid compartments of the body; however, the data collected may be affected by how hydrated or dehydrated people are at the time of measurements. Most BIA devices calculate percent body fat by factoring in weight, height, and gender. Perhaps the simplest and most effective resource is a common tape measure. Tape measures can be used to track body circumference changes (increases or decreases) to various areas of the body over time, depending on the purpose of the fitness training program.

Exergaming Technology

Exergaming, or interactive video, is becoming an increasing popular technology gadget for those who like to incorporate gaming entertainment with physical activity. Dance Dance Revolution, Wii Fit systems, and Game bikes are examples of exergaming programs. Some games transmit the actual movements of the person (e.g., boxing actions, tennis swings) to a visual screen, in addition to providing immediate feedback such as earned points or overall scores. Children tend to be motivated to participate in interactive games that allow them to be physically active (Epstein et al. 2007). These physical movements can help people expend around 2 to 7.5

An accelerometer tracks the time and intensity of physical activities.

Photo courtesy of Jane Shimon

The Taylor Body Fat Analyzer and Scale is one type of BIA device.

Photo courtesy of Jane Shimon

calories per minute in low- to moderate-intensity activity, depending on their motivation to engage in the game (Daley 2009; Haddock et al. 2008). Some physical education teachers are including exergaming in their programs, although the cost and ability to accommodate large classes remains an issue at this time (Mears and Hansen 2009).

Outfitting an exergaming room for physical education can be quite expensive, especially if a variety of equipment is purchased. An interactive light wall or floor alone can range from $15,000 to $22,000, and gaming bikes can be $3,000 each. Needless to say, a substantial funding source would be needed, along with a multiuse plan that would demonstrate a high rate of daily use to justify the costs. For example, some schools that have developed an exergaming room make it available to physical education teachers as well as classroom teachers during the school day and activity programs that are offered after school. Many schools make the gaming room available before school, during lunch, and after school with some community usage permitted as well, especially if the community has contributed funds to purchase the equipment. Some teachers go to their parent–teacher organization (PTO) to solicit funding, pointing out the interdisciplinary benefits of exergaming activities for the entire school. Other teachers write grants to secure funding. One such grant is the Carol M. White Physical Education Program grant, which is federally funded and has financially assisted many physical education programs throughout the years.

To offset the cost of exergaming equipment, one elementary physical education specialist in the Boise School District in Idaho modified a version of Dance Dance Revolution by designing a series of steps sequenced to music using PowerPoint. The PowerPoint Dance Revolution presentation is projected onto the gym wall so all students can see and perform the step patterns on each slide. Although students do not receive personal feedback on their successful steps as they would when stepping to the real version of Dance Dance Revolution, they are activity engaged in following the slides. This is a wonderful and inexpensive way to bring a type of exergaming into the gymnasium.

Handheld Computers

Many physical education teachers use handheld devices, such as PDAs, Palm Pilots, iPhones, BlackBerries, and tablet PCs). Many handheld devices run a variety of common software programs (e.g., Microsoft Word and Excel) that allow teachers to access their lesson plans or use spreadsheets for assessment purposes in the gymnasium or while teaching outdoors. Original lesson plans and assessment sheets can be created on an office computer and linked to the handheld device. Whatever information is collected on the device during class can be downloaded back to the office computer, eliminating the need for clipboards, paper, and pencils. In schools that are wireless, teachers use PDAs to take attendance and send the information directly to the front office with a quick touch of the computer screen (as long as the software is compatible).

> Based on the PowerPoint version of Dance Dance Revolution, how could you create modified versions of other exergaming programs? If limited exergaming equipment is available, how could you modify a lesson so all students could use it?

GPS

Global positioning systems (GPS) are handheld devices that help people navigate from a current position to another position via a triangulation of satellite transmissions. In schools, GPS systems are often used within an integrated curriculum, incorporating content from physical education with other subject areas such as geography and math. Students learn about distance and time by tracking their own speed, direction, and timing through geocaching (pronounced "geo cashing") activities. **Geocaching** is basically a technological game of hide and seek, in which teachers hide various objects (caches) and give students coordinates to find them using GPS units.

A search on the internet for *geocaching* will reveal a wide range of activities and information. In addition, a book called *Geocaching in Schools and Communities*, published by Human Kinetics (2010), is a wonderful resource that describes a variety of activities to use with GPS systems.

iPods

Although boom boxes and music CDs are still used in physical education classes across the United States, they are beginning to collect dust in some equipment rooms; teachers are now turning to their iPods. Any music can be downloaded off the Internet (e.g., from iTunes), stored in an iPod, and plugged into a speaker system for use during class. This technology allows you to choose and store large amounts of music on one small device. A genre of music can be selected and played based on the theme or purpose of the lesson (e.g., holiday music, fast-paced rhythms, popular hits, country, children's music).

Online Resources

There is more online information for physical education teachers to access than is imaginable. In addition to providing a wealth of content information, many physical education Web sites include lesson plan ideas and activities for all grade levels. Some Web sites also host forums or blogs, so teachers can stay connected to other professionals, voice concerns, and share teaching ideas. Spend some time browsing the Internet and you'll soon find information to help you with lesson and program planning, classroom management, content and instruction, assessment, equipment purchasing, and so much more. The following information available online is only a snippet of what is available to physical education teachers (refer to this chapter's online student resource for Web links to more information).

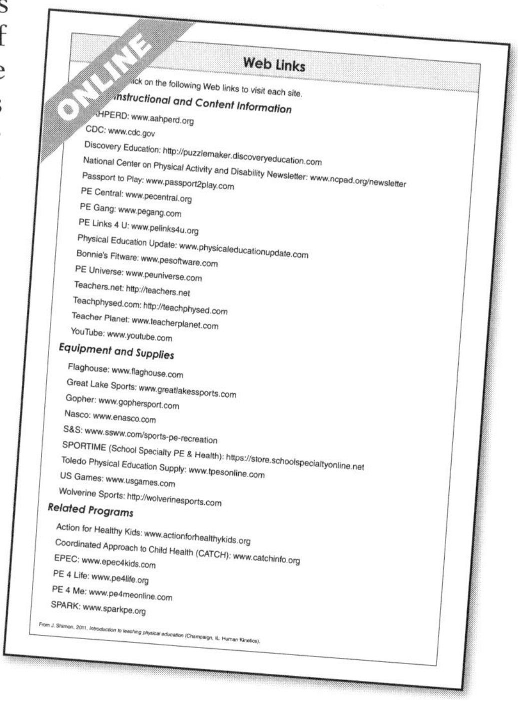

YouTube

Many classrooms and gymnasiums are connected to the Internet, allowing teachers access to all the positive online educational information that is available. One such resource is YouTube. This site is especially helpful when introducing a new activity or demonstrating how to do a skill during class. A video clip of just about any activity or skill can be found on YouTube. You can use this option to stimulate student interest or to provide demonstrations.

If your gymnasium is not wireless or accessible to online service, you can still show YouTube videos in class. Several free downloadable programs allow you to save video clips to the hard drive of your computer, including YouTubedownloadable, found in the address bar on the YouTube Web site, and www.realplayercafe.com. Once you download a video, all you need is your laptop computer and a projector to display the video in the gym.

You may also want to have students demonstrate their understanding of the content by creating an instructional video to upload to YouTube. For example, students could be required to develop a video that demonstrates how to perform a certain skill or activity (e.g., the set shot in basketball, throwing a ball in lacrosse, using pedometers). Students can upload videos from your YouTube account and display them during class. Of course, this assignment requires ample recording equipment and extended class time. Often, an assignment such as this is done in conjunction with another class. Make sure you have parental permission before any video is uploaded onto the Internet.

Professional and Educational Information

The American Alliance for Health, Physical Education, Recreation and Dance (AAHPERD) offers a wealth of information for all its disciplines. NASPE (National Association for Sport and Physical Education) is an alliance within AAHPERD that caters to physical educators and coaches. NASPE's Teacher Tool Box provides physical education teaching ideas, resource materials, and other information. You can find the Teacher Tool Box under the Publications and Resources link on NASPE's Web site. The Web site also includes the following:

- Current events, workshops, and conferences
- Relevant information and updates
- Career resources
- Available publications and journals
- A bookstore full of teaching materials and resources
- Grant opportunities
- Scholarship opportunities
- Advocacy ideas and materials

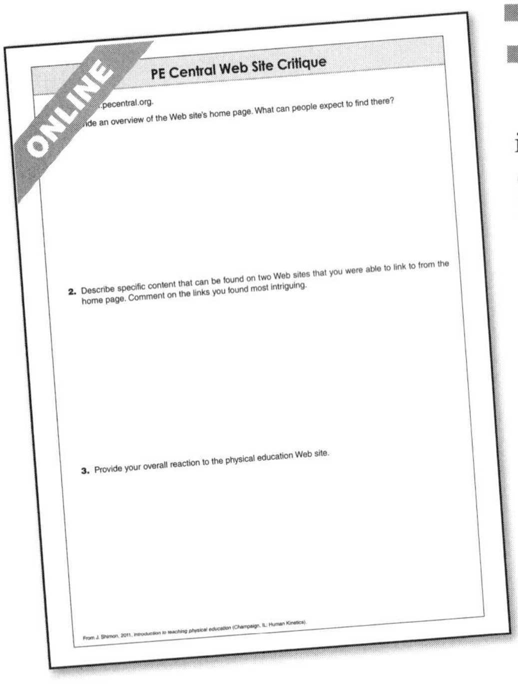
ONLINE

PE Central Web Site Critique

.pecentral.org.

ide an overview of the Web site's home page. What can people expect to find there?

2. Describe specific content that can be found on two Web sites that you were able to link to from the home page. Comment on the links you found most intriguing.

3. Provide your overall reaction to the physical education Web site.

From J. Shimon, 2011, *Introduction to teaching physical education* (Champaign, IL: Human Kinetics).

Numerous Web sites are available to help you improve your instruction and programs. Many, such as www.teacher.net, http://discoveryeducation.com, and www.teacherplanet.com, include lesson plan and activity ideas for all grade levels. Some Web sites also host forums or chat rooms that allow physical education teachers to share lessons, activities, and other ideas. PE Central's site (www.pecentral.org) is a premier Web site that contains an abundance of information for all involved in teaching physical education. Go online and check out PE Central. Use the reporting form found in the online resource to document your findings.

Professional Profile: *Theresa and Stephen Cone*

Photo courtesy of Steve and Theresa Cone

BACKGROUND INFORMATION

Dr. Theresa Cone and Dr. Stephen Cone are professors in the department of health and exercise science at Rowan University in Glassboro, New Jersey. They have coauthored the second edition of *Teaching Children Dance* (2005), *Assessing Dance in Elementary Physical Education* (2005), *Interdisciplinary Elementary Physical Education* (2009), and numerous papers. In addition, Steve coauthored *Seminar in Physical Education: From Student Teaching to Teaching Students* (2007). They have presented workshops and lectures at the international, national, regional, and state levels on arts education, interdisciplinary teaching, physical education, children's dance, leadership, and adapted physical education and dance. They have served as leaders and presidents of state, district, and national professional organizations. Theresa has served as president of the National Dance Association (NDA) and Steve has served as president of the American Alliance for Health, Physical Education, Recreation and Dance (AAHPERD). They have been recognized as outstanding educators and have both received the AAHPERD Honor Award.

Why did you decide to become college professors?

We teach because we want to make a difference in the next generation of educators. Every day we walk into the classroom, we are walking into the future. It is our way to give back and to share our passion and professional experiences. It also keeps us young.

What do you like most about your job?

We enjoy the students' energy, sharing personal experiences, witnessing the passion, and seeing future professionals grow. It is truly rewarding to see a diverse group of learners in action.

What is the most challenging part of your job?

It is difficult to consistently get students outside their comfort zone, to recruit them to be reflective thinkers, and to realize that they can be change agents. It is also difficult to get them to see the bigger education picture and to realize that it is not always appropriate to simply repeat what they have experienced in the past. They need to see themselves as future professionals who will be able to make real changes in teaching health and physical education to people of all ages.

How have you continued to grow professionally?

We continue to attend conferences and workshops, and we maintain a healthy writing and presentation agenda. We also know that, just as you would put on your own oxygen mask before you put one on a child on an airplane, you have to help yourself first before you can help another.

What advice would you give a college student who wants to become a health and physical education teacher?

It is essential to be passionate about your profession and to enjoy learning because it will strengthen you throughout a productive career. You must be articulate because you will need to be an eternal advocate for your profession. You can accomplish this if you understand the value of good writing, embrace service to the profession, and personify exemplary teaching.

Equipment

Physical education teachers are responsible for ordering equipment for their programs. Often, these orders must go out for bid to various companies. The Web sites in this chapter's online student resource provide a start to your search for popular physical education and sport equipment companies. You can also go online to request their catalogs. Alongside equipment, these catalogs often offer a variety of instructional materials such as books on lesson plans, games, activities, and music CDs to use during class. When purchasing equipment, make sure to also check out your local sporting goods stores; they often have wonderful deals for area schools and sport teams. Keep in mind that the equipment Web sites listed are not intended as advertisements or recommended companies, but rather as a starting point in your search for resources as you begin your career as a physical education teacher.

Summary

In addition to all of the available physical education–related textbooks, you can access a variety of free online resources when planning lessons, generating new ideas, developing assessments, and purchasing equipment. In addition, numerous technological tools can help you enhance your instructional efficiency and motivate students to learn and be physically active. Schools often provide some instructional technological equipment, such as laptop computers, projectors, and music or sound systems to use in the gym. Although most physical education departments have annual budgets to purchase supplies and equipment, it is usually not large enough to buy some of the more expensive technology, such as a classroom set of pedometers or heart rate monitors. You may have to be creative in finding additional funding sources to purchase those types of items.

Discussion Questions

1. What is the process for applying for a NASPE grant?
2. When might it be beneficial to use YouTube video clips in class? Are there certain skills or activities that are best suited to this technology?
3. What new or unique pieces of physical education equipment did you find after searching through some of the online catalogs of various sport equipment companies?
4. What are some interesting activities you could teach using pedometers to emphasize movement and physical activity?

CHAPTER 11

Careers in Physical Education

CHAPTER OBJECTIVES

After reading this chapter, you will be able to:

- Recognize alternative school settings that may include physical education programs in their curricula.
- Describe the advantages and disadvantages associated with substitute teaching.
- Recognize opportunities for employment in nonschool settings.
- Recognize possible certifications needed for various types of jobs.
- Explain the benefits of securing a graduate teaching assistantship to further your education.

KEY TERMS

alternative schools
charter school
graduate teaching assistantship

Students who pursue a teaching degree in physical education most often find employment teaching or coaching, or both, in public or private schools at the elementary, middle, or high school level. On occasion, however, such positions are not available upon graduation. What are other options you can pursue if a teaching position isn't open? With some added certifications and alternative searching, you can put your degree to good use.

Alternative School Settings

Don't limit your teaching possibilities to traditional public schools or teaching positions. Private schools, academies, charter schools, and alternative schools also include physical education programs in their overall curricula.

Private or Charter Schools

Teaching physical education at a private, charter, or alternative school is generally the same as teaching at a traditional public school; there is usually a curriculum to follow and skills for students to learn and develop. However, there are differences as well. Private and charter schools often have an added focus or increased academic rigor. For example, a private parochial, or religion-based, school may emphasize developing character and responsibility, prayer, and meeting explicit grading standards, whereas a specialized charter school or academy may focus specifically on dance forms (e.g., a charter school for the arts) or preparing students for health-related fields (e.g., a medical charter focus).

Sometimes, newly formed **charter schools** take up residence in portable units or buildings that do not have gymnasiums. As a result, physical education classes have to be taught outdoors or in a classroom or cafeteria when weather is less than favorable. Some charter schools do not have locker rooms for students to change in, or lack sufficient equipment. These situations make teaching physical education challenging, requiring that the teacher be resourceful and creative in developing meaningful lessons.

Alternative Schools

Teaching physical education at an alternative school often brings an added challenge. In general, **alternative schools** accommodate students who are not able to function within a traditional public school setting. For whatever reason, these students are often at risk of failing their classes, have behavior challenges, or require remedial programs. Needless to say, many adolescents who attend this type of school also have additional personal problems (e.g., drug issues, abuse, gang history, arrest record, pregnancy, single parenthood) and are often accompanied by poor attitudes and social skills. Physical education teachers who teach in an alternative school setting need to have the disposition to work with and help these students become responsible young adults. Many teachers in this position use physical activity as a way to develop self-esteem and positive social skills.

Night School or Summer School

Night school and summer school teaching positions are available in many cities throughout the United States. Those who teach night school often have an added daytime job to supplement the part-time teaching position. Night school for physical education credit may meet only twice a week for two to three hours at a time. If you teach in this setting, you will need to plan for a variety of learning activities to cover the length of each class meeting time. Keep in mind that you may be teaching classes in your minor field of study, or in both physical education and your minor field. For that reason, it is important that you complete a minor in some other area in education to make yourself as marketable as possible.

Physical education classes are usually available during summer school sessions. These classes are often taken by students who failed physical education during the regular school session and need the credit to graduate or by those wishing to complete their physical education requirement early. Needless to say, developing a motivational climate to help these students enjoy learning and participate in a variety of physical activities is important. In addition, summer school sessions can involve an entire morning or afternoon. As such, you will need to plan well and be well organized to keep students engaged.

Substitute Teaching

People who do not find teaching positions after graduating from college frequently contact school districts to request substitute teaching positions until permanent teaching positions become available. Long-term substitute positions are sometimes available (e.g., for maternity leave) and can be a good way to get your foot in the door and gain exposure within a school or district. There are possibilities to substitute daily, especially if substitute teachers are in high demand. This option is always a good way to help pay the bills for a time, even though benefits (e.g., health care, retirement) are not extended to those in substitute positions.

Unfortunately, many subs do not cover classes in their areas of expertise. In addition, teachers usually do not have detailed lesson plans for subs to follow. Thus, many substitute teachers get through the day by keeping students busy, happy, and good, often by showing a movie or having students do group work as outlined by the regular classroom teacher's notes. Some subs refer to this as baby-sitting. Finally, sometimes substitute teachers have to deal with the less-than-appropriate behaviors certain students display when their regular teachers are not there. This can become wearisome.

Coaching

Although most public schools hire head athletic coaches from their faculty, they often go outside the school to find assistant coaches if none are available within the school system. On the other hand, some private schools hire head coaches who do not work at the school. Sometimes coaches who do not have a teaching position take on substitute teaching jobs during the day and coach after school; others supplement a daytime job with a coaching stipend. As with most coaching positions, a current first aid and CPR card are normally required, along with a background check (if not teaching in the school) and the completion of any state requirements, such as an ASEP course (American Sport Education Program).

> Do you think coaches who are not a part of a school's faculty encounter player issues or difficulties that coaches who teach at that school do not?

Adapted Physical Education

Finding a position solely as an adapted physical education teacher may be difficult. Often, physical education teachers are asked to teach a period of adapted physical education during the school day if there is a need to do so, thereby eliminating the need for an adapted physical education specialist. Unfortunately, many physical education teachers do not have the unique skills and specialization needed for working

Do you have what it takes to be a good coach? Coaches are often role models and play an important part in helping kids develop good character along with sport skills.

© Ernest Prim

with students who have special needs. There are Adapted Physical Education National Standards (APENS) to help guide professionals in best practices, and you can also become nationally certified in adapted physical education (CAPE). Visit the APENS Web site (www.apens.org) for more information on adapted physical education.

Some schools have positions available for special education aides or resource teachers. Although such a position is usually not full-time, it may be a short-term alternative when physical education teaching positions are not available. Again, this is an avenue some recent graduates take to get their foot in the door of a school or district, knowing that, by being a known entity, they have a higher probability of securing a teaching position if one becomes available in the coming year.

Athletic Director

In addition to teaching, a physical education teacher can also become the athletic director (AD) for a school, either full-time for a school or district or part-time. Some schools require that ADs be currently employed at the school, whereas others hire them from outside the school if they meet the qualifications. The duties of an AD can be quite extensive, requiring that the person be well organized and demonstrate management savvy. In addition, some school districts require the AD to have certain certifications. For example, some school districts require high school ADs to take a specific ASEP course, be certified through the National Federation of Interscholastic Coaches Education Program (NFICEP), or have a CAA certification (Certified Athletic Administration).

One of the main duties of an AD is to schedule athletic contests for both girls' and boys' teams. This may include freshman, junior varsity, and varsity teams at the high school level or A, B, and C teams at the middle school level. Some high schools even hire assistant ADs as well. An AD not only schedules home athletic events, but also is responsible for securing game-day officials or referees. The duties of an AD may also include the following:

- Schedule transportation for away contests.
- Maintain game-day facilities (e.g., lines painted on fields, bleachers pulled out).
- Set up the management of concession stands and gate sales.
- Set up event management and safety control teams.
- Manage a purchase plan for new equipment and uniforms, and a maintenance plan for existing equipment.
- Coordinate and plan the athletic budget.
- Assess the athletic program and coaching performances.
- Issue coaching contracts.
- Maintain files on coaching requirements (e.g., current CPR and first aid certifications).
- Document athlete eligibility; administer National Federation of High School rules and regulations.
- Place advertisements, and print and sell event programs.
- Attend the school's athletic events whenever possible.

Clearly, the AD needs to be well structured and have financial skills to manage and maintain an athletic budget and program.

Other Career Avenues

If teaching positions are limited in your area and you are not in a position to move to another region or state to find employment, there are other employment possibilities to consider. A physical education degree may also be helpful in securing leadership or teaching positions in city recreation departments, YMCAs, fitness centers, Girls and Boys Clubs, and special programs such as Upward Bound that help high school students from low-income families work toward high school graduation and beyond. With a degree in physical education, you could be the director of youth programs or organize summer youth activities within many of these types of organizations. Some folks with physical education degrees and expertise in specific areas become teaching or coaching professionals, such as golf or tennis pros, strength and conditioning specialists, or speed training coaches.

With additional health education training, you may find a position in a hospital, clinic, or center as an outreach educator for various child or adult education programs. Another option is to use your physical education degree and expertise in an entrepreneurial venue. You may open a specialized physical training center, become involved in clothing or sport merchandise, develop specialized equipment for physical education programs, or act as a consultant. Many avenues are available to explore if teaching positions are hard to find.

Professional Profile: Rae Pica

Photo courtesy of Rae Pica

BACKGROUND INFORMATION

I am the founder and director of Moving and Learning, which is a physical fitness consultation service and Web site. I have also been a children's physical activity specialist since 1980. A former adjunct instructor with the University of New Hampshire, I am the author of 18 books, including *Physical Education for Young Children*. I served on the National Association for Sport and Physical Education task force that created Active Start, which are the national guidelines for early childhood physical activity. I was the 2009 recipient of the Margie R. Hanson Distinguished Service Award.

Why did you decide to become a physical education teacher?

No one grows up thinking about this as a career! It's definitely a path on which life led me. I started as a dancer and was asked to teach dance to preschoolers. Then I realized they didn't need dance technique as much as they needed basic body and spatial awareness. So I started studying movement education and it changed the course of my life!

What do you like most about your job?

The variety of ways in which I'm able to affect the lives of teachers and children! Between writing, consulting, speaking, and now hosting an Internet radio program, it's impossible to get bored.

What is the most challenging part of your job?

Having to advocate for the need for movement and physical activity in children's lives, even after 30 years! I keep waiting for the revolution in education, but it never seems to come. It's so very frustrating to have people believe that the mind and body are separate entities and that the functions of the mind are superior to the functions of the body!

How have you continued to grow professionally?

I'm always learning by reading as much as possible and by listening to what people are talking about. Mostly, though, I try to stay open to new challenges that come my way. Even if a new opportunity frightens me because I'm not sure I'm up to it, if it's something that intrigues me and that I believe will *make a difference*, I'll tackle it.

What advice would you give a college student who wants to become a PE teacher?

If you're going to enter this challenging field, you have to have a passion for it. Know that what you'll be doing is extremely important to the development of the *whole* child—physically, socially, emotionally, and cognitively—and that it can make a difference that lasts a lifetime! Most important, *never* stop moving and learning!

Fitness-Related Positions

Fitness-related options may be available in your area. You may be able to teach classes at a YMCA or fitness center if you have certain specializations (e.g., yoga, Pilates) or a training certificate. Most often, fitness-related facilities require their fitness training specialists to be ACE certified (American Council on Exercise). Following are the ACE fitness training certifications:

- Personal Trainer Certification
- Group Fitness Instructor Certification
- Lifestyle and Weight Management Consultant
- Advanced Health and Fitness Specialist Certification

Go to www.acefitness.org to find out more about ACE certifications. Some fitness centers look for those certified as strength and conditioning specialists (CSCS). This National Strength and Conditioning Association (NSCA) certification is popular with physical education graduates, because a good portion of the requirements for

Working as a personal trainer or fitness instructor is a feasible alternative if teaching positions are not available or if you decide to pursue a career path outside of teaching.
© Dmitry Ersler

a CSCS certification are met as part of a physical education degree. In addition to a CSCS certification, the association also offers a Certified Personal Trainer Certification. You can find more information on strength training and conditioning certifications by going to www.nsca-cc.org.

Safety-Related Positions

Teaching in adult education and safety education programs are other avenues for those with degrees in physical education. You might be able to teach health safety service courses through the American Red Cross (ARC), including first aid and CPR or AED classes. Of course, you will need to receive additional training to teach ARC courses. Visit your local ARC chapter to find out what courses are available, or go to www.redcross.org for more information.

Aquatics

With appropriate training and experience, you may be able to work as an aquatics director or in other aquatics-related positions. Positions in aquatics range from pool management director and lifeguard, to swimming and lifeguard training instructor. Of course, all of these positions require certifications.

The American Red Cross offers certifications for pool and waterfront lifeguards, water park lifeguards, and shallow water attendants. If teaching swimming or training lifeguards is appealing, the American Red Cross also offers certification for water safety instructors (WSI), lifeguard instructor (LGI), and lifeguard instructor trainer (LGIT). Some aquatics positions may require an additional Ellis certification, which involves a comprehensive aquatics risk management program, especially for

Physical education teachers can find employment as lifeguards or swimming instructors if they have the appropriate qualifications.

water parks, flat-water parks, and associated facilities. More information on the Ellis certification can be found at www.jellis.com. In addition, most positions that involve the management of a pool facility require a CPO certification (Certified Pool and Spa Operator). A CPO certification verifies that the person knows how to properly maintain pools in accordance with state regulations and industry standards. More information about a CPO certification can be found at www.nspf.org.

Continuing Your Education

If you want to increase your salary at the K-12 level, broaden your education, or teach or coach at a community college, college, or university, you will have to further your education. Typically, those who teach or coach at community or junior colleges hold master's degrees. Some smaller colleges hire faculty with master's degrees; however, a doctoral degree is usually preferred. To teach at most colleges and universities, a doctorate is required.

A master's degree can usually be obtained in two years, if going to school full-time. A graduate teaching, research, or coaching assistantship is one way to work toward an advanced degree. Plus, **graduate teaching assistantships** often include a tuition waiver, along with a stipend (payment for your work as part of the assistantship). This can be a wonderful way to defer the financial costs of pursuing a graduate degree. You can easily determine whether graduate programs and assistantships are available at your choice of colleges or universities by going online.

Summary

Numerous career options are available for those with a physical education teaching degree, ranging from teaching and coaching positions in public or private schools, to working in adult and outreach educational programs, recreational and fitness facilities, and entrepreneurial enterprises. You can also further your education by returning to school to obtain a master's degree in physical education or other related areas, such as sport or school administration.

▶ Discussion Questions

1. Do you know of any high school coaches who do not have a current teaching position in the school or district? What jobs do they do during the day that allow them to coach in the afternoons or evenings?
2. What are some advantages and disadvantages of being a substitute teacher?
3. How do physical education jobs in private, charter, and alternative schools differ from those in traditional schools?
4. What career positions in physical education may require further education, such as a master's degree?

Go online to complete a case study about job hunting.

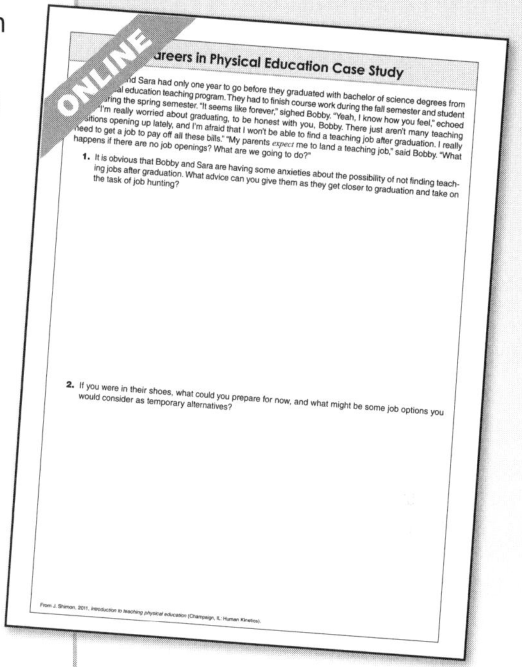

ONLINE
areers in Physical Education Case Study
nd Sara had only one year to go before they graduated with bachelor of science degrees from
al education teaching program. They had to finish course work during the fall semester and student
ring the spring semester. "It seems like forever," sighed Bobby. "Yeah, I know how you feel," echoed
"I'm really worried about graduating, to be honest with you, Bobby. There just aren't many teaching
sitions opening up lately, and I'm afraid that I won't be able to find a teaching job after graduation. I really
need to get a job to pay off all these bills." "My parents expect me to land a teaching job," said Bobby. "What
happens if there are no job openings? What are we going to do?"
1. It is obvious that Bobby and Sara are having some anxieties about the possibility of not finding teaching jobs after graduation. What advice can you give them as they get closer to graduation and take on the task of job hunting?
2. If you were in their shoes, what could you prepare for now, and what might be some job options you would consider as temporary alternatives?
From J. Shimon, 2011, Introduction to teaching physical education (Champaign, IL: Human Kinetics).

APPENDIX A

Example of Class Policies and Expectations

Radcliffe Junior High School Physical Education Policies and Expectations

The physical education program at Radcliffe Junior High School focuses on fitness and the refinement of individual, dual, and team sport skills. The goal of the program is to help students enhance their personal fitness levels, enjoy physical activity, and make it a part of their lifestyle now and in the future.

General Goals and Objectives of Physical Education

1. Motivate students to be physically active by making physical education fun!
2. Maintain or improve physical fitness through participation in regular exercise and conditioning.
3. Expose student to a wide range of activities and instruction.
4. Create an environment that promotes success for each student while encouraging social and emotional development and self-esteem.
5. Prepare students for further instruction and participation in high school physical education programs.

Basic Rules for Physical Education

1. Students are expected to *be on time and dressed* in the appropriate uniform or gym attire.
2. Students are expected to *treat others, equipment, and the facilities with respect*. This includes using appropriate language and speaking positively, helping others when needed, and listening when required.
3. Students are expected to *give their best effort* on all tasks.
4. Students are expected to *act appropriately* and do what is right.

Uniform

All students will be required to dress appropriately for each class. Proper uniform consists of (1) a uniform shirt or white T-shirt (no sleeveless T-shirts), (2) uniform shorts or blue or black athletic shorts (no cutoffs or jean shorts), (3) proper gym tennis shoes (no sandals, boots, etc.), and (4) and a notebook (with pencil). Clothes are available for students who do not have appropriate attire. For cold weather, it is strongly recommended that students wear sweatpants and sweatshirts. Students are responsible for their own uniforms and should make sure they are washed at least once per week. Students should take uniforms home on Friday and return them clean on Monday. Uniforms should not be shared with other students. Showers are strongly recommended, but not required. Students are to bring their own hygiene items (e.g., deodorant, hairbrush, wash cloth and towel, soap).

Students who are not dressed appropriately for class will lose points and be given an alternative assignment for the day(s) missed.

Lockers

Each student will receive a locker and lock at no cost. To guard against theft, students are not to share locker combinations or lockers with other students. Lost locks cost approximately $5.00 to replace. Students who lose a lock or discover that someone else knows their combination should see the physical education teacher right away.

Injury or Sickness

A written note from a parent or doctor is necessary to be excused from physical education; only serious injury or illness is considered a valid excuse. The note must state why the student cannot participate, list the dates involved, and have a parent's phone number. Alternate activities will be assigned for the missed day(s).

Grading Policy

Grade in physical education are determined as follows:

Participation, dress, and behavior	40%
Quizzes and tests	30%
Skill and fitness assessments	20%
Assignments	10%

Participation

Students earn daily participation and dress points for coming to class on time, wearing appropriate gym clothes and shoes, and exhibiting appropriate behavior. Not being dressed appropriately will result in the loss of *all* points for that day. A note from a parent does not excuse a student from dressing appropriately. Points are also withheld for insubordination (defiance of authority), vulgarity, profanity, and harassment or teasing.

1. After three nonparticipation days, the student will be counseled by the teacher and the parent or guardian will be notified.
2. After four nonparticipation days, the student will be referred for counseling and the parent or guardian will be notified.
3. After five nonparticipation days, the student will be referred to the assistant principal for possible disciplinary action.
4. After six nonparticipation days in a nine-week grading period or semester, the student will be removed from class and lose academic credit.

Fitness Assessment

Students are assessed using Fitnessgram, a program used throughout the New River Valley School District. Students are assessed on cardiorespiratory fitness (1-mile run or PACER), muscular strength (push-ups), muscular endurance (sit-ups), and flexibility (sit-and-reach). Students are tested in each of the fitness components at the beginning of the semester, at the end of the nine weeks, and at the end of the semester. Students are given a fitness report card after each assessment and will be guided in setting realistic goals for improvement. *There are no makeup days for students who miss fitness assessment days.* All students must complete fitness assessments, unless they are suffering from long-term illness or injury.

Makeup Policy

Physical education is like any other class; students who are absent or have in-school suspension must make up that day for credit to be awarded. A day can be made up before school, after school, or at lunch. Students must make prior arrangements with the teacher. Students are responsible for any makeup activities.

Acknowledgment

I understand the importance of participating in physical education and completing all program requirements. My participation and appropriate gym attire are required, and good effort is expected. Any medical conditions that may prevent me from participating must be verified by a written note from my parents or guardian, a doctor, or the school nurse.

I have read and understand the Radcliffe JHS Physical Education Policies and Expectations.

Student signature: ______________________________

Parent signature: ____________________ Date: __________

Phone or e-mail contact information (optional): ________________

APPENDIX B

Exercises for a Dynamic Warm-Up

Dynamic warm-ups include low-, moderate-, and then high-intensity hops, skips, jumps, lunges, and other upper- and lower-body movements to help elevate core body temperature, maximize active ranges of motion, and excite motor units and kinesthetic awareness (Faigenbaum & McFarlane, 2007).

Directions

Design an area that allows students to travel a certain distance (i.e., 30 to 60 feet, 10 to 20 yards, 9 to 18 meters) for warm-ups (or use the width of a basketball court). Place students in rows, two or three deep. The first person in each row goes first, followed by the next row, and so on. Have rows stop at the end line and wait for the return activity. This organization allows for a ratio of work to rest.

Low-Intensity Dynamic Warm-Up Exercises

1. *Walking arm circles.* Arms complete forward circles for half the distance; then switch to backward circles for the remaining distance (involves the overall shoulder capsule).
2. *Walking arm hugs.* Both arms fly out (open chest, pectoralis stretch); then cross to hug the chest (midtrapezius/rhomboid stretch).
3. *Walking fly swatters.* Both arms swing up and behind the head, touching the back of the neck or shoulder blades (swatting bugs) with each step. This exercise involves external rotation with a triceps stretch.

   Variations: *Cross-arm swatters,* moving one arm up and behind the neck, while the other arm travels low behind the back (top hand tries to touch bottom hand); *arm flutters,* moving both arms quickly out to the side, or moving both hands quickly forward and backward overhead.

Low-to Moderate-Intensity Dynamic Warm-Up Exercises

4. *Cheerleaders.* Lateral shuffle down the floor while swinging arms up and out to the side and back, like a jumping jack. At the halfway point, turn and face the other way and continue. This exercise involves the hip abductors (outer hip) and adductors (groin), as well as the shoulders.

5. *High knee lifts.* On each walking step, lift and hug one knee toward the chest while rising up on the toes.

   Variations: Swinging arms in opposition or extending leg out as if crossing a hurdle. This exercise involves the hip flexors and stretches the gluteus maximus.

6. *Stepping trunk turns.* On each high knee step, an elbow touches the opposite knee (right elbow to left knee; then left elbow to right knee). This exercise involves the hip flexors and core.
7. *Frankensteins* (toe touch and walk). On each step, extend one leg straight out in front of the body and touch knee or toes. Do the same with the other leg during the next step. This exercise involves the hip flexors and stretches the hamstrings.
8. *Airplanes.* On each step, bend over and touch the floor while raising the rear leg into the air. Laterally lift the arms out to the side to mimic the wings of an airplane. This exercise addresses hamstring flexibility.
9. *Inchworm.* Starting in a push-up position, walk feet toward the hands, keeping the legs straight. Then, walk the hands forward while keeping the arms and legs extended (plank to upside-down V to plank, and so on). This exercise addresses the core while the body is in a plank position, and the hamstrings, low back, and calves when in an upside-down V.
10. *X lunges.* Lunge sideways with the right foot; then step behind with the left (forms an X). Finish the movement with a forward bend at the hips. Try to keep the back leg (behind leg) straight. After half the distance has been completed, face the opposite direction (lunge with left foot, step behind with right foot). This exercise stresses the lateral hip/iliotibial band and hamstrings of the back leg.
11. *Giant lunge steps.* Take long steps forward and lunge with each step. After half the distance has been completed, turn around and continue stepping and lunging backward as far as possible.

    Variations: Raise arms overhead with each step. For higher intensity, add a knee hug between lunges. Make sure to keep the head and trunk upright, the front knee in line with the foot, and the back knee off the floor. This exercise stretches the hip flexors of the rear leg and involves the quadriceps of the front leg.

12. *Lunge trunk turns.* On each step, lunge and touch the opposite elbow to the opposite knee. Make sure to keep the head and trunk upright, the front knee in line with the foot, and the back of the knee off the floor. This exercise stretches the hip flexors of the rear leg and involves the quadriceps of the front leg and core.
13. *Lateral shuffles.* In a ready position (semisquat position), lateral shuffle with a long first step followed by a second quick step. After half the distance has been completed, face the opposite direction and continue. This movement stretches the groin (adductors) and works the lateral hip (gluteus medius).
14. *Cariocas.* Laterally step down the floor while alternating one foot in front of the body and the other behind. Halfway down the floor, switch position and face the opposite wall. Use the arms to horizontally swing in opposition to each step.

15. *Backpedal.* While keeping the feet under the hips, take small, quick steps backward.
16. *Backward run.* Reach back with one leg on each step.
17. *High knee skips.* While skipping, emphasize a high knee lift, alternating arm action and pushing up off the toes.
18. *Back-end kicks.* Kick the heel to the buttocks on each step.
19. *Run and go.* Jog into a run for the first half of the distance and finish with a sprint. Quickly stop by bending the knees and using short steps. Variations include doing a push-up first; then quickly jumping up to complete the exercise.

Stationary Dynamic Exercises

Crunch Punches

Begin in a sit-up position with knees bent and arms crossed at the chest. Crunch up and punch out arms past the knees; then lower the body and shoulders slowly back down to the floor. Repeat a desired number of times. Variation includes alternating punches across the body past the opposite knees.

Standing Crunch Rotations

Using a wide base of support, bring the arms laterally out to the side. While keeping the arms extended, slowly lower the body and rotate the arms one at a time to the opposite thigh, then knee, midcalf, and ankle. Each crunch rotation can include pivoting on the balls of the feet.

Standing Leg Cradles

While standing on one leg, lift the other leg using both hands. Turn the knee outward while lifting the lower leg up into a modified (standing) hurdler's stretch (ankle high). An easier position is supine on the ground.

Hamstring Rollovers

Lie on the back with arms pointing to the ceiling. Slowly curl up while assuming a modified hurdler's position and reach forward with the hands to stretch. Roll back down, and repeat with a curl and stretch to the opposite leg on the next repetition. The motion should be a continuous, slow, and controlled flowing motion. Stretch at the waist or hips, pretending to stretch over a bowling ball positioned in the lap. A variation includes both legs rising up to meet the hands at the start, and as the body slowly curls up, the legs assume a modified hurdler's position prior to final the stretch.

Hurdler's Twist

Begin in a modified hurdler's position. Reach out to stretch one leg; then lean back into a V-sit position while stretching out the other leg into position. Repeat. The motion should be slow and continuous. Stretch at the waist or hips, pretending to stretch over a bowling ball positioned in the lap.

Wave Push-Ups

At the end of a push-up (plank position), lift one hand up and reach out in front of the body or lift one hand off the ground and wave to a partner. Repeat with the opposite hand before going back down for another push-up. Keep shoulders level during the wave.

GLOSSARY

accelerometer—A device worn around the waist that measures the amount of active time and the intensity of movements throughout the day to determine daily physical activity levels.

accountability—Being responsible and answerable to a certain role.

affective domain—A domain of learning that taps into attitudes, values, and feelings.

alternative schools—Schools that accommodate students who cannot function successfully in a traditional public school setting, usually because of personal issues related to drugs, abuse, gang history, arrest records, pregnancy, or single parenthood.

American gymnastics—Systems that evolved as modifications of early German and Swedish systems and developed by early American leaders in physical education.

anthropometric measurements—Measurements of specific dimensions of the body such as height, weight, skinfold thickness, and body circumference.

anticipatory set—A quick introduction or opening statement that informs students about the day's lesson; also referred to as a set induction.

application activities—Activities that involve employing (applying) skills in a variety of situations.

assessment—The measurement and evaluation of a performance.

assumption of risk—An understanding that participating in an activity involves the potential risk of injury.

augmented feedback—Feedback that is obtained from an external source, such as a teacher or one's own performance.

axial skills—Stability skills that develop static and dynamic balance while the body rotates about an axis (e.g., spine, shoulder, hip).

charter schools—Schools that cater to a specific field of study or focus and often adhere to higher academic standards.

closed-skill practice—A practice in which skills are practiced in a stable and predictable environment so that dynamic factors do not affect the performance.

cognitive domain—A domain of learning that involves the intellectual understanding of content.

command style—A direct teaching style in which the teacher has complete control over what is taught, how it's taught, and when it's practiced.

concepts-based model—A teaching model that emphasizes the reasons for learning movement skills, based on concepts from various subdisciplines such as biomechanics, exercise physiology, sport psychology, and motor learning.

consequences—A behavior management strategy that involves a penalty (e.g., loss of points, time-out, detention, call to parent) resulting from an inappropriate behavior choice.

corrective, specific feedback—A type of augmented feedback used to correct specific movement errors.

criterion-referenced standards—Test scores that measure and compare scores to a preexisting set of norms or criteria.

distributed practice—A practice in which limited amounts of skill practice are scheduled over extended periods of time.

divergent style—A teaching style that allows for student choice, creativity, and a wide possibility of outcomes based on a teacher-designed question or task.

dynamic movements—Multijoint or multimuscle warm-up movements that prepare students or athletes for activity by increasing heart rate, body core temperature, and neuromuscular stimulation.

ego orientation—A motivational focus that describes someone who is extrinsically motivated by self-comparison and outperforming others.

evaluation—The analysis and interpretation of test scores or data.

exergaming—Physically active video games.

extensions—Learning tasks that are modified to change the difficulty, complexity, or variation of the task.

existentialism—A traditional philosophy based on the views of Jean-Paul Sarte. It centers on an individualistic process that allows students to learn through their choice of activities and the consequences of those choices.

extrinsic motivation—Motivation that comes from outside a person, from someone or something in the environment.

fitness education model—An education model in which the main emphasis is on the understanding and development of health-related fitness skills.

foreseeability—The ability to determine and act on possible dangerous situations based on an awareness of one's surroundings.

formative assessments—Assessments that are conducted throughout a unit of instruction or course of study to determine student progress in learning the material or mastering tasks.

fundamental movements—Movements that involve two more body segments and allow for the development of basic locomotor, manipulative, or stability skills.

general and positive feedback—A type of augmented feedback used to encourage and motivate.

German gymnastics—A prominent system in the early development of physical education in the United States that was based on vigorous calisthenics, heavy lifting, and the use of gymnasium apparatus.

geocaching—A technological game of hide-and-seek using a hand-held electrical global positioning system (GPS) and specific coordinates.

graduate teaching assistantship—An opportunity to work toward a master's or doctoral degree while teaching various undergraduate courses for the department. Assistantships often include a stipend and tuition waiver.

guided discovery style—A teaching style in which students arrive at an answer to a teacher-generated question or problem.

health-related fitness—A type of fitness that addresses five components related to enhancing health: cardiorespiratory endurance, muscular endurance, muscular strength, flexibility, and body composition.

heart rate monitor—A device usually worn around the chest as a strap (transmitter) and wrist as a watch (monitor or receiver) that indicates a level of intensity by measuring heart rate during physical activity.

hygiene—A term used during the early American period that mirrors the current meaning of health and wellness.

idealism—A traditional philosophy of the Greek philosopher Plato that centers on the importance of knowledge and how knowledge helps develop the mind and provides us with the ability to reason.

Individuals with Disabilities Education Act (1990)—Changed the terminology of the previous Education for All Handicapped Children Act (1975) to include individuals with disabilities instead of handicapped children, and indicated that children with disabilities be placed in the least restrictive environment.

informative feedback—A type of augmented feedback that informs students of what they are doing well and helps reinforce correct form on future repetitions. Also called evaluative or instructional feedback.

instant activity—A fun, quick, low-organized game or activity used at the beginning of class to help increase heart rate and motivate students to be active.

instructional tasks—Tasks that occur during a lesson that contribute to student learning, such as skill demonstrations and explanations, using teaching cues, and providing feedback to students.

intrinsic motivation—Motivation that comes from within, such as the motivation to satisfy one's own personal desires.

invasion games—A game form that requires a team to invade an opponent's territory in order to score. Games such as soccer, flag football, basketball, and lacrosse are examples of invasion games.

inverted supports—Stability skills that involve the development of static and dynamic balance while in an upside-down position.

knowledge of performance—A type of augmented feedback in which an external source informs a person about his or her performance.

knowledge of results—A type of augmented feedback in which the outcome, or result, of the performance is the source of feedback.

lead-up games—Gamelike activities that do not resemble the actual game, but allow students to practice skills in a more competitive environment.

liability—A legal responsibility. Physical education teachers are liable for providing a safe learning environment for students.

locomotor skills—Fundamental movements in which the body moves, or travels, from one location to another in a variety of ways.

malfeasance—A type of negligence that is brought about by doing something against the law.

manipulative skills—Fundamental movements that allow the body to direct or control an object in a variety of ways.

massed practice—A type of practice in which skills are practiced in a condensed period of time.

measurement—Administration of a test and collection of the scores.

misfeasance—A type of negligence resulting in actions that were done incorrectly based on a standard of care.

modified games—Adapted versions of actual games.

motivation—Factors that contribute to why people choose to act.

movement concepts—A method of developing fundamental movement skills by allowing the body to move in a variety of ways (effort and space) while in a variety of situations (relationships).

movement education—An education model that helps children enhance fundamental movement skills and learn through movement.

naturalism—A traditional philosophy based on the views of Jean-Jacques Rousseau. It centers on the importance of individual development and experiences gained by exploring one's environment; learning occurs through self-activity.

negligence—A legal wrong that results in physical injury, property damage, or harm to someone's reputation.

net and wall games—A game form that requires the use of a net to separate playing areas or walls as boundaries. Games such as tennis, badminton, pickleball, racquetball, and handball are examples of net and wall games.

new physical education—A new focus of physical education during the early 20th century that encompassed developing not only the physical person, but also character, intellect, and movement skills.

No Child Left Behind (1991)—Schools and teachers across the United States were required to show improvements in test scores in core academic subjects such as math, science, history, and English. Physical education was and is currently not part of the core academic subjects of NCLB.

nonfeasance—A type of negligence resulting in the failure to provide a standard of care that should have been provided.

noninstructional tasks—Tasks that occur during a lesson that do not contribute to learning, such as taking attendance, getting students' attention, placing students into groups or teams, or distributing and collecting equipment.

normal schools—Schools designed to train teachers (i.e., teachers' colleges).

objective assessments—Formalized assessments that involve standardized scoring systems in which only one answer is possible for each question.

objectivity (of a test)—The quality of a test that is impartial to different people scoring the same test; everyone scoring the test arrives at the same score.

open-skill practice—A practice in which skills are practiced in a constantly changing, dynamic, and unpredictable environment.

part skill practice—A setting in which skills are broken down and practiced in parts before the entire skill is practiced as a whole.

pedometer—A device worn on the waistband that records the number of steps taken as a way to measure physical activity.

performance objectives—Specifically stated learning outcomes that describe what students should be able to do by the end of a lesson.

performance-related fitness—A type of fitness that addresses five components related to enhancing performance: speed, power, agility, coordination, and balance.

personal interest— A motivational concept where one is motivated by something that has personal meaning or appears appealing or exciting.

PETE—An acronym for physical education teacher education programs offered at colleges or universities.

physical activity—Bodily movements that increase energy expenditure and have a role in enhancing health-related fitness.

physical education—A process of learning that revolves around participating in physical activities.

physical training—A precursor to the term *physical education*. Other terms with similar meaning during the early American period were *physical culture, calisthenics*, and *gymnastics*.

pinpointing—A behavior management strategy whereby teachers verbally recognize those students or groups who are demonstrating appropriate behaviors.

practice style—A teaching style that allows students some freedom and choice when practicing preassigned tasks determined by the teacher.

pragmatism—An American philosophy developed through John Dewey's ideas of progressive education. It centers on the importance of successful experiences and social cooperative interactions. The phrase *learn by doing* is consistent with this philosophy.

Premack principle—A behavior modification method in which positive extrinsic rewards are given for good behavior.

process—Assessment of a skill that addresses the form or technique of the skill (e.g., stepping with the opposite foot while throwing; wrist snap on a follow-through).

product—Assessment of a skill that addresses the outcome of performing the skill (e.g., a serve lands in the proper court; a basket or shot on goal is made).

proximity control—A behavior prevention strategy whereby teachers position themselves near students who are off task or behaving inappropriately to encourage better behavior.

psychomotor domain—A domain of learning that addresses the nerve–muscle (neuromuscular) connection in the performance of physical skills and movements.

realism—A traditional philosophy of the Greek philosopher Aristotle. It centers on the importance of demonstrating evidence; if something can be proven and makes sense, it is real.

reciprocal, or peer, style—A teaching style in which students are in charge of teaching their peers a task or assessing their peers' performance, based on criteria outlined by the teacher; also called peer teaching.

reliability (of a test)—The quality of a test that demonstrates consistency.

responsibility model—A teaching model that uses a series of responsibility levels to enhance personal and social skills.

role model—A person who serves as a positive example of attitudes, behaviors, and values.

rubric—A scoring system or rating scale used to assess a variety of learning tasks.

scope—The extent of the subject matter or content to be taught.

self-check style—A teaching style in which students select, complete, and check off various tasks arranged by the teacher.

self-efficacy—A belief in one's ability to accomplish a certain task or skill.

sequence—The order in which content is taught.

situational interest—A motivational concept referring to a circumstance, condition, or attention-getter that sparks initial motivation.

social domain—A domain of learning that addresses the social skills needed to work cooperatively and fairly with others.

specialized movements—Fundamental movements used when performing a variety of games, sports, and physical activities.

springing movements—A stability skill involving movements that cast the body in an airborne state.

sport education model—A model that offers students in physical education an opportunity to experience the various facets of sports while developing skills and learning how to play the game.

static movements—Movements that are done in a stationary position, often by holding a specific position for a certain time.

subjective assessments—Assessments that allow for more than one answer or several ways to express an answer.

summative assessments—Assessments that are administered at the conclusion of a unit of study or the end of a term to determine students' overall understanding of the content.

Swedish gymnastics—A prominent system in the early development of physical education in the United States based on a progression of well-defined movements to enhance strength and heart and lung capacity.

striking and fielding games—A game form that requires teams to hit or kick a ball to advance runners to score or field a ball to get runners out. Games such as softball and baseball, kickball, and cricket are examples of striking and fielding games.

tactical games approach—A teaching model that focuses on helping students understand the tactics or strategies of playing the game, more so than the physical skills needed for playing the game. Also referred to as teaching games for understanding.

target games—A game form that requires teams to hit a target in order to score. Activities such as golf, archery, bocce ball, and bowling are examples of target games.

task orientation—A motivational focus that describes someone who is intrinsically motivated by hard work and effort to improve.

teacher–coach role conflict—A conflict experienced by teachers who also have the role of coach; involves issues of time, energy, and priority.

teaching cues—Descriptive words or short, catchy phrases used during a demonstration that help describe a relevant movement or action in a meaningful way.

teaching styles—Various teacher-centered (direct) or student-centered (indirect) approaches to teaching and learning.

time on task—The time students are actively engaged or involved in productive learning-task activities.

time-out—A consequence for misbehavior that involves removing the student from the learning environment for a short time.

Title IX—A 1972 U.S. federal law that mandates equal sport and physical education opportunities for females.

upright supports—Stability skills that involve the development of static and dynamic symmetrical (both sides of the body doing the same thing) and asymmetrical (both sides of the body doing something different) balance skills.

validity (of a test)—The quality of a test that measures what it is supposed to measure.

verbal prompts—Quick verbal reminders used to bring about appropriate student behaviors.

wait time—A period of silent observance by the teacher, indirectly sending a message to the class to stop talking and pay attention.

whole skill practice—A setting in which skills are practiced in their entirety (the whole skill).

with-it-ness—An attitude that demonstrates that the teacher is alert and aware of what is happening during the lesson.

REFERENCES

American Alliance for Health, Physical Education, Recreation and Dance (AAHPERD). 1981. *Basic stuff series I and II*. Reston, VA: AAHPERD.

American Alliance for Health, Physical Education, Recreation and Dance (AAHPERD). 1987. *Basic stuff series I and II*. Reston, VA: AAHPERD.

Adams, S.H. (1993). Duty to properly instruct. *Journal of Physical Education, Recreation and Dance* 64 (2): 22-23.

Adams, J.B., and J.B. Adams. 2009. Practical applications and limitations of tracking body mass index in schools. *Journal of Physical Education, Recreation and Dance* 80 (4): 14-17, 54.

Alderman, B.L., A. Beighle, and R.P. Pangrazi. 2006. Enhancing motivation in physical education. *Journal of Physical Education, Recreation and Dance* 77 (2): 41-45, 51.

Ames, C. 1992. Achievement goals, motivational climate, and motivational processes. *Motivation in sport and exercise*, ed. G.C. Roberts, 161-176. Champaign, IL: Human Kinetics.

Arbogast, G.W., and D.L. Kizer. 1996. *Case study workbook for physical education teacher preparation*. Dubuque, IA: Kendall/Hunt Publishing.

Bailey R. 2006. Physical education and sport in schools: A review of benefits and outcomes. *Journal of School Health* 76 (8): 397-401.

Bandura, A. 1977. Self-efficacy: Toward a unifying theory of behavior change. *Psychological Review* 84 (2): 191-215.

Bandura, A. 1986. *Social foundations of thought and action: A social cognitive theory*. Englewood Cliffs, NJ: Prentice Hall.

Baumgartner, T.A., A.S. Jackson, M.T. Mahar, and D.A. Rowe. 2007. *Measurement for evaluation in physical education and exercise science*, 8th ed. New York: WCB McGraw-Hill.

Beecher, C.E. 1867. *Physiology and calisthenics for schools and families*. New York: Harper & Brothers.

Belka, D.E. 2002. A strategy for improvement of learning-task presentations. *Journal of Physical Education, Recreation and Dance* 73 (6): 32- 35, 42.

Bennett, B.L. 1984. Dudley Allen Sargent: The man and his philosophy. *Journal of Physical Education, Recreation and Dance* 55 (9): 61-64.

Blaufarb, M. 1976. Title IX and physical education: A compliance overview. Washington, DC: U.S. Office of Education, Department of Health, Education, and Welfare.

Bloom, B.S., ed. 1956. *Taxonomy of educational objectives, handbook I: Cognitive domain*. New York: McKay.

Bouchard, C., and T. Rankinen. 2001. Individual differences in response to regular physical activity. *Medicine & Science in Sports & Exercise* 33 (6): S446-S451.

Boyce, B.A., and G.L. Rikard. 2008. A comparison of supply and demand for PETE faculty: The changing landscape. *Research Quarterly for Exercise and Sport* 79 (4): 540-545.

Brink, B.D. 1916. *The body builder, Robert J. Roberts*. New York: Association Press.

Buck, M.M., J.L. Lund, J.M. Harrison, and C. Blakemore Cook. 2007. *Instructional strategies for secondary school physical education*, 6th ed. New York: McGraw-Hill.

Burke, R.K. 1963. Pragmatism in physical education. In *Philosophies fashion—Physical education*, ed. E.C. Davis, 6-15. Dubuque, IA: Wm. C. Brown.

Buschner, C. 2006. Online physical education: Wires and lights in a box. *Journal of Physical Education, Recreation and Dance* 77 (2): 3-5.

California State Department of Education. 2005. California physical fitness test: A study of the relationship between physical fitness and academic achievement in California using 2004 test results. www.cde.ca.gov/ta/tg/pf/documents/2004pftresults.doc.

Carbarino, M.S. 1976. *Native American heritage*. Boston: Little, Brown and Co.

Cardinal B.J. 2001. Role modeling attitudes and physical activity and fitness promoting behaviors of HPERD professionals and preprofessionals. *Research Quarterly for Exercise and Sport* 72 (1): 84-90.

Castelli, D.M., C.H. Hillman, S.M. Buck, and H.E. Erwin. 2007. Physical fitness and academic achievement in third- and fifth-grade students. *Journal of Sport and Exercise Psychology* 29: 239-252.

Centers for Disease Control and Prevention. 2007. NCHS data brief: *Obesity among adults in the United States—No statistically significant change since 2003-2004*. Division of Health and Nutrition Examination Study. www.cdc.gov.nchs/data/databrief/db01.pdf.

Centers for Disease Control and Prevention. 2009a. *How much physical activity do children need?* www.cdc.gov/physicalactivity/everyone/guidelines/children.html.

Centers for Disease Control and Prevention. 2009b. Press release. *Study estimates medical cost of obesity may be as high as $147 billion annually.* www.cdc.gov/media/pressrel/2009/r090727.htm.

Chase, M.A. 2001. Children's self-efficacy, motivational intentions, and attributions in physical education and sport *Research Quarterly for Exercise and Sport* 72 (1): 47-54.

Chen, A. and P.W. Darst. 2001. Situational interest in physical education—A function of learning task design. *Research Quarterly for Exercise and Sport* 72 (2): 150-163.

Clements, R. 2009. Four considerations for urban physical education teachers. *Journal of Physical Education, Recreation and Dance* 80 (8): 29-31.

Coe, D., J. Pivarnik, C. Womack, M. Reeves, and R. Malina. 2006. Effect of physical education activity levels on academic achievement in children. *Medicine & Science in Sports & Exercise* 38 (8): 1515-1519.

Colcombe, S., and A.F. Kramer. 2003. Fitness effects on the cognitive function of older adults: A meta-analytic study. *Psychological Science* 14 (2): 125-130.

Cooper Institute. 2009. Texas Education Agency News Release. March 9, 2009. www.cooperinstitute.org/ourkidshealth/index.cfm.

Cooper Institute. 2010. *Fitnessgram/Activitygram: Test administration manual,* updated 4th ed., eds. M.D. Meredith and G.J. Welks. Champaign, IL: Human Kinetics.

www.cooperinstitute.org/ourkidshealth/index.cfm.

Corbin, C.B. 1987. Youth fitness, exercise and health: There is much to be done. *Research Quarterly for Exercise and Sport* 58 (4): 308-314.

Corbin, C.B., and R. Lindsey. 2007. *Fitness for life*, 5th ed. Champaign, IL: Human Kinetics.

Cowell, C.C., and W.L. France. 1963. *Philosophy and principles of physical education*. Englewood Cliffs, NJ: Prentice Hall.

Crouter, S.C., P.L. Schneider, M. Karabulut, and D.R. Bassett, Jr. 2003. Validity of 10 electronic pedometers for measuring steps, distance, and energy costs. *Medicine & Science in Sports & Exercise* 35 (8): 1455-1460.

Daley, A.J. 2009. Can exergaming contribute to improving physical activity levels and health outcomes in children? *Pediatrics* 124 (2): 763-771.

Darden, G.F. 1997. Demonstrating motor skills—Rethinking that expert demonstration. *Journal of Physical Education, Recreation and Dance* 68 (6): 31-35.

Darst, P.W., and R.P. Pangrazi. 2009. *Dynamic physical education for secondary school students*. San Francisco: Pearson Benjamin Cummings.

Davis, E.C. 1963a. Idealism and physical education. In *Philosophies fashion—Physical education,* ed. E.C. Davis, 58-83. Dubuque, IA: Wm. C. Brown.

Davis, E.C. 1963b. *Philosophies fashion—Physical education*. Dubuque, IA: Wm. C. Brown.

Deci, E.L., and R.M. Ryan. 1985. *Intrinsic motivation and self-determination in human behavior*. New York: Plenum.

Deci E.L., and R.M. Ryan. 2000. The "what" and "why" of goal pursuits: Human needs and the self-determination of behavior. *Psychological Inquiry* 11 (4): 227-268.

Doolittle, S., and T. Fay. 2002. *Authentic assessment of physical activity for high school students*. Reston, VA: National Association for Sport and Physical Education.

Dougherty N.J. 2010. Legal responsibility for safety in physical education and sport. In *Principles of safety in physical education and sport,* 4th ed., ed. N.J. Dougherty. Reston, VA: National Association for Sport and Physical Education.

Downing, J., T. Keating, and C. Bennett. 2005. Effective reinforcement techniques in elementary physical education: The key to behavior management. *Physical Educator* 62 (3): 114-122.

Enebuske, C.J. 1890. *Progressive gymnastic day's orders*. New York: Silver, Burdett & Company.

Epstein, J. 1988. Effective schools or effective students? Dealing with diversity. In *Policies for American's public schools*, eds. R. Haskins and B. MacRae, 89-126. Norwood, NJ: Ablex.

Epstein, L.H., M.D. Beecher, J.L. Graf, and J.N. Roemmich. 2007. Choice of interactive dance and bicycle games in overweight and nonoverweight youth. *Annals of Behavior Medicine* 33 (2): 124-131.

Ernst, M.P., R.P. Pangrazi, and C.B. Corbin. 1998. Physical education: Making a transition toward activity. *Journal of Physical Education, Recreation and Dance* 69 (9): 29-32.

Faigenbaum, A., and J.E. McFarlane, Jr. 2007. Guidelines for implementing a dynamic warm-up for physical education. *Journal of Physical Education, Recreation and Dance* 78 (3): 25-28.

Freeman, W.H. 2001. *Physical education and sport in a changing society,* 6th ed. Boston: Allyn & Bacon.

Fronske, H.A. 2001. *Teaching cues for sport skills*. Needham Heights, MA: Allyn & Bacon.

Gallahue, D.L. 1996. *Developmental physical education for today's children,* 3rd ed. Dubuque, IA: Brown & Benchmark.

Gallahue, D.L, and F. Cleland-Donnelly. 2003. *Developmental physical education for today's children,* 4th ed. Dubuque, IA: Brown & Benchmark.

Gentile, A.M. 2000. Skill acquisition: Action, movement, and neuromotor processes. In *Movement sciences: Foundations for physical therapy,* 2nd ed., eds. J.H Carr, and R.B. Shepherd. Rockville, MD: Aspen.

Gibson, A.M. 1969. *The American Indian: Prehistory to the present*. Lexington, MA: D.C. Heath.

Goodsell, W. 1931. *Pioneers of women's education in the United States*. New York: McGraw-Hill Book Company.

Gordon, T. 2003. *Teacher effectiveness training*. New York: Three Rivers Press.

Graham, G.M., S.A. Holt/Hale, and M. Parker. 2010. *Children moving*, 8th ed. New York: McGraw-Hill.

Green, K.B. 1979. *Test item construction in the cognitive domain*. Washington, DC: Home Economics Education Association.

Griffin, L.S., S.A. Mitchell, and J.L. Oslin. 1997. *Teaching sports concepts and skills: A tactical approach*. Champaign, IL: Human Kinetics.

Gulick, L.H. 1920. *A philosophy of play*. New York: Charles Scribner's Sons.

Haddock, B.L., A.M. Brandt, S.R. Siegel, L.D. Wilkin, and H. Joung-Kyue. 2008. Active video games and energy expenditure amount overweight children. *International Journal of Fitness* 4 (2): 17-24.

Halsey, E. 1961. *Women in physical education: Their role in work, home, and history*. New York: B.P. Putnam's Sons.

Harter, S. 1982. The perceived competence scale for children. *Child Development* 53: 87-97.

Hawkins, A. 2008. Pragmatism, purpose, and play: Struggle for the soul of physical education. *Quest* 60: 345-356.

Heitmann, H.M., and M.E. Kneer. 1976. *Physical education instructional techniques: An individualized humanistic approach*. Englewood Cliffs, NJ: Prentice Hall.

Helion, J.G. 2009. Professional responsibility. *Journal of Physical Education, Recreation and Dance* 80 (6): 5-6, 62.

Hellison, D. 2003. *Teaching responsibility through physical activity*, 2nd ed. Champaign, IL: Human Kinetics.

Henderson, H.L., R. French, R. Fritsch, and B. Lerner. 2000. Time-out and overcorrection: A comparison of their application in physical education. *Journal of Physical Education, Recreation and Dance* 71 (3): 31-35.

Henry F. 1964. Physical education: An academic discipline. *Journal of Health, Physical Education, and Recreation* 37 (7): 32-33.

Heron, T.E. 1987. Time-out from positive reinforcement. In *Applied behavior analysis*, eds. J.O. Cooper, T.E. Heron, and W.L. Heward, 439-453. Columbus, OH: Merrill.

Hetherington, C. 1910. Fundamental education. *American Physical Education Review* 15: 629-635.

Hewett, T.E., K.R. Ford, and G.D. Myer. 2006. Anterior cruciate injuries in female athletes: Part 2, a meta-analysis of neuromuscular interventions aimed at injury prevention. *American Journal of Sports Medicine* 34 (3): 490-498.

Hewett, T.E., G.D. Myer, and K.R. Ford. 2006. Anterior cruciate ligament injuries in female athletes: Part 1, mechanisms and risk factors. *American Journal of Sports Medicine* 34 (2): 299-311.

Hidi, S. 2000. An interest researcher's perspective: The effects of extrinsic and intrinsic factors on motivation. In *Intrinsic and extrinsic motivation—The search for optimal motivation and performance,* eds. C. Sansone and J.M. Harackiewicz, 309-339. San Diego, CA: Academic Press.

Hiliman, C.H., S.M. Buck, J.R. Themanson, M.B. Pontifex, and D.M. Castelli. 2009. Aerobic fitness and cognitive development: Event-related brain potential and task performance indices of executive control in preadolescent children. *Developmental Psychology* 45 (1): 114-129.

Holbrook, L. 1963. The philosophy of realism in physical education. In *Philosophies fashion—Physical education*, ed. E.C. Davis. Dubuque, IA: Wm. C. Brown.

Jewett, A.E., L.L. Bain, and C.D. Ennis. 1995. *The curriculum in physical education*, 2nd ed. Dubuque, IA: Brown & Benchmark.

Johnson, R. 1999. Time out: Can it control misbehavior? *Journal of Physical Education, Recreation and Dance* 70 (8): 32-35.

Johnson, R. 2008. Overcoming resistance to achievement-based unit grading in secondary physical education. *Journal of Physical Education, Recreation and Dance* 79 (4): 46-49.

Kounin, L.S. 1970. *Discipline and group management in classrooms*. New York: Holt, Rinehart & Winston.

Kraus, H., and R.P. Hirschland. 1953. Muscular fitness and health. *The Journal of the American Association of Health, Physical Education, and Recreation* 24 (10): 17-19.

Kraus, H., and R.P. Hirschland. 1954. Minimum muscular fitness tests in school children. *Research Quarterly* 25 (2): 178-188.

Kretchmar, R.S. 2005. *Practical philosophy of sport and physical activity*. Champaign, IL: Human Kinetics.

Lakka, T.A., and C. Bouchard. 2004. Genetics, physical activity, fitness and health: What does the future hold? *The Journal of the Royal Society for the Promotion of Health* 124: 14-15.

LaSalle, D. 1951. Thomas D. Wood, M.D.—A great leader. *The Journal of the American Association for Health, Physical Education, and Recreation* 22 (9): 28-30.

Latham, G. I. 1998. *Keys to classroom management*. North Logan, UT: P&T Publisher.

Lavay, B.W., R. French, and H.L. Henderson. 1997. *Positive behavior management strategies for physical educators*. Champaign, IL: Human Kinetics.

Lee, M. 1978. *Memories beyond bloomers*. Washington, DC: American Alliance for Health, Physical Education and Recreation.

Lee, M. 1983. *A History of physical education and sports in the U.S.A.* New York: John Wiley & Sons.

Leonard. F.E. 1915. *Pioneers of modern physical training*. New York: Association Press.

Leonard, F.E., and R.T. McKenzie. 1927. *A guide to the history of physical education*. Philadelphia: Lea & Febiger.

Lewis, D. 1864. *The new gymnastics for men, women, and children*. Boston: Tricknor & Fields.

Lewis, J.J. 2009. *Gerda Lerner Quotes*. http://womenshistory.about.com/cs/quotes/a/gerda_lerner.htm.

Lund, J.E. 2000. *Creating rubrics for physical education*. Reston, VA: National Association for Sport and Physical Education.

Lynn, S., and T. Ratliffe. 1999. Grouping strategies in physical education. *Strategies* 12 (3): 13-15.

Mager, R.F. 1997. *Preparing instructional objectives: A critical tool in the development of effective instruction*, 3rd ed. Atlanta, GA: The Center for Effective Performance.

Maggard, N.J. 1984. Upgrading our image. *Journal of Physical Education, Recreation and Dance* 55 (1): 17, 82.

Magill, R.A. 2007. *Motor learning and control—Concepts and applications*, 8th ed. New York: McGraw-Hill.

Mahle, B.1989. *Power teaching: Stay sane and enjoy your job even though you teach adolescents*. Carthage, IL: Fearson Teacher Aids.

Maier, S.F., and M.E. Seligman. 1976. Learned helplessness: Theory and evidence. *Journal of Experimental Psychology: General* 105 (1): 3-46.

Martin, E.H., M.E. Rudisill, and P.A. Hastie. 2009. Motivational climate and fundamental motor skill performance in a naturalistic physical education setting. *Physical Education and Sport Pedagogy* 14 (3): 227-240.

McCloy, C.H. 1930. Professional progress through research. *The Research Quarterly of the American Physical Education Association* 1 (2): 63-73.

McKenzie, R.T. 1936. Benjamin Franklin—Illustrious pioneer in physical education. *Journal of Health and Physical Education* 7 (2), 67-72, 125.

McKenzie, T.L., J.F. Sallis, and P. Rosengard. 2009. Beyond the stucco tower: Design, development, and dissemination of the SPARK physical education program. *Quest* 61 (1): 114-127.

Mears D., and L. Hansen. 2009. Active gaming: Definitions, options and implementation. *Strategies* 23 (2): 26-29.

Mechikoff, R., and S. Estes. 1993. *A history and philosophy of sport and physical education*. Madison, WI: Brown & Benchmark.

Melograno, V.J. 2007. Grading and report cards for standards-based physical education. *Journal of Physical Education, Recreation and Dance* 78 (6): 45-53.

Merriman, J. (1993). Supervision in sport and physical activity. *Journal of Physical Education, Recreation and Dance* 64 (2): 20-21; 23.

Metheny, E. 1954. The third dimension in physical education. *Journal for the American Association for Health, Physical Education and Recreation* 25 (3): 27-28.

Millslagle, D., and L. Morley. 2004. Investigation of role retreatism in the teacher/coach. *Physical Education* 61 (3): 120-130.

Mintah, J.K. 2003. Authentic assessment in physical education: Prevalence of use and perceived impact on students' self-concept, motivation, and skill achievement. *Measurement in Physical Education and Exercise Science* 7 (3): 161-174.

Mitchell, M. 2009. Content development—Using application tasks to celebrate and calibrate. *Journal of Physical Education, Recreation and Dance* 80 (5): 47-50, 60.

Mohnsen, B. 2003. *Concepts of physical education—What every student needs to know*, 2nd ed. Reston, VA: National Association for Sport and Physical Education.

Morgan, Jr, C.F., R.P. Pangrazi, and A. Beighle. 2003. Using pedometers to promote physical activity in physical education. *Journal of Physical Education, Recreation and Dance* 74 (7): 33-38.

Morrow, Jr., J.R., Z. Weimo, B.D. Franks, M.D. Meredith, and C. Spain. 2009. 1958-2008: 50 years of youth fitness tests in the United States. *Research Quarterly for Exercise and Sport* 80 (1): 1-11.

Morse, R.C. 1913. *History of the North American men's Christian associations*. New York: Association Press.

Mosston, M., and S. Ashworth. 2002. *Teaching physical education,* 5th ed. San Francisco: Benjamin Cummings.

Nash, J.B. 1960. Luther Halsey Gulick. *Journal of Health, Physical Education, and Recreation* 31 (4): 60, 114.

National Association for Sport and Physical Education (NASPE). 1995. *Moving into the future: National standards for physical education,* Boston, MA: MCB/McGraw-Hill.

National Association for Sport and Physical Education (NASPE). 2004. *Moving into the future: National standards for physical education,* 2nd ed. Boston, MA: MCB/McGraw-Hill.

National Association for Sport and Physical Education (NASPE). 2008. *PE metrics: Assessing the national standards, standard I: Elementary*. Reston, VA: NASPE.

National Association for Sport and Physical Education (NASPE) and American Heart Association (AHA). 2010. *Shape of the nation report: Status of physical education in the USA*. Reston, VA: NASPE. http://iweb.aahperd.org/naspe/ShapeOfTheNation/PDF/ShapeOfTheNation.pdf.

Nicholls, J.G. 1984a. Achievement motivation: Conceptions of ability, subjective experience, task choice, and performance. *Psychological Review* 91 (3): 328-346.

Nicholls, J.G. 1984b. Striving to demonstrate and develop ability: A theory of achievement motivation. In *The development of achievement motivation*, ed. J.G. Nicholls, 328-346. Greenwich, CT: JAI.

Nichols, R., K.L. Davis, T. McLord, D. Schnidt, and A.M. Stezak. 2009. The use of heart rate monitors in physical education. *Strategies* 22 (6): 19-23.

No Child Left Behind. 1991.www.edu.gov/nclb.

Ogden, C.L., M.D. Carroll, and K.M Flegal. 2008. High body mass index of age among U.S. children and adolescents, 2003-2006. *Journal of the American Medical Association* 299 (10): 2401-2405.

Okely, A., M. Booth, and J.W. Patterson. 2001. Relationship of physical activity to fundamental movement skills among adolescents. *Medicine & Science in Sports & Exercise* 33: 1899-1904.

Ortega, F.B., J.R. Ruiz, M.J. Castillo, and M. Sjöström. 2008. Physical fitness in childhood and adolescence: A powerful marker of health. *International Journal of Obesity* 32: 1-11.

Oslin, J.L. 1996. Routines as organizing features in middle school physical education. *Journal of Teaching Physical Education* 15 (4): 319-337.

Oslin, J.L., and S.A. Mitchell. 1998. Teaching form follows function. *Journal of Physical Education, Recreation and Dance* 69 (6): 46-49.

Owens, L. 2006. Teacher radar: The view from the front of the class. *Journal of Physical Education, Recreation and Dance* 77 (4): 29-33.

Owens, L.M., and C.D. Ennis. 2005. The ethic of care in teaching: An overview of supportive literature. *Quest* 57 (4): 392-425.

Pangrazi, R.P., and A. Beighle. 2010. *Dynamic physical education for elementary school children*, 16th ed. San Francisco: Pearson Benjamin Cummings.

Pangrazi, R.P., A. Beighle, and C.L. Sidman. 2007. *Pedometer power: Using pedometers in school and community*, 2nd ed. Champaign, IL: Human Kinetics.

Petersen, S.C., and L.M. Cruz. 2000. Using small-sided games in traditional activities. *Strategies* 14 (2): 19-21.

Placek, J.H. 1983. Conceptions of success in teaching: Busy, happy, and good? In *Teaching in Physical Education*, eds. Templin, T.J., and J.K. Olsen, 46-56. Champaign, IL: Human Kinetics.

Plowman, S.A., C.L. Sterling, C.B. Corbin, M.D. Meredith, G.J. Welk, and J.R. Morrow, Jr. 2006. The history of Fitnessgram. *Journal of Physical Activity and Health* 3 (Suppl. 2): S5-S20.

Premack, D. 1965. Reinforcement theory. In *Nebraska symposium on motivation*, ed. D. Levine. Lincoln: University of Nebraska Press.

Ransdell, L.B., K. Rice, C. Snelson, and J. DeCola. 2008. Online health-related fitness courses: A wolf in sheep's clothing or a solution to some common problems? *Journal of Physical Education, Recreation and Dance* 79 (1): 45-52.

Rauschenbach, J. 1994. Checking for student understanding. *Journal of Physical Education, Recreation and Dance* 65 (4): 60-63.

Reilly, J.J. 2006. Diagnostic accuracy of the BMI for age in pediatrics. *International Journal of Obesity* 30: 595-597.

Rink, J.E. 2009. *Designing the physical education curriculum—Promoting active lifestyles*. New York: McGraw-Hill.

Rink, J.E. 2010. *Teaching physical education for learning*, 6th ed. New York: McGraw-Hill.

Rowlands, A.V., and R.G. Eston. 2005. Comparison of accelerometer and pedometer measures of physical activity in boys and girls, ages 8-10 years. *Research Quarterly for Exercise and Sport* 76 (3): 251-257.

Rudisill, M.E. 1989. Influence of perceived competence and casual dimension orientation on expectations, persistence, and performance during perceived failure. *Research Quarterly for Exercise and Sport* 60 (2): 166-175.

Ryan, T.D. 2008. Antecedents for interrole conflict in the high school teacher/coach. *Physical Educator* 65 (2): 58-67.

Sabo, D., K. Miller, M. Melnick, and L. Heywood. 2004. *Her life depends on it: Sport, physical activity and health and well-being of American girls*. East Meadow, NY: Women's Sports Foundation.

Sage, G.H. 1987. The social world of high school athletic coaches: Multiple role demands and their consequences. *Sociology of Sport Journal* 4: 213-228.

Sallis, J.F., T.L. McKenzie, B. Kolody, M. Lewis, S. Marshall, and P. Rosengard. 1999. Effects of health-related physical education on academic achievement: Project SPARK. *Research Quarterly for Exercise and Sport* 70 (2): 127-134.

Sargent, D.A. 1900. The place for physical training in the school and college curriculum. *Physical Educator Review* 5 (1): 1-17.

Sargent, L.W. 1927 *Dudley Allen Sargent: An autobiography*. Philadelphia: Lea & Febiger.

Schmidt, R.A., and C.A. Wrisberg. 2008. *Motor learning and performance—A problem-based learning approach*, 4th ed. Champaign, IL: Human Kinetics.

Secretary, Department of Physical Education for Women, Oberlin College. 1941. Brief outline of life and work of Delphine Hanna—Pioneer women in physical education. Supplement to *Research Quarterly of the American Physical Education Association* 12 (3): 646-652.

Shen B., and A. Chen. 2006. Examining the interrelations among knowledge, interests, and learning strategies. *Journal of Teaching Physical Education* 25 (2): 182-199.

Shen, B., A. Chen, H. Tolley, and K.A. Scrabis. (2003). Gender and interest-based motivation in learning dance. *Journal of Teaching Physical Education* 22: 396-409.

Shephard, R. 1997. Curricular physical activity and academic performance. *Pediatric Exercise Science* 9: 113-126.

Sibley, B.A., and J. Etnier. 2003. The relationship between physical activity and cognition in children: A meta-analysis. *Pediatric Exercise Science* 15: 243-256.

Siedentop, D. 1994. *Sport education: Quality physical education through positive sport experiences*. Champaign, IL: Human Kinetics.

Siedentop, D. 2009. *Introduction to physical education, fitness, and sport*, 7th ed. New York: McGraw-Hill.

Siedentop, D., P.A. Hastie, and H. van der Mars. 2004. *Complete guide to sport education*. Champaign, IL: Human Kinetics.

Siedentop, D., and D. Tannehill. 2000. *Developing teaching skills in physical education*, 4th ed. Mountain View, CA: Mayfield.

Simons-Morton, B.G., N.M. O'Hara, D.G. Simons-Morton, and G.S. Parcel. 1987. Children and fitness: A public health perspective. *Research Quarterly for Exercise and Sport* 58 (4): 295-302.

Solmon, M.A. 2006. Creating a motivational climate to foster engagement in physical education. *Journal of Physical Education, Recreation and Dance* 77 (8): 15-16, 22.

Spencer A. 1998. Physical educator: Role model or roll out the ball? *Journal of Physical Education, Recreation and Dance* 69 (6): 58-63.

Standage, M., J.L. Duda, and N. Ntoumanis. 2003. Predicting motivational regulations in physical education: The interplay between dispositional goal orientations, motivational, climate and perceived competence. *Journal of Sports Sciences* 21 (8): 631-647.

Stiehl, J., D. Morris, and C. Sinclair. 2008. *Teaching physical activity—Change, challenge, and choice*. Champaign, IL: Human Kinetics.

Treasure, D.C., and G.C. Roberts 1995. Applications of achievement goal theory to physical education: Implications for enhancing motivation. *Quest* 47 (4): 475-489.

Trout J., and D McColl. 2007. Vocal health for physical educators. *Journal of Physical Education, Recreation and Dance* 78 (8): 12-15.

Tudor-Locke, C., R.P. Pangrazi, C.B. Corbin, W.J. Rutherford, S.D. Vincent, A. Raustorp, et al. 2004. BMI-referenced standards for recommended pedometer-determined steps/day in children. *Preventive Medicine* 38: 857-864.

Van Dalen, D.B., and B. Bennett. 1971. A *world history of physical education*, 2nd ed. Englewood Cliffs, NJ: Prentice Hall.

Vincent, D.S., and R.P. Pangrazi. 2002. An examination of the activity patterns of elementary school children. *Pediatric Exercise Science* 14 (4): 432-441.

Walsh, K.M., B. Bennett, M.A. Cooper, R.L. Holle, R. Kithil, and R.E. Lopez. 2000. NATA position statement: Lightning safety for athletic and recreation. *Journal of Athletic Training* 35 (4): 471-477.

Weiner, B. 1979. A theory of motivation for some classroom experiences. *Journal of Educational Psychology* 71 (1): 3-25.

Weiner, B. 1985. An attribution theory of achievement motivation and emotional. *Psychological Review* 92 (4): 548-573.

Werner, P., R. Thorpe, and D. Bunker, D. 1996. Teaching games for understanding—Evolution of a model. *Journal of Physical Education, Recreation and Dance* 67 (1): 28-33.

Weston, A. 1962. *The making of American physical education*. New York: Appleton-Century-Crofts.

Williams, N.F. 1992. The physical education hall of shame. *Journal of Physical Education, Recreation and Dance* 63 (6): 57-60.

Williams, N.F. 1994. The physical education hall of shame, part II. *Journal of Physical Education, Recreation and Dance* 65 (2): 17-20.

Woods, M.L., G. Goc Karp, and D. Feltz. 2003. Positions in kinesiology and physical education at the college or university level. *Quest* 55: 30-50.

Woods, M.L., G. Goc Karp, and M.R. Judd. 2009. Chair's perceptions of PETE candidates. PowerPoint presentation at the 2009 AAHPERD National Convention, Tampa, FL.

Woody, T. 1929. *A history of women's education in the United States, volume II*. New York: Science Press.

Zeigler, E.F. 1964. *Philosophical foundations for physical, health, and recreation education*. Englewood Cliffs, NJ: Prentice Hall.

INDEX

Note: The italicized *f* and *t* following page numbers refer to figures and tables, respectively.

ABOUT THE AUTHOR

Photo courtesy of Carrie Quincy, Photographic Services Photographer at Boise State University

Jane M. Shimon, EdD, ATC, is an associate professor in the department of kinesiology at Boise State University in Boise, Idaho. She was named Outstanding College Educator of the Year in 2006 by Idaho AHPERD, University Educator of the Year in 2007 for AAHPERD's Northwest District, and received an Outstanding Teaching Award in 1998 from Radford University.

Shimon has firsthand experience in teaching physical education and health at the secondary level and has been teaching an introduction to physical education class since 2000. She has supervised student teachers in rural, urban, and suburban areas in many states across the country. These experiences have broadened her views of PE programs and teaching practices.

Shimon has been a member of various state Alliance for Health, Physical Education, Recreation and Dance organizations and has served on the *Journal of Physical Education, Recreation and Dance* editorial board and on a subcommittee for the National Association for Sport and Physical Education. She is also a certified athletic trainer and a member of the National Athletic Trainers' Association. She enjoys road and mountain cycling, watercolor painting, and reading mysteries and historical fiction.

I'VE GOT THE BEAT